THE TRICKSTER AND THE SYSTEM

For centuries, the trickster has been used in various narratives, including mythological, literary and cinematic, to convey the idea of agency, rebellion and, often turbulent, progress. In *The Trickster and the System: Identity and agency in contemporary society*, Helena Bassil-Morozow shows how the trickster can be seen as a metaphor to describe the psycho-anthropological concept of change, an impulse that challenges the existing order of things, a progressive force that is a-structural and anti-structural in its nature. The book is about being able to see things from an unusual, even 'odd', perspective, which does not coincide with the homogeneous normality of the mass, or the social system, or a political ideology, or some other kind of authority.

The Trickster and the System offers an analytical paradigm that can be used to examine relationships between tricksters and systems, change and stability, in a wide range of social, political and cultural contexts. It covers a range of systems, describes different types of tricksters and discusses possible conflicts, tensions and dialogues between the two opposing sides. One of the central ideas of the book is that social systems use shame as a tool to control and manage all kinds of tricksters – individuality, agency, creativity, spontaneity, innovation and initiative, to name but a few. The author argues that any society that neglects its tricksters (agents of change), ends up suffering from decay, stagnation – or even mass hysterical outbursts.

The Trickster and the System provides a fresh perspective on the trickster figure in a variety of cultural contexts. It covers a range of psychological, cultural, social and political phenomena, from personal issues to the highest level of society's functioning: self-esteem and shame, lifestyle and relationships, creativity and self-expression, media, advertising, economy, political ideology and, most importantly, human identity and authenticity. The book is essential reading for scholars in the areas of psychoanalysis, analytical psychology, myth, cultural and media studies, narrative analysis, cultural anthropology, as well as anyone interested in critical issues in contemporary culture.

Helena Bassil-Morozow is a cultural philosopher, film scholar and academic writer whose many publications include *Tim Burton: The monster and the crowd* (Routledge, 2010) and *The Trickster in Contemporary Film* (Routledge, 2011). Helena is currently working on another Routledge project, *Jungian Film Studies: The essential guide* (co-authored with Luke Hockley). Her principal academic affiliation is to the University of Bedfordshire, Faculty of Creative Arts, Technologies & Science.

THE TRICKSTER AND THE SYSTEM

Identity and agency in contemporary society

Helena Bassil-Morozow

Routledge
Taylor & Francis Group

LONDON AND NEW YORK

First published 2015
by Routledge
27 Church Road, Hove, East Sussex, BN3 2FA

and by Routledge
711 Third Avenue, New York, NY 10017

Routledge is an imprint of the Taylor & Francis Group, an informa business

British Library Cataloguing in Publication Data
A catalogue record for this book is available from the British Library

Library of Congress Cataloging in Publication Data
Bassil-Morozow, Helena Victor, 1978-
The trickster and the system: identity and agency in contemporary society/
Helena Bassil-Morozow.
pages cm
1. Social change. 2. Social evolution. 3. Tricksters. 4. Stigma (Social
psychology) 5. Progress. I. Title.
HM831.B373 2014
303.4—dc23
2014015470

ISBN: 978-0-415-50793-6 (hbk)
ISBN: 978-0-415-50794-3 (pbk)
ISBN: 978-1-315-75810-7 (ebk)

Typeset in Bembo
by Swales & Willis Ltd, Exeter, Devon, UK

MIX
Paper from
responsible sources
FSC
www.fsc.org   FSC® C013056

Printed and bound in Great Britain by
TJ International Ltd, Padstow, Cornwall

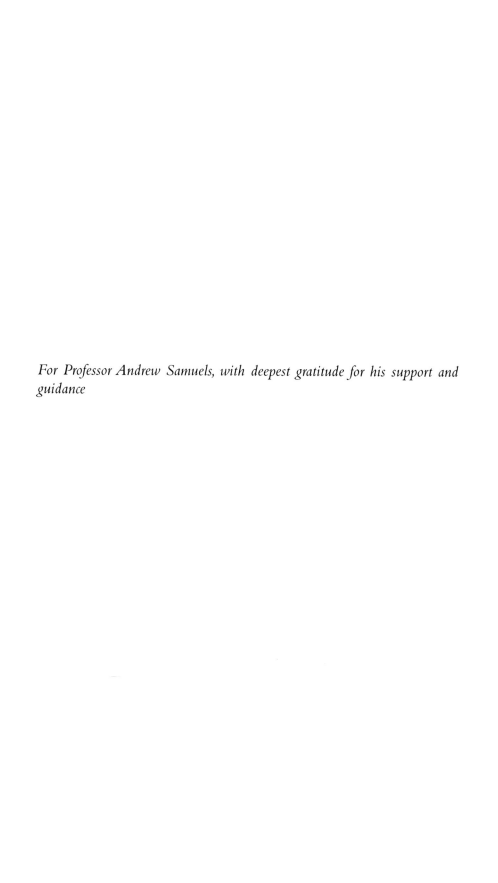

For Professor Andrew Samuels, with deepest gratitude for his support and guidance

CONTENTS

ACKNOWLEDGEMENTS

I would like to thank Routledge, and particularly my editor Kate Hawes, for her patience and understanding, and for her continued help and support.

I am grateful to the Centre for Applied Jungian Studies and Stephen Anthony Farah for providing me with occasional inspiration (mostly in the form of quotes), and to my friend, the documentary director and author Agnieszka Piotrowska, for reminding me about the importance of the female trickster.

I am also greatly indebted to my teachers, Professors Avril Horner and Irina Kabanova. Finally, I would like to thank Alexey for providing me with inspiration, criticism and feedback, and the Russian photographer Ruslan Nugraliev for allowing me to use his artwork to illustrate my concepts.

Permissions

I am very grateful to Routledge/Taylor & Francis for the permission to quote from *The Collected Works of C.G. Jung* (hereafter CW), edited by Sir Herbert Read, Dr Michael Fordham and Dr Gerhardt Adler, and translated by R.F.C. Hull, London.

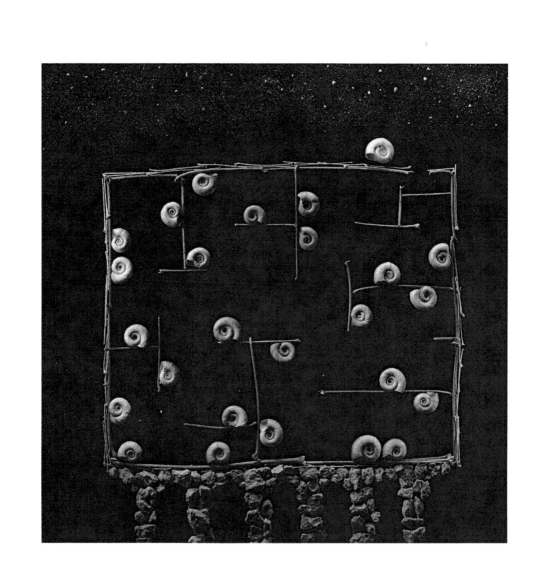

INTRODUCTION

A healthy and progressive society requires both central control and individual and group initiative: without control there is anarchy, and without initiative there is stagnation.

(Bertrand Russell, *Authority and the Individual*)

This book is about similarity and difference. It is about being different and being able to see things from an unusual, even 'odd', perspective, which does not coincide with the homogeneous normality of the mass, or the social system, or a political ideology, or some other kind of authority.

This book is also about systems and tricksters in different political and social contexts. It covers a range of systems, describes different types of tricksters and discusses possible conflicts, tensions and dialogues between the two opposing sides. It closely examines the miracle that is human identity, which is forever stuck between the systemic and the personal, between the individual and the social, between difference and similarity, between being unique and being one of the many – 'like everyone else', 'normal'. Human identity, to use the British anthropologist Victor Turner's expression, is forced to exist 'betwixt and between' the two opposites, and is therefore a volatile and fragile concept. It is a liminal concept. As such, it falls under the jurisdiction of the trickster.

My interest in tricksters began very early – at the nursery. The Soviet nursery, I can tell you, was a rather weird place where toddlers were expected to sing communist songs with piano accompaniment, make identical cows out of plasticine manufactured by the Soviet industry in a limited range of dull colours, and recite patriotic poems at state holiday celebrations. Children grew up with the idea that spontaneity was an undesirable quality, and that anyone expressing it would be punished. At the age of four we already knew that it was dangerous to be different, or to explore the world in ways that were not officially approved. The ruling ideology despised and repressed the concept of choice. Variety was a despicable trickster that smacked of Western consumerism, and could spoil the pure minds of young Soviet citizens.

The children's regime, therefore, had to be dull and predictable, and the group had to be intellectually, socially and psychologically homogeneous. The 'play' element of our development was curtailed, both financially and ideologically: there was no choice of clothes thanks to the limitations of the Soviet production (which meant that we all ended up looking more or less the same), we all had the same 'approved' books, and the nursery could offer very few toys. In fact, the good toys were kept on the top shelves because they were too expensive for us to play with. It would simply have been too difficult for the nursery to find replacements if the originals got broken. From the point of view of the Soviet regime, the trickster (choice, play, spontaneity, change, difference, non-compliance) was an element of the capitalist ideology.

However, even in the circumstances when self-expression was a problem, we still managed to find alternative ways of getting creative. For instance, we transformed 'found' objects into improvised toys. Twigs, leaves, stones and pieces of coloured glass were particularly good for this purpose. Even better were long feathers, pulled out of pillows during the boring obligatory 'quiet hours'. Unfortunately, this type of self-expression was seriously frowned upon. Whereas transforming twigs into various objects was seen as a mad yet relatively innocent activity, making dolls out of feathers was considered a near-criminal act as it resulted in 'the damage of government property'. The punishment for this 'crime' was rather original: whenever we were caught pulling feathers out of pillows, nurses tied our hands together with wet towels. This is how my acquaintance with the trickster started – with my hands bound by a piece of 'government property' for ruining another piece of 'government property', I was supposed to learn a lesson about the dangers of spontaneous creativity. I must admit, the lesson was wasted on me, otherwise I would not be writing this book now. The power of the individual, whose internal trickster is alive, lies in the refusal to be shamed by the system; in the refusal to be ashamed of doing things differently from the majority of people; it resides in the impulse to deviate from the official prescriptions. To defy the system is to laugh at it, and laughter is the trickster's main tool.

In fact, this punishment was suitably metaphorical, wonderfully ridiculous and emblematic of mythological tricksters' adventures in the world of authority and prohibition. Such measures as stopping the flow of creativity by physically tying people's hands or covering their mouths with duct tape are simultaneously brutal and funny. They are narratively and ideologically similar to the myth of Zeus chaining Prometheus to a Caucasian rock or the story of the Norse gods locking the trickster Loki in a cave to prevent him from causing Ragnarök ('the doom of the gods'). Both these tricksters dared to challenge the power of the pantheon, and both were physically restrained (which, of course, is only one of the many forms of restraint by systemic structures).

My task in this book is to create a loose analytical paradigm that could be used to examine relationships between tricksters and systems, change and stability, in a wide range of social, political and cultural contexts. In order to assess the fragile balance between the tricksterish-individualistic on the one hand, and the cultural-systemic on the other, I employ a set of anthropological, psychotherapeutic and sociological theories. As far as psychology concepts are concerned, I use an integrative approach in my examination of the trickster, and bring together the work of several theorists including Heinz Kohut, Carl Jung and Donald Winnicott. Each psychology theory is a system in itself, and therefore has its limitations, gaps and shortcomings. My belief is that, as a complex psycho-anthropological concept and cultural phenomenon, the trickster cannot be trapped within a single theoretical framework, and it is therefore important to leave him some room for (theoretical) manoeuvre.[1] For instance, I employ the Jungian concept of the shadow to describe the personal, social and political effects of repressing the trickster; but equally I need Kohut's idea of the selfobject to show what happens to the individual or a group of people when elements of spontaneity and genuineness – essentially, trickster qualities – are absent from their lives.

Throughout this book I also use the trickster as a metaphor to trace the emergence and development of human identity as well as to examine the role of individuality in society. The trickster's childish impatience, his rapture and joy, his determination to break out of the narrow frame into which he was placed by the system, are all linked to the desire to become oneself – a psychological and intellectual entity that is independent from the social structure. Mythological tricksters are traditionally punished by gods for introducing havoc and change into what is otherwise a well-organised, tightly controlled and well-preserved order. Gods like to be in charge of the world, and therefore any aspiring trickster has to tread carefully when trying to introduce change into it. Authority has always wrestled with change – particularly with unplanned, sudden, unpredictable transformation.

Systems and structures prevalent in Western contexts differ greatly from both the ones used in pre-industrial settings and the ones employed by non-capitalist ideologies. Indeed, on the surface, modernity's systems seem to propagate freedom of choice and identity, and uphold independent thinking. Yet, their influence on the individual is not that dissimilar from their oppressive counterparts. Carl Jung did not write about 'the archetype of the system', and yet the system is such a universal entity that it can be promoted to the status of an archetype. Its aims remain the same throughout centuries, in different cultures, in different economic conditions and in different political climates. The system can be very oppressive or rather moderate, but its main purpose is always to keep the individual in check. In fact, it represents the Rousseauian social contract, which states that we exchange our illusory freedom for the safe and secure existence within a social structure.

---

[1] I should note that I use 'he' as a gender-neutral pronoun throughout this book when I refer to the trickster and the individual. This allows me to avoid clumsy grammatical constructions.

In a world that has shrunk thanks to the power of mass communications, and is now drowning in news, opinions, pictures and videos, the relationship between the individual and society is particularly acute. Even more acute in this unstable world, however, is the issue of identity – the problem of the self. The abundance of lifestyle choices does not help the individual to achieve better self-knowledge or self-reflection. Moreover, the choice further fragments and destabilises the individual. Expert systems (to use Anthony Giddens's term) exist to pull this broken individual together, to help him choose from the wide range of possible lifestyles and consumer choices the right one – yet they often lead to further confusion and bewilderment. Modernity has not resolved the conflict between systemic thinking and individual freedom. Modern contexts are populated by tricksters of all kinds, and it is these tricksters that I explore in this book.

Each chapter examines different aspects of the relationship between authority and the trickster. Chapter 1, 'The birth of shame', discusses the psycho-social origins of human personality through the trickster paradigm. It explores the importance of shame and other trickster-controlling and personality-framing devices both on the individual and societal levels. In this chapter I argue that human identity is the tricksterish by-product of the tension between individualist-narcissistic tendencies on the one hand, and the 'civilising' influence of society on the other. In order to 'tame' the 'primary omnipotence' (which can be destructive as well as creative), society uses limit-setting and boundary-creating tools such as shame, duty and morality. The result is the individual torn between self-expression on the one hand, and society's expectations on the other. For, after all, humans are social animals and cannot live without the support of the framework.

'The birth of shame' integrates a range of theoretical approaches. It uses anthropology and sociology (Victor Turner, Clifford Geertz and Pierre Bourdieu) as well as psychotherapy concepts, including Freudian and Jungian theories, the ideas of Melanie Klein, Donald Winnicott, Heinz Kohut and Mario Jacoby. This chapter prepares the base for further discussion of the trickster as an important element of society, as well as tracing its place in the psychology of the individual.

In Chapter 2, 'The arrival of Ragnarök', I further develop the argument (started in Chapter 1) that post-modernity is the age of the trickster as it is characterised by psychological fragmentation and the diminished roles of systems and frameworks. This chapter outlines the trickster's principal areas of influence in modern contexts. It argues that, on the surface of it, modernity is that very Ragnarök – the reign of the trickster – which Odin and other gods were so keen to prevent, and that the trickster permeates the interstices of western societies and inhabits their hidden corners. At the same time, I aim to show that the trickster's power in modern contexts is only illusory, and the system still reigns supreme.

Chapter 3, 'The trickster and the capitalist system' argues that capitalism is based on trickster psychology, and aims to show that it exploits the trickster for economic purposes. It discusses the concepts of choice, advertising, consumerism, objectification and narcissism in Western industrialised societies as well as linking the emergence of the middle class to the growing influence of trickster values (such as mobility – geographical as well as social) in society. This ability of the capitalist system to harvest creative trickster energies has always mesmerised me – primarily because in the Soviet Union the trickster had been consistently discarded as an undesirable element as it challenged the uniformity of prescribed thinking.

'The trickster and the capitalist system' links the themes of identity, emotional security and confidence started in Chapter 1, to the way the individual feels in a status-obsessed society. The system cannot operate or generate income when every human being has the same unchanging self-image throughout his life. Change – the economic trickster – is the foundation of the market economy. To analyse the role of the trickster in capitalism, I employ a range of anthropological concepts as well as Andrew Samuels's astute description of the market economy as the realm of Hermes, the Greek god of messengers, thieves and tradesmen.

Chapter 4, 'The media trickster', extends the trickster metaphor to mass communications, and traces its complex influence – including celebrity culture – on individual identity. In this chapter I argue that the media trickster, on the one hand, fragments and confuses individuals by offering them a multitude of lifestyles and identities. On the other hand, it provides people with temporary replacement identities in the form of celebrity figures and role models. In other words, it both destabilises and 'rebuilds' the individual using 'synthetic' identity parts. This chapter also contains discussion of the female trickster, and her creative and political impact on contemporary culture. In my analysis of the relationship between the individual and mass media I primarily employ the ideas of psychoanalyst Heinz Kohut (selfobjects), cultural philosopher Jean Baudrillard ('the system of objects' and the simulacrum) and Jungian analyst Mario Jacoby.

In Chapter 5, 'Creative rebellion', I explore the psychological origins of creativity and the trickster's impact on the life of the creative artist. I argue that the artist's mission in society is that of the trickster, challenging social, political and religious views, and renewing stale societal structures. In this chapter I employ a variety of psychoanalytic perspectives, including Freud and Jung's views on creativity, Melanie Klein's idea of the creative-destructive impulse, and Heinz Kohut's discussion of talent and charisma.

I believe that complex concepts are best explained using narratives; and films, being visual narratives, are particularly suitable for this purpose. Thus, in Chapter 1 I use Peter Weir's *The Truman Show* (1998) to illuminate the role of the trickster in human development. Chapter 2 uses Steve McQueen's *Shame* (2011) to discuss the issues of identity and relatedness. In Chapter 3, David Fincher's cult film *Fight Club* (1999) helps me examine the connection between the trickster and the market economy. Chapter 5 uses Milos Forman's masterpiece *Amadeus* (1984), which creatively rethinks the relationship between Mozart and his contemporaries to explain exchanges between the genius and the system.

Apart from the terminology borrowed from psychological, philosophical and anthropological theories (I did my best to integrate them and to ensure that they work well together, for some of them are conflicting), I invented my own discourse. It uses the trickster as a metaphor to describe the psycho-anthropological idea of change, an impulse that challenges the existing order of things, a progressive force that is a-structural and anti-structural in its nature. Throughout the book, and depending on the context, I call it 'the trickster' or 'trickster impulse'. I also interchangeably use the terms 'system', 'structure', 'framework', 'habitus', 'order' and 'authority' to indicate a generic, rule-making, power-containing, controlling construct of any size as opposed to the creative impulse, originating on the individual level and intrinsically lacking the mass-systemic degree of power and control. The construct can be as big and influential as a political ideology, or as small as a self-oppressive mind that stifles its own creative instincts and eliminates desire for change because these are 'dangerous' things.

Any framework needs executors of its will, and keepers of its rules and regulations. These executors are uncreative as well as blind in their intention to follow the existing rules. They tend to be unbending and lack empathy towards individual ambition and individual differences. I decided to call these elements of the system 'the frameworkers'. They are the trickster's main enemies. Some of them actively support and defend the framework; others sustain it inadvertently, by simply blindly obeying the rules. For instance, in the story about the Soviet nursery, the cruel nurses are the typical frameworkers, for (even though the systemic rules did not contain any directives requiring the use of wet towels as behaviour-modifying tools) they correctly understood and realised the principal aim of the political order – which was the creation of an obedient, passive individual. Their interpretation of the aims and objectives of the Soviet education was technically correct.

Throughout the book I attempt to explain why anyone would agree to become 'a frameworker'. The reasons to become the executor of a structure's will are very human and even understandable – it is a fast track to regaining or acquiring control over the outside world. Control lies at the heart of being human; it forms the base of human identity. Being 'a mature individual' means surrendering much of your control over the world to the familial/social/political habitus. Creativity – the ability to influence the world in a positive and constructive manner – is one way of regaining mastery over one's environment. Another way – uncreative and often destructive – is to control others via a pre-existent system of rules; to become a frameworker; to use the system to gain confidence at the expense of others. The frameworkers' narcissism is supported by the narcissism of the system. By contrast, the trickster is someone who prides himself on being out of control as well as creating havoc in the well-ordered world.

At the same time, this book is not a hymn to the trickster impulse. As anyone who is terrified of flying will confirm, we do not want 'an accidental', unpredictable impulse to govern our world. As children of modernity, we want to feel safe in the increasingly tricksterised, fragmenting world. We want to rely on the transport system to get us to work every morning. We want to know that, in case of a serious disaster, man-made and well-organised structures such as the police, healthcare systems and fire emergency services will respond effectively and on time. We want to live in a world in which criminals are punished and aggressive impulses are not openly expressed. We expect people to control their sexual instinct in public because we do not want to be harassed or raped. Modern public places are complex and dangerous, as is the hectic modern life, which implies that our behaviour should be regulated by a number of social protocols. In other words, we are supposed to subscribe to the Kantian Imperative that forms the moral base of any Western society. We want to feel protected and looked after, and the trickster impulse is certainly not a 'good enough parent' (to use Winnicott's term), for its aim is to destabilise – not to soothe or to protect. As such, the trickster is neither a positive nor an entirely negative psychological phenomenon. And neither, by the way, is its adversary – the system. The key is to create a balance between the two.

Two other terms invented to complete my trickster paradigm are 'narcissistic capital' and 'narcissistic exchange'. The first means the sum of the individual's achievements; an 'outward' price by which others judge the individual's social importance, and the second describes social interaction that takes into consideration the profitability or non-profitability of contact between the individuals. Both are meant to describe the different types of economic and personal relationships prevalent in modern contexts. These terms are helpful in examining close connection between the economic and the personal, as well as in tracing the strong influence of the socio-economic order on identity formation. Narcissistic capital is directly linked to identity issues and the problems of hierarchy, status and success. These are traditional 'trickster' values as mythological and folk tricksters typically show little respect for the existing hierarchy, often attempt to redefine success and like to reverse or challenge social status. They sometimes do this by criminal means (and in any case, any act of aggressive defiance would be deemed as criminal by the established framework). For instance, the baby Hermes steals fifty cattle from his famous half-brother Apollo, Prometheus snatches fire from Zeus, and Loki engineers the death of Odin's son Baldr. Their actions are spontaneous and unpredictable as compared to the smooth operation of systemic hierarchy, which they challenge.

All in all, my aim in this book was not to create a 'perfect', all-encompassing theory – for the trickster is the very opposite of all things perfect, ideal, absolute and flawless. The idea was to write a theory that would lend itself to a number of interpretations, and that could be applicable to a number of contexts. It is practical, applied, live – and therefore changeable and changing. As William Hynes, the co-editor of *Mythical Trickster Figures: Contours, Context and Criticisms* (Hynes and Doty, 1997) remarks, 'to define (de-finis) is to draw borders around phenomena, and tricksters seem amazingly resistant to such capture, they are notorious border breakers' (Hynes, 1993a: 33). Hynes also complains that his attempt to capture the trickster failed as the 'trickster theory' stubbornly refuses to be set in stone: 'the trickster is constantly disassembling and deconstructing this book' (1993a: 35). In trickster language, 'perfect' means 'imperfect', and vice versa. Nothing ideal could ever be alive.

Perfection is a narcissistic word. The trickster is the opposite of the never-attainable, dead narcissistic ideal. Besides, his genuine, spontaneous creativity is incompatible with the empty dream of perfection. The trickster is the process, not the final product.

Definitions of the trickster

Before we delve deeper into the psychology of the trickster impulse, its role in the formation of identity and its place in society, it is worth having a look at the history of 'trickster criticism' and sketching out the trickster's principal attributes.

Predictably, there have been numerous attempts to define the trickster. Scholars from all branches of the humanities have been trying the capture the essence of the stubborn psychosocial phenomenon and, to a degree, they were successful. Many of them agree that the trickster has a dual nature and is a sort of oxymoron combining opposing qualities.

For Carl Jung, the trickster is an archetype – that is, an archaic, universal image regularly occurring in myth, folk tales and dreams. In his seminal essay 'On the psychology of the trickster figure', Jung defines him as a creature of the unconscious, the wise fool, the clown, the delight-maker who has a dual nature: half-animal, half divine. Tricksters reverse the hierarchic order, are capable of changing shape and are famous for their malicious tricks and pranks. Jung also mentions the strong link between the trickster figure and the tradition of carnival, where the Devil appeared as *simia dei* – the ape of God (CW9/I: paras. 465–472). The trickster is both 'subhuman and superhuman, a bestial and divine being, whose chief and most alarming characteristic is his unconsciousness' (CW9/I: para. 472). Phylogenetically and anthropologically, he designates the dawn of civilisation and the origins of human consciousness; ontogenetically he symbolises a pre-conscious child, a creature who cannot be responsible for what he does because he is unaware of his actions. As such, he 'is a faithful reflection of an absolutely undifferentiated human consciousness, corresponding to a psyche that has hardly left the animal level' (CW9/I: para. 471).

The duality of the trickster's nature and his mutability are also emphasised by several cultural anthropologists. Paul Radin writes in the preface to *The Trickster: A Study in American Indian Mythology* (1956) that the trickster 'knows neither good nor evil yet he is responsible for both. He possesses no values, moral or social, is at the mercy of his passions and appetites, yet through his actions all values come into being' (Radin, 1972: xxiii). He also foreshadows 'the shape of man' (1972: xxiv).

Like Radin, Karl Kerenyi calls attention to that paradoxical 'creation through destruction' quality of the trickster. Mythological tricksters are silly and irresponsible; they may walk into an existing order of things and thoughtlessly ruin it – yet out of their careless actions a new life is born. As Kerenyi notes in his analysis of tricksters in Greek mythology, often the folk prankster 'approximates to the figure of a beneficent creator and becomes what the ethnologists call "a culture hero"' (cited in Radin, 1972: 180–181). Greek tricksters combine the sly and the stupid in them; in their behaviour we can discern both intention and lack of it. They symbolise the twilight of human consciousness:

> Prometheus, the benefactor of mankind, lacks self-interest and playfulness. Hermes has both, when he discovers fire and sacrifice before Prometheus

did – without, however, bothering about mankind. In the playful cruelties which the little god practiced on the tortoise and the sacrificial cows at his first theft, and which conferred no benefit on mankind, . . . we see the sly face of the trickster grinning at us, whereas in the deeds of Prometheus we see the sly and the stupid at once.

(1972: 181)

The French anthropologist Laura Makarius seeks to explain the trickster's contradictory nature by linking him to the sphere of ritual magic. According to her, he is a taboo-breaker and violator of prohibitions, and 'can only retain the contradictions inherent in the violation itself' (Hynes and Doty, 1997: 73).

Apart from the Promethean (and oxymoronic) role as an inadvertent culture hero, the mythological trickster has other functions in society. Most scholars agree that the trickster figure serves as a chaos-inducing element intent on challenging the existing order of things. As such, it is neither good nor bad but is a weapon that can be used to modify a rotten order or to destroy a good one. Dealing with the trickster is like a balancing act. For instance, the folklorist Barbara Babcock-Abrahams argues that the trickster is responsible for 'the tolerated margin of mess'; he is the kind of creature who does not respect rules, restrictions and regulations: 'Although we laugh at him for his troubles and his foolishness and are embarrassed by his promiscuity, his creative cleverness amazes us and keeps alive the possibility of transcending the social restrictions we regularly encounter' (Babcock-Abrahams, 1975: 147). Likewise, Andrew Samuels calls attention to the trickster's ability to revive the 'civilizing forces' of society by shaking them up (either in a positive or a negative sense). As such, this figure 'acts as a yardstick and spur to consciousness' (Samuels, 1993: 83).

An interesting point is brought forth by Mac Linscott Ricketts who writes that the trickster figure is 'the symbol of the self-transcending mind of humankind and of the human quest for knowledge and the power that knowledge brings' (Hynes and Doty, 1997: 88). Interestingly enough, Ricketts calls the trickster 'a primitive humanist' whose structure-challenging antics are psychosocially equal to the democratic attitude characteristic of modernity:

Unlike the shaman, the priest, and the devotee of supernaturalistic religion, the trickster looks to no 'power' outside himself, but sets out to subdue the world by his wits and his wit. In other words, as I see him, the trickster is a symbolic embodiment of the attitude today represented by the humanist.

(1997: 88–89)

Other scholars recognise the trickster's role in identity formation: by challenging the structure, by rejecting it and by laughing at it, we find our own unique way of living and of doing things. For instance, Robert Pelton emphasises the positive outcomes of the trickster's ability to challenge dominant structures, which can be destructive and oppressive. He notes in *The Trickster of West Africa* that the trickster can be regarded as a 'process designed to *combat* darkness by bringing to light the causes of disorder' (1980: 286). Pelton brings together the creative and destructive traits of the trickster when he states that this figure represents the human race both phylogenetically and ontogenetically. Moreover – more than anything it is also an all-encompassing metaphor of human development and learning. Both individually and communally, the trickster seizes the fragments of his experience and discovers in them 'an order sacred by its very wholeness' (1980: 21).

Thus, the trickster describes the process of individual development and meaning-making in relation to a socialising and civilising structure. As a psycho-anthropological phenomenon, it is of paramount importance for the balance between the social and the personal in the individual's life. In her book *The Female Trickster: the Mask that Reveals* (2007), Ricki Stephanie Tannen links this figure to Jung's idea of 'individuation' – the process 'by which individual beings are formed and differentiated' (CW6: para. 757). In particular, it is 'the development of the psychological individual as a being distinct from the general, collective psychology. Individuation, therefore, is a process of differentiation, having for its goal the development of the individual personality' (CW6: para. 757). Tannen writes: 'Trickster energy is the archetypal energy of individuation – for a culture as well as an individual' (Tannen, 2007: 3).

In *Wild/Lives: Trickster, Place and Liminality on Screen* (2009) Terrie Waddell expresses a similar view when she argues that the trickster is 'an archetypal agent of change with the potential to guide us through each jolting shift in the process of growing up' (Waddell, 2009: 1). As such, it is an important narrative element because 'with its enthusiasm for peeling away outer facades and exposing emotional vulnerabilities, trickster, as a conductor of change, is a potent driver of stories dabbling in enforced self-examination' (2009: xi).

Common motifs in trickster narratives

Most trickster narratives (mythological, literary or cinematic) share a number of stock themes and motifs that serve as the backbone for the plot. Usually, a trickster narrative starts with the cunning creature being or feeling restricted (often physically), goes on to describe the trickster's escape and his adventures, and ends with the dissolution/transformation of the trickster. The most common structural elements of trickster narratives are being trapped, boundary-breaking, creativity, licentious behaviour, scatological humour, bodily transformations (shapeshifting), the presence of animals (which I prefer to call 'the animal connection'), naming issues, loss of control over one's body and mind, and the trickster's dissolution/death/transformation at the end of the story. Not all of the elements can be present in one story, film or myth, and their place in the narrative sequence is certainly not fixed. However, the 'end result' of trickster narratives is invariable: forced transformation of the protagonist via chance and loss of control. In other words, the protagonist achieves a new 'status' via sudden destructuralisation and change.

Being trapped

Physical entrapment in narratives is an allegory of control and order. It symbolises the structure's desire for being in charge. The trickster that is not controlled is a menace as, unrestrained and therefore unpredictable, it can damage or even destroy the system. Neither the systemic control nor the trickster's actions aimed at blocking it are intrinsically good or bad. In fact, the 'being trapped' motif foregrounds the balance between stability and change. Tricksters can be trapped at any stage throughout the narrative, and when they are locked up, this is usually as a punishment for some misbehaviour such as theft, lying or murder. When a narrative starts with the trickster freeing itself from his prison, the rest of the narrative is devoted to the characters' efforts to regain control over the situation and to recapture or tame him.

Restrained tricksters can be presented as suffering and heroic, malevolent and dangerous or playful and stupid – but their task is always to defy and dupe the system. Their transgressions are also of differing importance. For instance, Prometheus is an example of a heroic prisoner; Loki, who directly threatens to bring down the pantheon, is a malevolent one; and the Native American tricksters Wakdjunkaga and Coyote, who find themselves trapped inside a dead animal's skull, are foolish and impudent. Imprisonment inside the belly of a monster, giant fish or whale, with subsequent escape, is one of the most popular versions of this motif.

The entrapment metaphor also describes the destructive potential of the trickster, who becomes more powerful the longer he is kept inside his cage. If neglected by the system, change tends to accumulate and grow. The Arabic trickster, Sakr al-Jinni from *One Thousand and One Arabian Nights* is stuffed into a jar and sent drifting in the open ocean for rebelling against King Suleiman. There he remains for two thousand years during which time he is 'washed and swashed like a lake squeezed into a cup or a whale squeezed into an egg'. When a fisherman happens to catch the bottle with his net and break its seal, Jinni describes to him how his rage and despair increased with time:

> For the first hundred years I swore that if anyone freed me from the copper bottle I would grant him three wishes – however greedy.
>
> But nobody came.
>
> For the next two hundred years I swore that if anyone freed me from the copper bottle I would give him and all his tribe everlasting riches.
>
> But nobody came.
>
> For the next five hundred years I swore that if anyone freed me from the copper bottle I would make him ruler and owner of all the people of earth!
>
> But nobody came.
>
> For the next thousand years I swore . . . and I swore, but now my oaths were terrible. My patience was gone, my fury was bigger than the ocean I was

floating in. I swore that if anyone freed me from the copper bottle (*unless, of course, it was the all-powerful lord Suleiman*) I would make him the first to feel the scourge of my revenge! My old enemies are long since dead. You will have the honour of standing in their place while I cut you to atoms! I have sworn it.

(McCaughrean, 1999: 35–36)

The folk tradition of depicting the birth of the trickster as a powerful and uncontrollable event is astutely noted by the French humanist writer François Rabelais (1494–1553) in his book *Gargantua and Pantagruel*. The story of the giant Gargantua begins with his birth 'in a strange manner' wherein he escapes his mother's body through the ear because the lower part of her body is rendered intractable by an anti-diarrhoeal drug:

Then suddenly came the midwives from all quarters, who groping her below, found some peloderies, which was a certain filthy stuff, and of a taste truly bad enough. This they thought had been the child, but it was her fundament, that was slipped out with the mollification of her straight entrail, which you call the bum-gut, and that merely by eating of too many tripes, as we have showed you before. Whereupon an old ugly trot in the company, who had the repute of an expert she-physician, and was come from Brisepaille, near to Saint Genou, three score years before, made her so horrible a restrictive and binding medicine, and whereby all her larris, arse-pipes, and conduits were so oppilated, stopped, obstructed, and contracted, that you could hardly have opened and enlarged them with your teeth, which is a terrible thing to think upon; seeing the Devil at the mass at Saint Martin's was puzzled with the like task, when with his teeth he had lengthened out the parchment whereon he wrote the tittle-tattle of two young mangy whores. By this inconvenient the cotyledons of her matrix were presently loosed, through which the child sprang up and leaped, and so, entering into the hollow vein, did climb by the diaphragm even above her shoulders, where the vein divides itself into two, and from thence taking his way towards the left side, issued forth at her left ear. As soon as he was born, he cried not as other babes use to do, Miez, miez, miez, miez, but with a high, sturdy, and big voice shouted about, Some drink, some drink, some drink, as inviting all the world to drink with him. The noise hereof was so extremely great, that it was heard in both the countries at once of Beauce and Bibarois. I doubt me, that you do not thoroughly believe the truth of this strange nativity. Though you believe it not, I care not much: but an honest man, and of good judgment, believeth still what is told him, and that which he finds written.

(Rabelais, 2004: 56)

Rabelais is well aware of the profanity of this image and its references to the Virgin Birth, and hurries to put forth a disclaimer:

Is this beyond our law or our faith—against reason or the holy Scripture? For my part, I find nothing in the sacred Bible that is against it. But tell me, if it had been the will of God, would you say that he could not do it? Ha, for favour sake, I beseech you, never emberlucock or inpulregafize your spirits with these vain thoughts and idle conceits; for I tell you, it is not impossible with God, and, if he pleased, all women henceforth should bring forth their children at the ear.

(Rabelais, 2004: 56)

Meanwhile, Loki the Norse trickster should be locked up because his rebellious-ness and unpredictability might cause Ragnarök. When it arrives, 'the world will be in uproar, the air quaking with booms and blares and their echoes', and all the monsters and giants will be released from Hel, the 'realm of the dead' (Crossley-Holland, 1993: 171). Therefore, Loki is captured, placed into a cave, strapped to stone slabs, and a snake is placed above him which keeps dripping poison onto his face. For all his cleverness and wit, Loki has lost the fight and has to surrender. All he can do now is wait for the right moment to escape:

Sigyn [his wife] holds a wooden bowl over Loki's face and slowly it fills with the snake's venom. When it is brimming, Sigyn carries the bowl away and empties it into a rock basin – a fermenting pool of poison.

Loki is left unguarded. He screws up his eyes. The snake does not wait. Its venom splashes on to Loki's face and in torment he shudders and writhes. He cannot escape and the whole earth quakes.

Loki lies bound. This is how things are and how things will remain until Ragnarök.

(1993: 169–170)

Overall, 'being trapped' is an important structural element that embodies a psycho-anthropological counterweight to the system's authoritativeness and exactitude.

Boundary-breaking

Tricksters are notorious boundary-breakers. In myth, folk tales and literary and cinematic narratives they cross all kinds of boundaries, from physical (such as property borders) to metaphysical (for instance, sacred cultural values and taboos). Metaphorically, this means that the trickster has no respect for the structural aspect of the social. Neither does he respect the *structuring* function of the system. He does not accept 'the way things are', and keeps attempting to re-draw the map. Civilisation is born with the emergence of boundaries, physical as well as psychological: rules of decency and propriety, property borders, psychological boundaries, etc. Boundaries separate the unconscious, pre-civilised man (or child) from an adult member of community, conscious of his actions and prepared to take responsibility for them. It is these boundaries that the trickster keeps challenging and disregarding.

In classical mythology, the trickster is often depicted as a *psychopomp*, a mythical conductor of souls to the nether regions. The Greek Hermes and the Roman Mercurius are both psychopomps; in many other trickster stories the right to cross the boundary between life and death is designated as immortality. The role of the psychopomp emphasises the trickster's transcendent qualities, among which is the ability to transgress the frontier between consciousness and the unconscious.

The trickster's boundary-breaking and map re-drawing activities can be malicious, playful or heroic – and sometimes all three at once. For instance, the Yoruba trickster Eshu makes two sworn friends quarrel when he paints one half of his cap white and the other black, and then rides between the two men on his horse so that each of them can only see one side of the cap. The neighbours, naturally, start arguing about the cap's colour (Pelton, 1980: 141).

The tricksters are also notorious taboo breakers. Taboo-breaking in fairytales ensures that no corners of the structure remain unexplored (and therefore too tempting and attractive for visitors). For instance, in one Lipan Apache fairytale, the trickster Coyote breaks two taboos simultaneously: incest and necrophilia. He makes a powder out of his dead wife's genitals, puts it in a pouch and uses it for masturbation. One day his sons find the keepsake and start experimenting with the powder too:

> They stood around and sprinkled the powder on their penises. It caused erections and orgasms, and they were ejaculating in all directions. Just then Coyote came in and found them at it. He was very angry. He scolded them and beat them. 'It was just for myself', he said. 'You had no business taking it'. Which of you did it work on?
>
> 'It didn't work on me', the smallest son said. 'No white stuff came out, though my penis grew big. I had only a pouch'.
>
> *(Erdoes and Ortiz, 1999: 65–66)*

In this profoundly Oedipal story several levels of authority are defied and several kinds of outrageous tricksterism take place: the father breaks a social taboo and has 'sex' with his dead wife, and the sons 'copulate' with their mother in a sort of 'group sex' session. As the boys grow up, they 'challenge' the father who promptly punishes them and leads them back into the social order. Thus, the order is restored and civilisation is 'saved' from the ruinous influence of the trickster.

Many tricksters are shameless thieves – which means transgressing one of the basic frontiers ever invented by civilisation – private property. Hermes steals Apollo's cattle and Prometheus steals Zeus's fire. A Native American trickster Yehl the Raven is lazy and greedy. He appropriates a whole load of treasures – food, finest furs and walrus ivory – which he finds on a seemingly abandoned island. For his misdeeds he is grabbed by invisible hands that start suffocating him with supernatural strength as a hundred voices whisper: 'Give it back, give it all back!' (Erdoes and Ortiz, 1999: 249).

Theft of fire is a popular motif that is shared by trickster cycles all around the world. Apart from the Greek Prometheus, there are numerous tricksters who dare to steal fire (a metaphor representing knowledge and civilisation) from a powerful deity and deliver it to the people. The boundary separating the little trickster from the celestial keeper of fire is enormous – but tricksters, being fearless and shameless are generally prepared to cross it. For instance, Coyote from a Klamath tale plucks up courage to challenge the highest and most powerful deity – Thunder, despite the latter being a 'fearful being'. Moreover, Coyote chooses the worst possible time for his cunning deed:

> There was a time when people had no fire. In winter they could not warm themselves. They had to eat their food raw. Fire was kept inside a huge white rock and belonged to Thunder, who was its caretaker. Thunder was a fearful being. Everybody was afraid of him. Even Bear and Mountain Lion trembled when they heard Thunder's rumbling voice.
>
> Coyote was not afraid of Thunder. He was afraid of nothing. One day, Thunder was in an angry mood and roared and rumbled his loudest, so that the earth trembled and all animals went into hiding. Coyote decided that this was the time to get the fire away from Thunder.
>
> *(Erdoes and Ortiz, 1999: 18)*

Tricksters' compulsive desire to cross and break boundaries has both 'high' and 'low' meanings. On the one hand, the trickster is a pre-civilised, shameless creature incapable of belonging to the system and following the rules laid out for everyone. On the other, he is someone capable of challenging a structure precisely because he does not know its true value and is not afraid of its power. The trickster simply has no respect for the structure.

Shapeshifting

Tricksters are notorious shapeshifters. They frequently change their appearance, transform into various animals and objects – even change their sex. Parts of their bodies fall off, but they grow back or can be reattached onto the body. The trickster's hands, legs, penis and anus all have minds of their own and 'do what they want'. Tricksters' bodies are fluid and malleable, and it is hard to damage them 'permanently'. For instance, the trickster Veeho from a Cheyenne tale loses his buttocks for 'giving unasked advice' and being too curious. One day he passes a giant who is uprooting trees in order to make arrows out of them. Veeho is curious as to how trees can be used as arrows, and asks the giant for a demonstration. The tree hits Veeho on the bottom, and his buttocks fall off. The giant kindly collects them and slam them against Veeho's backside. They grow back into their place instantly.

The only problem is – he now has his left buttock on the right side, and his right buttock on the left side (Erdoes and Ortiz, 1999: 152).

Following Radin's and Joseph Henderson's argument, the trickster is an incomplete individual, a fluid transitory path from animal to human (Jung and von Frantz, 1964: 103–104). A creature steeped in 'primary omnipotence', he thinks he is part of the world, and therefore can hardly be expected to be fully responsible for his body's actions. While a fully-fledged individual (ideally) feels psychologically complete, the trickster is not entirely aware of his physical and psychological fragmentedness. The Winnebago trickster Wakdjunkaga, for instance, becomes very surprised when different parts of his body behave as if they were autonomous. One night he wakes up and realises that the blanket is missing:

> He sees it floating above him, and only gradually recognizes that it is resting on his huge penis erectus. Here we are brought back again to the Wakdjunkaga whose right hand fights with his left, who burns his anus and eats his own intestines, who endows the parts of his body with independent existence and who does not realize their proper functions, where everything takes place of its own accord, without his volition. 'This is always happening to me' – he tells his penis.
>
> *(Radin, 1972: 136)*

It is not easy to damage a trickster permanently, for his very power lies in his unconsciousness. When murdered or challenged by gods, giants or natural powers, tricksters tend to spring back to life or rebuild themselves from scratch. For instance, the Argentinean trickster Tokwa transforms into a tree and a gourd in an attempt to escape the great flood he accidentally caused. The water uproots the tree, and smashes the gourd into pieces. But 'such beings as he' – the tale goes – 'can't stay dead'. Naturally, he revives himself and goes on to introduce other big changes to the world, including the invention of fire (Sherman, 1996: 100–101).

Many tricksters lack a stable sense of sexual identity. Coyote, Loki, Wakdjunkaga, Nixant and Uncle Tompa all change into women (usually to fool other women, and then catch them off guard). Some of them just cross-dress; others undergo 'proper' transformations. The shapeshifter Loki transforms into an old woman in order to catch the goddess Frigg off guard, and find out from her what object might hurt the otherwise indestructible Balder (it is mistletoe) (Crossley-Holland, 1993: 149).

Loki's Northern American colleague Nixant puts a on a woman's dress and approaches two young women crossing a stream. They are amazed to see a female with very hairy legs and something big dangling under her dress. When they question Nixant about the strange dangling thing, he replies:

'It's a love root'.

They got to the other bank of the river. They laid down to rest. 'This love root of yours', said one of the girls, 'what do you use it for?'

'Oh, it's good for whatever ails you – aches and pains, a sickness. Even if you're not sick, it makes you feel good'.

'Do you cook it or eat it raw?'

'No, no, it only works if you stick it up between your legs. Here, let me show you'.

He showed it to them. He did this several times. 'You are right', said the girls. 'This root makes one feel good'.

(Erdoes and Ortiz, 1999: 162)

If need be, tricksters can also pretend to be 'professional people'. This is usually happens when tricksters are in a survival mode. For instance, the European trickster Tyl Eulenspiegel runs out of money and presents himself as a famous painter to a group of unsuspecting aristocrats. He shows them a blank wall and claims that those who bear at least one drop of lowly blood, peasant blood, will not be able to see the paintings. Needless to say, none of the aristocrats dares to admit that the paintings do not exist. In another tale of survival, belonging to the Liberian Vai people, Lion captures two friends – Cat and Goat. Cat proclaims himself to be a dancer, and escapes over the wall; while Goat claims to be a doctor, and sends Lion to kill Leopard in order to create a special 'medical pendant'. He also escapes while the stupid Lion is away trying to catch Leopard (Abrahams, 1983: 197).

Shapeshifting is closely linked to the issues of shame and identity, while the theme of resurrection metaphorically represents the individuating, identity-making component of the trickster impulse. The 'simple' tricksters such as Coyote and Raven have no concept of shame and no stable vision of themselves, and therefore lie and deceive without any qualms. However, the tricksters who use deception and shapeshifting for survival purposes (such as Tyl) – and particularly in tales discussing the matters of social class – discard shame in order to reclaim their identity from the system.

The problem of the name

Another common moment that trickster narratives tend to share is preoccupation with the way human identity is formed. Tricksters – as they are pre-conscious creatures – are often obsessed with their name and status. The trickster's name (or names) is his passport into the world. Paul Radin links the process of naming, and the name as a concept, to the individual's status in his community. He postulates that the Winnebago trickster Wakdjunkaga takes much interest in his name, which translates as 'a foolish one'. 'In Winnebago society', Radin writes, 'a child has no legal existence, no status, until he receives a name' (Radin, 1972: 135). Throughout his silly adventures, Wakdjunkaga keeps repeating his name to himself as if asserting his – albeit low – existence. For instance, after mistaking a tree stump for a man, he says: 'Yes indeed, it is on this account that the people call me Wakdjunkaga, the foolish one! They are right!' (1972: 134).

Similarly, Anansi the Spider from a Jamaican tale does not like the fact that he is 'a nobody', and that 'nothing at all is named after him', for he is only small and insignificant compared to other animals. Meanwhile, it is Tiger who is considered to be the greatest of all the animals:

> 'This will never do', Anansi said to himself. 'I won't stay a nobody, not me!'
>
> And he went to Tiger, and told him, very politely, 'I have a favour to ask of you, Mighty One'.
>
> Tiger yawned, showing off his sharp fangs. 'What would you ask?'
>
> 'Many things are named after you because you are such a powerful beast. I would like something to be named after me, too'.
>
> 'And what is that?' Tiger asked, flicking his tail impatiently.
>
> 'Oh, I would like something very small, very unimportant. I would like to have stories named after me'.
>
> Stories? How silly, Tiger thought, how very weak and small and silly! Just as weak and small and silly as this spider!
>
> *(Sherman, 1996: 140)*

What Anansi the Spider wants, in fact, is popularity and fame. He wants to be noticed. He wants his name to be known. This is certainly pertinent for our discussion of the mass media and its influence on the celebrity culture, and of the contemporary individual's compulsion to become visible in a mass of people. The impulse 'to be someone', to be visible, to have an impact on the world is a big part of the trickster impulse. On the one hand, the trickster is psychologically backwards and still swimming in the darkness of primary omnipotence. On the other, he starts to realise, albeit still dimly, that he is one of the many, and that being visible in this world would involve making serious efforts. Becoming an individual is also a difficult task because the individuating force, mighty and impulsive as it is, the minute it bursts out, is met with the cold and secure wall of systemic thinking. To show to your community or society that you have a name, or that you truly stand out from the crowd, might prove to be a serious feat. Anansi the Spider does it, though, when he completes the difficult tasks set to him by Tiger, and gains the right to have stories named after him.

Creationism

Tricksters tend to be madly, unstoppably creative. Often their creative activities are linked to the birth of the world. Their creativity is not human – not directed, conscious and framed – but spontaneous, wild and random. It is the opposite of the system in that it is free and unframed. Like their endless tricks, it is part of their playful attitude towards the world. They are capable of re-arranging their surroundings, and adapting them to suit themselves. The new order is born out of mischief and play.

For instance, in a short Yokuts tale, Coyote and Eagle create the earth and people, and teach humans to fend for themselves. In a Zuni tale, Coyote accidentally 'invents' winter by opening a box he is prohibited to open. The box contains the moon (Erdoes and Ortiz, 1999: 6). In another tale, belonging to Miwok, Coyote steals the sun, thus creating day and night. He is also responsible for designing human beings (1999: 6–16). The Argentinian Tokwa 'changes the face of the world' by freeing the waters encased within one mighty bottle (Sherman, 1996: 100). Often tricksters create new power arrangements by stealing fire from assorted gods and giants – Prometheus is the best known example of this but there are also numerous ethnic tricksters who do the same, for instance, the Filipino prankster Lam-ang (1996: 85). Thus they empower people and re-draw the power balance between gods and humans (and between the unlimited powers of the unconscious and the still frail human consciousness).

William Hynes in *Mythological Trickster Figures* (Hynes and Doty, 1997) links the 'creationist' motifs in trickster tales with scatological references also prevalent in them:

> [A]ll creative intentions are ultimately excreta. Like the mystic who constantly reminds us that no words or doctrinal construct can express adequately the ineffable nature of God, the trickster reminds us that no one creative ordering can capture life. In so far as an ordering continues to express life, it continues to be viable. If not viable, such ordering will drop away, be replaced with new productivities, or this ordering will work to repeal their potential replacements.
>
> *(Hynes, 1993b: 216)*

The randomness of the creative process is related to the trickster's ability to challenge the system – and, particularly, to his ability to renew it when it goes into the stale mode. As Christopher Vecsey argues, 'by breaking the patterns of culture the trickster helps define those patterns. By acting irresponsibly, he helps define responsibility. He threatens, yet he teaches too. He throws doubt on realities but helps concentrate attention on realities' (cited in Hynes and Doty, 1997: 106). The trickster's use of playful creativity to 'change reality' by creating new rules is further discussed in Chapter 5, which examines the various kinds of stand-offs between the frameworkers and the creative impulse.

Loss of control

On the one hand, the trickster's psyche and body are so fluid that he does not always have control over them. On the other hand, he can play tricks with human beings and cause *them* to lose control over *their* minds and bodies. The 'loss of control' metaphor renders the idea of the interdependence of consciousness and the unconscious. The undercivilised trickster is silly and childlike, and therefore can be easily deceived; but the very adult-like 'consciousness' can become so confident in its over-inflated 'wisdom' and 'maturity' that its vision becomes dangerously narrow. A stagnant vision and loss of perspective makes consciousness vulnerable for the traps set up by the unconscious.

The problem of control is symbiotically connected with the issue of shame. Mythological tricksters, being metaphorically pre-individual, do not claim to have control over their bodies or actions. Things always happen to the trickster – like they do to the Winnebago trickster Wakdjunkaga who regularly loses control over his body and does not take responsibility for his actions. He does a number of stupid things and is not ashamed of looking silly or being considered stupid by his social environment, primarily because the concept of the social environment – the world of separate 'objects' – is not yet known to him. Paul Radin writes:

> The cycle begins with an incident found in no other version, namely Wakdjunkaga pictured as the chief of the tribe, giving a warbundle feast on four different days. He, although host and consequently obligated to stay to the very end, is described as leaving the ceremony in order to cohabit with a woman, an act which is absolutely forbidden for those participating in a warbundle feast. On the fourth day he stays to the end and invites all the participants in the feast to accompany him by boat. Hardly has he left the shore when he returns and destroys his boat as useless. At this piece of stupidity some of his companions leave him. He then starts on foot, but after a short time destroys his warbundle and his arrowbundle and finds himself eventually deserted by everyone and alone; alone, that is, as far as human beings and society are concerned. With the world of nature he is still in contact. He calls all objects, so our text tells us, younger brothers. He understands them; they understand him.
>
> *(Radin, 1972: 132–133)*

Wakdjunkaga often experiences problems with various body parts being unruly and even quarrelsome. For instance, his hands start fighting with each other in the middle of killing a buffalo:

> In the midst of these operations suddenly his left arm grabbed the buffalo. 'Give that back to me, it is mine! Stop that or I will use my knife on you!' So spoke the right arm. 'I will cut you to pieces, this is what I will do to you', continued the right arm. Thereupon the left arm released its hold. But, shortly after, the left arm grabbed hold of the right arm. This time it grabbed hold of his wrist just at the moment that the right arm had commenced to skin the buffalo. Again and again this was repeated. In this manner did the Trickster make both his arms quarrel.
>
> *(Radin, 1972: 8)*

Tricksters play practical jokes on their victims, but are often deceived and duped in return. For instance, Odysseus, despite being a famously cunning fellow, repeatedly falls prey to women's fatal charms (including the Sirens and the enchantress Circe). Similarly (albeit in a more low-brow key), the Native American tricksters Nixant, Coyote and Wakdjunkaga often fail to control their male organs whenever they see a pretty female – or sometimes *any* female. Uncontrolled tricksters not 'framed' by boundaries are often presented in tales as dangerous: in a Wayao tale from East Africa a leopard abuses the hospitality of a bushbuck by gradually pushing her boundaries. He starts off by pretending to be ill and asking to be taken into her home. Then he begins to ask for small favours, his appetites grow, and he eventually eats everyone in the antelope's house, including the hostess (Abrahams, 1983: 197).

When tricksters play their tricks on humans, gods and 'powerful persons', they show the power of chance and choice over rational frameworks and established orders. They also remind people that the individual is never truly perfect or complete, and that control over one's mind and body – as well as control over one's surroundings – has to be constantly maintained and observed.

The trickster's dissolution

In many trickster tales – and this is particularly noticeable in large cycles containing a series of trickster transformations – the trickster spirit is dissolved at the end of the narrative. After the creative, chaotic unconscious energy has been woken up for the purpose of disrupting the stale (personal or social) order, it must go back to its dark wellspring. The trickster impulse does not die but is absorbed by the personality structure, and becomes an essential part of the individuating forces that would later closely guard the balance between the personal and the social in the individual's life. The trickster energy is still alive underneath the structuring forces of the social order.

One of the common narrative sequences in the trickster genre is 'trickster tamed'. The narrative opens with the release of the trickster from a small and stifling place, and ends with the trickster being under control again. The story of the jinni, in all its varieties, is a good example of this. Prometheus and Loki are imprisoned by the gods because their actions are potentially lethal for the existing order. Native American tricksters Coyote, Raven, Wakdjunkaga, Veeho and Nixant are often punished by what the tales indicate as 'powerful people'. The dissolution of the trickster at the end of a tale or cycle of tales is linked to his shapeshifting and boundary-crossing abilities. For instance, in one particular story Coyote plays the role of the psychopomp, visits the land of the dead and attempts to revive all the spirits he finds there. He takes them to the land of the living, but they escape on the way (Erdoes and Ortiz, 1999: 15). Coyote grows sad, but eventually accepts the limitations to his magic abilities (sheds his 'primary omnipotence').

Radin notes that, as the Wakdjunkaga cycle progresses, the protagonist acquires more human traits, starts scrutinising and analysing his actions, and the raconteur begins to define his physical appearance and character traits with better precision:

He is now to be shown emerging out of his complete isolation and lack of identity, and as becoming aware of himself and the world around him. He has learned that both right and left hands belong to him, that both are to be used and that his anus is part of himself and cannot be treated as something independent of him. He realises, too, that he is being singled out, even if only to be ridiculed, and he has begun to understand why he is called Wakd-junkaga. [...] He is now to be given the intestines and anus of the size and shape which man is to have.

(Radin, 1972: 136)

The 'taming of the trickster', or his dissolution, signifies the victory of the civilising forces over the dark powers of the unconscious. It also shows that the trickster impulse can be dangerous, needs to be used sparingly – and only for the purposes of regeneration and renewal.

The trickster's licentiousness

Another prominent feature of the trickster is his obsession with sex. Because he is a shapeshifter and breaker of taboos, he is capable of having sex with virtually any object. For the trickster, sex is a very vague notion and is certainly not subject to control or prohibitions – or even the strictest taboos. Most cultures have a cata-logue of 'indecent' fairytales containing the sexual adventures of rogues and fools. For instance, both Northern American Coyote and Wakdjunkaga cycles include stories that depict the tricksters as oversexed owners of uncontrollable penises, whereas Russian fairytales of the 'indecent' kind often portray cunning peasant males duping unsuspecting females into having sex with them.

The trickster's hyper-virility, which he cannot control, has several psycho-social functions. The trickster is a pre-conscious, pre-shame creature incapable of managing his own instincts and systematically failing to tame his unruly body parts. Psycho-logically he is an 'omnipotent' baby – hence his indifference to the behaviour-framing tools (primarily shame) employed by the civilising forces of the habitus. As such, he is both a fool and a revolutionary – depending on the context and on the qualities of the structure he rejects in a particular narrative. On the one hand, the sexual motif shows to the audience the difference between the proper, adult behav-iour and the behaviour before the onset of shame. The audience laughs at the stupid trickster because they can clearly see the 'civilising' boundary, which protects them from the dark contents of the unconscious, thus ensuring the safety and stability of the social structure. On the other hand, many trickster narratives employ the sexual motif to challenge a social structure whose oppressiveness stretches beyond the essen-tial rules of decency and propriety. In this case the trickster uses the power of sexual-ity metaphorically. As a fundamental anti-structural force with unlimited destructive potential, the sexual instinct is a constant threat to the structuring forces of society.

Often, however, the virility motif in fairytales and myths depicts defiance that is stupid and unwise, and therefore has to be punished and tamed by behaviour-modifying tools (usually by exposure and shame). For instance, Nixant the trickster from a fairytale belonging to the Northern American tribe Gros Ventre, is endowed with a giant talking penis, which has the inconvenient habit of speaking at the wrong moments and giving away its owner. The chatty penis is a punishment for misusing a hunting song that was supposed to be used only once during the hunting months, and that Nixant foolishly sang all the time. Every time Nixant says a lie, he is immediately confronted by his penis:

> Nixant felt like copulating. He noticed some young women digging wild turnips. He called out to them: 'You girls, come over here. I want to dance for you'.

> His penis stood up and shouted: 'You girls, do not come. He only wants to abuse you! Stay away'. The young women ran off. Nixant was angry and embarrassed.

> Nixant sat among a circle of warriors. He boasted of the great deeds he had done.

> The penis swelled up and said: 'Nixant had not done these things. He is a liar. He never fights'. The penis laughed. Then everybody laughed. Nixant was ashamed.

> *(Erdoes and Ortiz, 1999: 161)*

Curiously, it is the trickster-penis that performs the shaming function and therefore has the boundary-making influence of civilisation. Eventually, the acceptance into society is achieved via the taming of sexuality as well as the taming of primary psychological omnipotence: Nixant goes to the sorcerer who had made his penis talk in the first place, repents and asks for a remedy. The sorcerer (or 'the powerful man', as he is described in the narrative) prescribes him to co-habit with a very ugly woman. Not surprisingly, it works very well, and the penis becomes obedient – although, because the loss of omnipotence motif is psychologically equal to the loss of paradise, both Nixant and his penis are described as being sad and depressed. Being civilised is no fun:

> Nixant went to the ugly woman's tipi. He went inside. He stayed there for a long time. They did something in there. Nixant was not smiling when he came out of the ugly woman's tipi. He looked grim, but after that his penis never talked again.

> 'How did the ugly woman cure you?' a friend asked.

> 'I don't want to talk about it', said Nixant.

> *(Erdoes and Ortiz, 1999: 161)*

Other Native American tricksters are as sexually voracious as Nixant. Wakdjunkaga from the Winnebago cycle has an enormous penis that he carries on his back

(Radin, 1972: 142), and Coyote transforms his male organ into various harmless things such as fish and stalks, which tend to penetrate unsuspecting women (Erdoes and Ortiz, 1999: 55). Wakdjunkaga's penis is eventually gnawed down by a chipmunk and attains its human size, which, like the story about Nixant's unruly penis, symbolises crossing the boundary into consciousness and becoming fully human (Radin, 1972: 142).

Ancient Greek culture also linked the idea of virility to the idea of laughter. Greek comedy actors of the classical age (the fifth century BC) wore costumes that were generally gross and uncouth. People in the audience had nothing against the fact that costumes incorporated, as a basic element, a large leather phallus. This is because, as Richard Green explains, 'the comic performer stands outside the accepted norm, and this is doubtless part of the convention which allows the characters of comedy to behave in ways and to say things which also fall outside the accepted norms of public behaviour' (cited in Easterling and Hall, 2002: 104). Phallus was used as a symbol of transgression and defiance.

In Ancient Greece, comedy was often indecent and openly criticised politics (as it does in the work of the great playwright Aristophanes). Virility in this context means defiance of oppression and defence of one's own individuality and opinion. It is less about sex per se as it is about libido as Jung understood it – as psychic energy, 'the total force which pulses through all the forms and activities of the psychic system and establishes a communication between them' (Jacobi, 1973: 52). It is nothing other than 'the intensity of the psychic process, its *psychological value*, which can be determined only by psychic manifestations and effects' (1973: 52). Whereas the noble art of tragedy (as it was defined by Aristotle in his monumental work of literary criticism, *Poetics*) portrayed human beings as being oppressed, tortured and murdered by forces beyond their control, from envious gods to thickheaded politicians, comedy insisted on the individual's right to stick up his middle finger at them. This action, of course, is potentially calamitous (as it is foolish to disobey authority), but its dangerousness is part of the appeal. Comedy demonstrated resurrection of the spirit of freedom, and survival of individuality. Its aim was to show that human beings had the right to be themselves regardless of what the authorities wanted them to be.

The sexual motif in trickster tales often has powerful social and political undertones. Many 'indecent' Russian fairytales, recorded before the abolition of serfdom, involve members of the clergy, aristocracy and other representatives of authoritative structures. For instance, a peasant in one Russian fairytale grows a crop of penises, harvests them and takes them to town to sell on a marketplace. A rich aristocratic woman sends her servant to buy a couple of male organs 'for private use'. Each of them costs a lot of money. The organs seem to work very well – so well, in fact, that the woman does not know how to stop them as they are capable of having sex perpetually. The peasant tells her how to 'switch them off', but charges extra for this piece of information. Figuratively speaking, the peasant duped ('fucked up') a representative of the upper class in more than one way (Afanasiev, 1994: 102–109).

In another Russian tale, a cunning son of a well-off peasant uses his virility and sexual prowess to attract an aristocratic woman, and teases her until she offers him money to have sex with her (1994: 121–124). In both these stories, sex is the great 'equaliser'; a powerful instinct, it erases man-made structures such as class boundaries and social distinctions. Moreover, because both the ladies end up appreciating the sexual services offered by the peasants and begging for more, the whole power structure is turned upside down. The peasants use sex to regain control whereas the aristocrats become dependent on them for sexual satisfaction, and are prepared to pay for it.

In a similar vein, the Tibetan trickster Uncle Tompa sells penises at a nunnery and manages to sleep with the King's daughter (Dorje, 1997: 19–23). The laughter these tales generates is aimed at the inflexible system. This kind of carnivalesque defiance – although passive and only superficial – still manages to damage the social order by defiling it.

Scatological references

Scatology is a regular guest in trickster tales. This kind of basic humour – alongside sexual references – is another fundamental way of deflating the system and dragging it off its high horse. It works because the trickster is unaware of the shameful aspect of all things scatological. In fact, the more 'basic' tricksters such as Wakdjunkaga and Coyote start off with not being able to recognise that certain bodily functions should remain private. Recognition of privacy, and the birth of shame and decency, constitute the boundary which separates the pre-civilised trickster, jubilant in its omnipotence and brandishing its giant penis, from the human being who has surrendered a big chunk of his freedom to the social order as part of the contract.

The trickster has not yet reached the stage when he feels the need to hide his bodily processes from others, therefore he freely burps, farts, belches, hiccups, defecates, urinates and vomits. The chipmunk who nibbled down Wakdjunkaga's long penis and the ugly woman who tamed Nixant's wild sexual organ metaphorically represent the civilising forces of the habitus. The loss of the right to celebrate and exercise one's bodily functions freely is taken away with the signing of the social contract.

Native American trickster cycles are full of stories about skunk monsters farting other animals to death, animals that defecate money and tricksters eating forbidden fruit, which makes them sick. For instance, Coyote from a Lipan Apache tale is stupid enough to eat rose hips that warn him not to eat them:

'What will happen if someone eats you?

'Oh, if someone eats us, he will have to break wind so hard that it will toss him up into the sky'.

(Erdoes and Ortiz, 1999: 87)

Needless to say, Coyote eats the berries (which are clearly sour and not sweet) and ends up flying off into the sky. To be human – these tales are saying – means to be prudent and belong to a culture. It also means using the accumulated cultural knowledge. Scatological stories describe learning through mistakes – a civilising process in itself.

Wakdjunkaga's adventures include a story of the trickster eating a talking laxative bulb. As he prides himself on being called 'the foolish one', he does not listen to the bulb's warning that eating it would trigger an uncontrollable urge to defecate. Predictably, the bulb happens to be right:

> 'Well, this bulb did a lot of talking,' he said to himself, 'yet it could not make me defecate.' But even as he spoke he began to have the desire to defecate, just a very little. 'Well, I suppose this is what it meant. It certainly bragged a good deal, however.' As he spoke he defecated again. 'Well, what a braggart it was! I suppose this is why it said this.' As he spoke these last words, he began to defecate a good deal. After a while, as he was sitting down, his body would touch the excrement. Thereupon he got on top of a log and sat down there but, even then, he touched the excrement. Finally, he climbed up a log that was leaning against a tree. However, his body still touched the excrement, so he went up higher. Even then, however, he touched it so he climbed still higher up. Higher and higher he had to go. Nor was he able to stop defecating. Now he was on top of the tree. It was small and quite uncomfortable. Moreover, the excrement began to come up to him.
>
> *(Radin, 1972: 26–27)*

After his ordeal, Wakdjunkaga ends up covered in his own excrement – which does not embarrass him in the least as he generally is not sensitive or capable of feeling shame. He is yet to acquire the human capacity for self-reflection.

Like the sexual motif, scatological references in trickster tales sometimes have social and political allusions. This is common in canons describing a well-established class system (feudalism and up). The trickster in these tales tends to be conscious of his actions, and his choice to ignore shame is also deliberate and conscious. For this type of trickster, profanity and lewdness are some of the few ways of challenging the immobility of the social system. For instance, in the Tibetan tale 'Uncle Tompa Drops Shit on the Ruler's Lap', the trickster restores justice and literally makes his cruel and hypocritical master 'eat shit'. The tale starts with Uncle Tompa nearly freezing to death because the ruler took away his clothes in punishment for a misdeed. The cunning servant devises a clever response: he mixes human excreta with some lime dust, freezes it, and scrapes some words on the bottom. He then proceeds to drop his creation from the rooftop onto the lap of the ruler who is meditating before a splendid altar of Buddha:

> The ruler woke up from his meditation and was very surprised.
>
> When he looked at this object more carefully, he saw there was some writing on the bottom.

Since he could not read, he ordered his servants to bring Uncle down into his presence. Uncle, still shivering from the cold, was served a hot breakfast.

Soon after, the ruler ordered Uncle to read the 'Miracle Shit'. Uncle bowed down three times in respect and sat below the ruler's throne in a very humble posture. He picked up the shit and read the writing on the bottom very loudly:

> 'WOODEN HANDLED AND WHITE BOTTOMED.
> THIS IS THE SHIT FROM HEAVEN. HE IS THE
> LUCKIEST RULER WHEN IT DROPS ON HIS LAP!'

Uncle stood up in amazement and said: 'Ah! You are very fortunate because this is shit from heaven and when it drops on someone like you, you're the luckiest person on the earth. You should eat a little bit of it to get its blessings.'

The ruler touched it to his forehead, ate a piece of it, and put the rest on his altar. Uncle Tompa saluted and was dismissed.

(Dorje, 1997: 41–43)

Here Uncle Tompa approaches the most well-known type of literary trickster – *servus callidus*, the cunning slave, examples of which include Plautus's Pseudolus and Tranio, Carlo Goldoni's Arleccino and Beaumarchais's Figaro. The clever slave/servant has a low position in the social structure, and is forced to stay in his little 'underworld', which is far too constraining for his abilities, projects and, most importantly, for his social ambition.

Bodily functions and excreta are the first 'victims' of the civilising efforts of the system in ontogenetic development. This makes profanity an effective tool of protest because it shakes the founding principles of social existence; it transgresses the basic rules of decent behaviour. Civilisation, the trickster discovered, can be challenged and scared to death with something as innocuous as a bare ass.

The animal connection

Animals are frequent guests in trickster myths. In fact, they symbolise the trickster's connection with the 'underworld' of instincts and animal behaviour. Many mythological and folkloric tricksters are animals, and even when they are not, some association with the animal kingdom is often present. The African trickster club boasts a spider (Kwaku Anansi), a hare and a tortoise; the Northern American group includes a raven, a coyote, a rabbit and Wakdjunkaga's numerous animal transformations. The fox is the principal trickster of Russian fairytales; India has the monkey called Hanuman (one of the heroes of Ramayana); the most-known Chinese trickster is also a monkey – the hero of the novel *The Journey to the West* (1590); in Peruvian fairytales the trickster's role is played by a guinea pig; Argentinian folklore has Tokwah who is neither human nor animal; Japanese folktales mention Hare and Badger as cunning transformers.

Some trickster tales – such as the one authored by the Ilocano people of the Philippines – start with the description of a paradisiacal state in which humans and animals share a common language:

> In the long-ago days, humans and animals could speak with each other and be understood. Back then, humans had no fire, no way to warm themselves or cook their food. Fire did exist, but it was owned by two giants who kept it for themselves only and would not let so much as a single spark get away.
>
> Lam-ang did not like the giants' greediness, not at all. Not even the bravest or strongest of heroes could defeat those giants in battle, but Lam-ang thought: 'There are other ways to win than in battle'.
>
> *(Sherman, 1996: 85)*

In all ages and cultures professional and amateur 'fool' entertainers have included 'the animal connection' into their performances and had it reflected in their dress. Horse-tailed Greek satyrs and goat-like hoofed fauns of the Roman mythology; eared hoods, feathers, fox-tails, cockscombs and calf-skins of medieval jesters (Welsford, 1936: 123; Willeford, 1969: 3–4); little dogs accompanying circus clowns and participating in clown acts – all these traditional elements emphasise the trickster's role as a culture hero, as a 'mediator' between the world of humans and the 'underworld' of instincts.

Moreover, many canons do not even draw a clear boundary between the trickster's human and animal characteristics. For instance, in some Native American tales Coyote seems to be an animal; in others he looks like a man. Sometimes he transforms from animal to man within the space of one story. Like his shapeshifting habits, this lack of clarity signifies the transitionality of the trickster's psyche. He is still enjoying his 'primary omnipotence' – yet is gradually becoming a human being. Jung writes in his essay about the trickster archetype:

> [H]e is no match for the animals either, because of his extraordinary clumsiness and lack of instinct. These defects are the marks of his 'human' nature, which is not so well adapted to the environment as the animal's but, instead, has prospects of a much higher development of consciousness based on a considerable eagerness to learn, as is duly emphasized in myth.
>
> *(CW 9/I: para. 473)*

In a story by the Hoh and Quileute tribes, Raven transforms from a human into a bird because he is too stupid and greedy to be a man. It does not befit a decent man to try 'to get something for nothing': 'Long ago, Raven was a man, a human being. He was lazy and he was a thief. He stole rather than fend for himself. He was always trying to scavenge, to get something without working for it' (Erdoes and Ortiz, 1999: 246). One day Raven stole a woman's clams because he did not want to dig for them himself. Little did he know that she was a powerful sorceress, and in revenge she made water disappear whenever Raven felt thirsty. In order to fool her, Raven covered his body with feathers and made himself look like a bird:

> And so Raven changed himself into a bird. He flew all over the country to find a place where he could get a drink of water. When he was far enough from the powerful woman (and her powers reached very far), he at last found such a place. Raven has been a bird ever since. But his nature did not change. He is still a thief and he is still lazy.
>
> *(Erdoes and Ortiz, 1999: 246)*

Social structures, cultural systems and the human agency

The psycho-anthropological concept of the trickster is closely related to the idea of the human agency. At the core of the trickster principle lies the dynamic between the individual and society. The trickster embodies the tension between the established order and any innovations that might threaten its stability and internal self-congratulatory coherence. The principal aim of the system is to keep its contents and structures intact for as long as possible, while the main task of new ideas is to replace portions of the system for the purpose of renewing and improving it. The trickster is the raw energy of the new struggling to break through the surface of old structures. It is a metaphor for change. A healthy system has an in-built trickster as a necessary chaotic element, a menacing but important nuisance, ensuring the system's renewal within a controlled framework. The systems (personal, cultural, social or political) that do not let out the steam and suppress the innovative impulse end up crumbling from without or from within. Thus, in dealing with the trickster impulse, balance and careful consideration are paramount as they determine the ability of the system to survive, perpetuate and sustain its principles.

Perhaps not surprisingly, the human agency is one of the central problems of cultural anthropology. From the point of view of the British anthropologist and semiotician Gregory Bateson, the individual is permanently caught in the developmental tug of war – the process of fission and fusion (which he termed *schismogenesis*), the rivalry between individual initiative and cultural imperatives (Bateson, 1936: 195–196).

Another British anthropologist, Victor Turner (1920–1983), also explored the relationship between the individual and the system. He theorised that all systems were structures with an in-built internal conflict, triggered by communitas, or counter-structures. Communitas is 'over and above any formal social bonds' (Turner, 1975: 45). It can be organised and led by a group of disgruntled individuals whose vision of the system's operation and functioning differs from that upheld by those in power. The psycho-anthropological task of communitates is to counterbalance the solidifying actions of the official structure. As a result of this destabilising tension – the cultural equivalent of the trickster – the system renews itself as the fresh ideas 'feed back into the "central" economic and politico-legal domains and arenas, supplying them with goals, aspirations, incentives, structural models and *raisons d'etre'* (Turner, 1979: 21). Communitas is an inhabitant, and spokesperson, of liminal situations in which 'new symbols, models, paradigms, etc., arise – as the seedbeds of cultural creativity in fact' (1979: 21).

Turner employed the term *liminal* to describe the situations in which the structure was challenged, altered or destroyed. Liminality (from Latin *limen* – threshold) was initially mentioned by the French ethnographer Arnold Van Gennep in his work, *The Rites of Passage* (1909), and later developed by Turner into a set of political and social concepts. It denotes lack of stability, temporary absence of order – a transitional, twilight state. In his analysis of liminality, Turner uses Van Gennep's tripartite rite of passage: *separation, transition* and *incorporation*.

The first phase, *separation,* marks the end of the old state of things and the beginning of a new 'order'. The second phase is the liminal period during which 'the ritual subjects pass through ... an area of ambiguity, a sort of social limbo which has few ... of the attributes of either the preceding or subsequent profane social statuses of cultural states' (Turner, 1979: 16). The concluding phase is the time of healing of the developmental rift, when 'the ritual subjects' (initiates, candidates, whole communities in social, political or economic transition) return to their new, 'relatively stable, well-define position in the total society' (1979: 16). 'Liminality' – Turner points out – refers to 'any condition outside or on the peripheries of everyday life' (Turner, 1975: 47).

Turner also sub-divides liminal happenings into accidental and 'planned' (the 'in-built trickster'). Depending on whether they are sudden or expected, the liminal forces could be sudden or pre-planned and they alter the system either by force or in a controlled fashion (controlled by the system). Liminal moments are part of the healthy life of any social group, and include, for instance, calendrical changes, wartime, birth and death, and communal celebrations (such as coming-of-age rites). Such moments may or may not involve a status advancement: life-cycle rituals always involve a change of status whereas seasonal celebrations usually don't (Turner, 1979: 16). Between the points of 'detachment' and 'reattachment' lies a grey middle area of uncertainty, turbulence and chanciness. From the point of view of the system, liminal moments are always potentially destabilising regardless of whether they are controlled or uncontrollable.

Naturally, there is a big difference between an earthquake as a liminal force and a radical political group. Communitates can only be organised by humans; and liminal happenings created by human beings have a different character from those brought about by nature (a simple change of seasons or a more disturbing event such as an earthquake, a tsunami, a volcano eruption). At the same time, there is a clear parallel between the two types of liminality: they have a similar effect on the system. In both these cases, the system, which preserves itself by following a tried and tested routine, loses control over its actions, and its routine is derailed. Often during liminal times new routines emerge, new sets of rules are created, and mistakes are corrected and taken into consideration.

Communitates are not simply reversed mainstream structures, Turner theorises; rather, they are the source and origin of all structures, and at the same time their critique (1975: 202). Monastic life, pilgrimage, bonds of friendship formed among the group of young initiates, contemporary teenage counter-culture movements and even hippie camps are all good examples of communitates. Turner links communitates with spontaneity and freedom, while the 'official' structure means 'obligation, jurality, law, constraint and so on' (1975: 49). Both the warring sides are neutral, and interdependent in their survival.

As Turner argues in his book *The Ritual Process: Structure and Anti-Structure* (1969), there is something very attractive and magical about the power of the communitas (Turner, 2009: 139). On the one hand, spontaneous or uncontrolled liminal moments can be very destructive and might seriously damage or destroy the system. On the other, any system that stifles or ignores the trickster force sooner or later is faced with internal decay and staleness. Turner argues for a balance between these two opposing attitudes:

> [S]tructural action swiftly becomes arid and mechanical if those involved in it are not periodically immersed in the regenerative abyss of communitas. Wisdom is always to find the appropriate relationship between structure and communitas under the *given* circumstances of time and place, to accept each modality when it is paramount without rejecting the other, and not to cling to one when its present impetus is spent. Gonzalo's commonwealth, as Shakespeare appears ironically to indicate, is an Edenic fantasy. Spontaneous communitas is a phase, a moment, not a permanent condition.
>
> *(Turner, 2009: 139–140)*

Turner adds that no society can function adequately without this dialectic:

> Exaggeration of structure may well lead to pathological manifestations of communitas outside or against 'the law'. Exaggeration of communitas, in certain religions or political movements of the levelling type, may be speedily followed by despotism, overbureaucratisation, or other modes of structural rigidification.
>
> *(Turner, 2009: 129)*

At the same time, structure is important for civilisation as well as physical and emotional survival of human beings. There is no life without the structure as it guarantees safety, security and mutual understanding of individuals. It provides common ground for understanding between human beings: 'Communities cannot stand alone if the material and organisational needs of human beings are to be adequately met' (2009: 129).

The trickster metaphor communicates that, for the structure to operate smoothly, the liminal force needs to be constrained, contained and framed in a certain way. Its outbursts should be controlled, regulated and used for renewal of stale structural parts, traditions and rules. Therefore, control (whose psycho-social nature and main properties will be discussed in detail in the next chapter) plays a central role in the relationship between the trickster and the system.

Turner's view seems to be pro-individualist as he starts off with applying his liminality concept to Ndemby and Tallensi rituals and medieval Christianity, but gradually branches into discussions of hippy communes, the Dharma Bums and Hell's Angels. Turner seems to be fascinated by the very trickster whom he discovered lurking in the social structure; by the trickster that frees the individual from the tenets of systemic behaviour and thinking. He explores the complexities of communitates; he looks into the issues of hierarchy and status reversal in order to get a clearer understanding of the energy-generating tension between singularity and plurality in social contexts. He seems to have a neutral, balanced view of the relationship between the system and the trickster force. His recommendation is to be wise in regulating system–trickster conflicts in order to avoid 'Ragnarök' on the one hand, and dictatorship on the other.

By contrast, the French cultural philosopher Pierre Bourdieu can be described as being more pro-trickster than having a neutral vision of the conflict. To outline the dynamic between the individual and his surroundings, Bourdieu devised the concept of *habitus*. It includes:

> [S]ystems of durable, transposable dispositions, structured structures predisposed to function as structuring structures, that is, as principles which generate and organise practices and representations that can be objectively adapted to their outcomes without presupposing a conscious aiming at ends or an express mastery of the operations necessary in order to maintain them.
>
> *(Bourdieu, 1977: 53)*

The *habitus,* Bourdieu argues, is a product of history as 'it produces individual and collective practices – more history – in accordance with the schemes generated by history' (1977: 54). These practices are 'collectively orchestrated without being the product of the organising action of a conductor' and ensure

> the active presence of past experiences, which, deposited in each organism in the form of schemes of perception, thought and action, tend to guarantee the 'correctness' of these practices and their constancy over time more reliably than all formal rules and explicit norms.
>
> *(1977: 53–54)*

Like an ancient god, the *habitus* tends to ensure its own constancy and 'its defence against change through the selection it makes within new information by rejecting information capable of calling into question the accumulated information, if exposed to it accidentally or by force, and especially by avoiding exposure to such information' (1977: 60). Its influence ranges from communal to centralised as the human propensity to belong to the *habitus* can be harvested by all kind of leaders, from local to global, from religious to financial and political. Being part of the homogeneous (and forcibly homogenised) *habitus*, agents mould their aspirations according to the ingrained notions of what is and is not 'for us'. Like this, the *habitus* effectively shapes its subjects' future success in life:

The relation of what is possible is a relation to power; and the sense of the probable future is constituted in the prolonged relationship with a world structured according to the categories of what is possible (for us) and impossible (for us), of what is appropriated in advance by and for others and what we can reasonably expect for oneself. The habitus is the principle of a selective perception of the indices tending to confirm and reinforce rather than transform it, a matrix generating responses adapted in advance to all objective conditions identical to or homologous with the (past) conditions of its production; it adjusts itself to a probable future which it anticipates and helps to bring about because it reads directly in the present of the presumed world, the only one it can ever know. It is thus the basis of what Marx calls 'effective demand' (. . . as opposed to 'demand without effect', based on need and desire), a realistic relation to what is possible, founded on and therefore limited by power. This disposition, always marked by its (social) conditions of acquisition and realisation, tends to adjust to the objective chances of satisfying need or desire, inclining agents to 'cut their coats according to their cloth', and so become the accomplices of the processes that tend to make the probable a reality.

(1977: 64)

Bourdieu does not see the ability of the structure to keep its frame as intact as possible for as long as possible as a well-justified virtue that protects the individual and civilisation from the unpredictable forces of change. Rather, he sees the very concept of structure as malevolent and ruinous for human identity because it restricts our freedom. The structure, according to Bourdieu, is as irrational as the chaos it aims to control, frame and organise. And the worst thing is that the individual is programmed to take seriously the 'performative magic of the social, that of the king, the banker or the priest' while the institutions, which these leaders represent, exploit the body's readiness to belong to an order (1977: 57).

Bourdieu does not differentiate between the various forms of authority, or between pre-modern 'gods', 'spirits' and 'powers' on the one hand, and modern variations of the *habitus* such as bureaucracy, the state or the so-called 'cultural norm' on the other. For him, any authority is bad for the individual. Biological individuals having the same *habitus*, and therefore being products of the same conditioning, tend to possess similar dispositions and social expectations. Bourdieu seems to suggest that, even though our social instinct is to merge with the rest of our community in order to appear 'normal', we must learn to question its values. One can infer from Bourdieu's position that human agents are deliberately limited by the 'keepers' of the *habitus* from exploring their possibilities and looking for opportunities, incidental or pre-planned. The system exploits its subjects' propensity for magnetic unification but should be challenged at every step by proactive individuals prepared to exercise their uniqueness, the right for self-expression and the right to modify their environment.

This view directly taps into the socio-political role of the trickster who questions any fixed position within the *habitus*, thus disputing its validity and supremacy. It does this by introducing chance and unpredictability into the otherwise stable and rational structure. From the point of view of the trickster impulse (or rather, from the point of view of its rebellious human carriers), rationality is a prison guard and a source of inequality because any hegemony is always structured and, as a rule, has a prescribed, 'logical' foundation. The system is always 'right'. To deal with it successfully, the individual must ensure that the trickster is kept alive and in fighting shape.

The trickster challenges or even destroys the local power, which offers limited social routes and curtailed paths of personal growth, by introducing into it chaos in the form of plurality of discourses, as well as accidents such as chances and opportunities. The natural, instinctual, unpredictable trickster is the enemy of the structure whose aims are the implementation of 'civilisation' and the blind instalment of social control (through law, tradition, religion, communal ties, cultural patterns, economic circumstances, etc.).

Not all cultural philosophers, however, are excited by the idea of an autonomous human agency, not dependent on the system and geared up for independent thinking, self-expression and proactive life position. The American anthropologist Clifford Geertz defends the cultural framework and argues that it has an important function – that of protecting the individual from ... well, himself. In his view, without highly particular, defining forms of culture, constrictive, conservative and prison-like as they are, the individual is incomplete, unfinished. Human beings cannot survive without the culture's structured prison. Men have a psychological necessity to belong to a collective identity – 'Dobuan or Javanese, Hopi and Italian, upper-class and lower-class, academic and commercial' (Geertz, 1973: 49). Only through their culture can individuals attain full completion (cf. Jung's individuation and 'wholeness') because culture is there to fill the 'information gap' between 'what our body tells us and what we have to know in order to function' (1973: 49).

Geertz also argues that culture should not be regarded as 'complexes of concrete behaviour patterns – customs, usages, traditions, habit clusters' – but as a set of 'programs' whose primary purpose is to govern the behaviour of the individual and to ensure attainment of a certain cultural norm. Thus, traditions, rules and laws exist because 'man is precisely the animal most desperately dependent upon such extragenetic, outside-the skin control mechanisms, such cultural programs for ordering his behaviour' (1973: 44). Geertz effectively advocates that human agents need culture to structure and organise their world; that the man is in need of pre-existent symbols, with fixed meanings attached to them by the system. These symbols are important for the individual because they put a 'construction upon the events through which he lives', thereby helping him to 'orient himself within the "ongoing course of things", to adopt a vivid phrase of John Dewey's' (1973: 45).

Geertz is critical of the West's attempts to present the individual experience as an end in itself; as something unique and potentially separable from its surroundings:

> [T]he Western conception of the person as a bounded, unique, more or less integrated motivational and cognitive universe, a dynamic center of awareness, emotion, judgement and action, organised into a distinctive whole and

set contrastively against a social and natural background is, however incorrigible it may seem to us, a rather peculiar idea within the context of the world's cultures.

(Geertz, 1984: 126)

For Geertz, individualism is an illusory concept, which, at best, is an anthropological oddity and, at worst, a dangerous psychological delusion.

Cultural imperatives are thus like parents, guiding the individual from the cradle into adulthood and providing the socio-cultural safety net whenever answers to fundamental life questions are needed. Without these parent-like forms of authority, man feels lost, enslaved by his physical frame, dominated by his own body and its powerful instinctual cravings. The individual can be confused by the trickster. Culture takes the man beyond the narrow frame of his body; alleviates his dependence on its intractable, base, brutish and strictly practical functions. The socio-cultural framework consisting of moral abstractions, protocol procedures and communal celebrations forces the individual to grow up, and it is important for taming the unpredictable and, essentially, wild and animalistic human nature. The unifying function of culture glues together the fragmented experience that is being human. In a way, the rigidity of a given culture is the guarantor of the individual's psychological stability because, undirected by cultural patterns – 'organised systems of significant symbols – man's behaviour would be virtually ungovernable, a mere chaos of pointless acts and exploding emotions'. His experience would be 'virtually shapeless' (Geertz, 1973: 46). In the next chapter we will link the phylogenetic component of this theory to its ontogenetic siblings provided by several psychotherapists including Donald Winnicott and Heinz Kohut. They all discuss the 'shapeless' experience of the pre-parented, pre-cultural baby – 'childhood omnipotence'. Ideally, this experience gradually wanes as the cultural and 'civilising' forces, initially represented by the parents, imprint themselves onto the young individual's mind.

Andrew Samuels presents a similar 'balanced' view of the trickster in his assessment of the role and function of qualities such as spontaneity and playfulness in the contemporary professional world. He argues that

> tricksters introduce us to more than a laudable and much needed visionary politics. Trickster politics involves bringing a dreamy and playful out-of-touch-with-reality viewpoint into politics. [. . .] We are talking about ingenuity, improvisation, flexibility, rule-breaking, seeing things differently, doing things differently, not being hidebound, being open to change, being open to failure.
>
> (Samuels, 2001: 94)

It is important to keep the trickster alive in order to counterbalance the rigidity of the system with its civilising tendencies and – often cold-blooded – rationalisations. Society neglecting, suppressing or destroying its tricksters would be dead: 'Western politics places great stress on the formal constitutional structures and decision-making processes. In its devotion to formality, mainstream politics has often lost the ability to access the vital and innovatory dimensions that Tricksters bring into play' (2001: 94). At the same time, Samuels aptly notes: 'Trickster leaders will fail ... because anybody who tries to live *exclusively* as a Trickster will simply and correctly not be trusted, and will be unlikely to achieve high office' (2001: 94). In other words, as the trickster despises social intricacies, formalities and masks, its presence on the professional scene would mean more open communication and creativity.

The idea of balancing order and control in human life on the one hand, and progress and change on the other, lies at the heart of all world religions and philosophies. This precarious balance also forms the (unstable and shaky) base of democratic capitalism and the whole Western way of living. It can be argued that the founding political and social principles of the West depend on the correct positioning of the trickster within the social, political, economic and cultural structures.

The Prussian philosopher and diplomat Wilhelm Von Humboldt notes in his seminal work, *The Limits of State Action* (written in 1791–2; published in 1850), that diversity and variety in human existence is the result of freedom from total systemic control – and yet *some* systemic control is important and necessary. Ideally, rationality should 'know' that the trickster is paramount to systemic survival in the long term:

> [R]eason cannot desire for man any other condition than that in which each individual not only enjoys the most absolute freedom of developing himself for by his own energies, in his own individuality, but in which external nature itself is left unfashioned by any human agency, but only receives the impress given to it by each individual by himself and of his own free will, according to the measure of his wants and instincts, and restricted only by the limits of his powers and his rights.
>
> From this principle it seems that reason must never retract anything except what is absolutely necessary. It must therefore be the basis of every political system [...].
> *(Humboldt, 1993: 15)*

Humboldt's vision of human nature and its ability to control itself, as well as to make change and routine co-exist and work harmoniously, is rather idealistic. For him, this contraption would primarily work because reason is self-regulating and is able to see the traps laid out for it by the unconscious. As industrialised societies developed throughout the nineteenth and the twentieth centuries, it was becoming clear that this kind of co-existence, mapped out by naive in their hopefulness Enlightenment thinkers, makes for a precarious and fragile balance because reason can be heavily influenced by a whole range of phenomena, and become oppressive and over-inflated. As a result, what was meant to be the genuine trickster full of innovation and life would be replaced with its horrifying counterpart – mass thinking (which leads to what Jung called 'the collective shadow'). Thus, the idealistic conglomeration of understanding, rational and self-regulating individuals who are wise enough to give freedom to their tricksters, might turn out to be an aggressive, irrational, easily influenced and easily governable mass with one brain. What Enlightenment thinkers – including Humboldt – did not take into consideration was the power of the unconscious over the conscious mind. In particular, they underestimated the power and attraction of unconscious processes such as mirroring and attunement, both of which will be discussed in detail in the next chapter.

Meanwhile, the principal instrument against systemic tyranny has always been laughter. Any system is an artificial construct, and laughter – the great equaliser – brings this fact to our attention. Any systemic contraption, be it large or small (or even global), can be reversed, deflated or challenged, the trickster implies. And if it resists change – well, in this case you just have to wait, and it will eventually rot from the inside and fall apart like a house of cards. As the great humanist writer François Rabelais (1494–1553) wrote in the preface to his famous *Gargantua and Pantagruel* (2004):

> One inch of joy surmounts of grief a span
> Because to laugh is proper to the man

1

THE BIRTH OF SHAME

Shame and the individual

The trickster impulse affects the human ability to be in control. Consequently, it is closely related to the problems of narcissism and shame. Meanwhile, shame is a framing device designed to limit the trickster's sphere of influence. Shame is also used by cultural frameworks to mould the individual into a certain kind of human being – standardised, normalised and knowing his limitations. It is thus a boundary-making tool whose task is to delimit the individual's sense of omnipotence in order to create a 'social being'. Seen in this light, structures use shame to tame the internal trickster; and by doing this, they take away our pre-conscious, paradisiacal sense of unity with the world.

Shame is one of the most – if not *the* most – powerful of all human emotions. It equals lack of control. It defines us as conscious, thinking, emotional human beings. It exposes our inner fragility. It reveals our helplessness in the face of hostile surroundings. It reminds us that, by becoming individuals – human beings with unique personalities, separate from our primary carers – we have lost the powerful, ecstatic, uroboric unity with the world. It tells us that the world is not kind and that it can reject us. Shame is a reminder that the world is not perfect – that it is not an ideal reflection of ourselves. The loss of unity with the world ('perfect mirroring') means that there is always going to be opposition, hostility, rivalry and struggle. Everyone is different, we all have our own plans, our own agenda, ambitions, frustrations and problems. We have to compete with others for resources, and competing and fighting makes us feel fragile and unprotected because a conflict might result in failure, anger and feelings of inadequacy. Conflicts trigger the shameful awareness of one's powerlessness and they lead to re-discovery of the feeling of embarrassment. The feeling of shame emphasises (or, rather, symbolises) the world's imperfection.

In his book *Shame and the Origins of Self-Esteem*, Mario Jacoby explains the etymology and evolution of the word:

> Etymologists have linked the modern English word 'shame' with the Indo-Germanic root *kam/kem* meaning 'to cover'. The idea of covering oneself with a garment seems to have been implicit in the concept of shame for a long time (Wurmser, 1981: 29). Later, the word 'shame' was also used as an oblique reference to 'private parts'. Shame is also related to disgrace, and is often used in literature – for example, by Shakespeare – to signify dishonour. [. . .]
>
> When one falls into disgrace, resulting in a loss of honour, one is degraded or demeaned, marked by a stigma or stain.
>
> *(Jacoby, 1996: 2)*

This means that sense of shame is born simultaneously with the realisation of the need to protect oneself from public eyes – with the realisation of the difference between 'You' and 'I', with the idea of an autonomous self, separate from the rest of its environment. The birth of the individual is the birth of shame. The starting point of many mythological tricksters, as we remember, is the blissful state of being at one with the world – a state in which there is no place for shame. The trickster does not have to cover his penis or his 'buttocks' – he has no psychological need for it. It is only when he starts to acquire mastery over them that he learns about the close link between embarrassment and control. He learns that control is one of the few effective devices for alleviating the sense of shame.

Thus, civilisation begins with shame; and with shame the trickster's absolute freedom ends. From now on the trickster impulse will only be allowed to express itself within specially designed frameworks (works of art; public celebrations). Modern society has learned to deal with relative efficiency with chance and change, and manage essentially tricksterish and unpredictable phenomena such as, for instance, weather disasters and accidents. Abstract systems such as health and safety regulations provide rational and logical frameworks for controlling the trickster.

In fact, Jacoby argues, civilisation would be impossible without the framing functions provided by shame on all levels of human existence:

> Shame exercises an essential function; without shame and the restraint it imposes, even the most rudimentary form of civilization would be unthinkable. Shame is a highly complex phenomenon, promoting an individual's adaptation to collective norms and morals no less than the protection of his privacy. In this respect, shame can be likened to a border guard who punishes those who overstep a particular moral code's sense of dignity and respectability.
>
> *(Jacoby, 1996: 46)*

The Bible makes the loss of paradisiacal infant omnipotence the basis of what it means to be human. The Biblical story of Adam and Eve places shame at the heart of human experience: we are born out of self-recognition, out of experiencing the world as 'the other', as different, out of the realisation that others exist separately from us. Shame is part of the process of seeing oneself as separate from one's surroundings – it is about connecting, making contact, reaching out, going outside one's frame of subjective perception. When faced with the irreversible difference and foreign nature of the world, we become intent on establishing ourselves in it and on making our impression on our surroundings. People need to conquer, seduce, lure and, when all else fails, manipulate and threaten the world into understanding us, because, if we do not, a sense of shame will remind us about our loneliness and lack of visible, recognisable, strong, resilient, acceptable and loveable identity. Being accepted and being loved reduces the sense of shame in human beings because it covers the gap between the private and the public, between self and other, between I and Thou. The ideal world is the mirror reflecting the self's desires and thoughts, reflecting one's inner core – thereby confirming one's existence as an individual.

The metaphor of the loss of Paradise has profound political and social undertones. Any autonomy, even the smallest attempt at autonomy, is regarded by the system as aggression. Erich Fromm writes in his essay 'Disobedience as a Psychological and Moral Problem' (1960):

> Human history began with an act of disobedience, and it is not unlikely that it will be terminated by an act of obedience. [. . .]
>
> Adam and Eve, living in the Garden of Eden, were part of nature; they were in harmony with it, yet they did not transcend it. They were in nature as the foetus is in the womb of the mother. They were human, and at the same time not yet human. All this changed when they disobeyed an order. By breaking the ties with earth and mother, by cutting the umbilical cord, man emerged from a pre-human harmony and was able to take the first step into independence and freedom. The act of disobedience set Adam and Eve free and opened their eyes. They recognised each other as strangers and the world outside them as strange and even hostile. Their act of disobedience broke the primary bond with nature and made them individuals. 'Original sin', far from corrupting man, set him free; it was the beginning of history. Man had to leave the Garden of Eden in order to learn to rely on his own powers and to become fully human.
>
> *(Fromm, 2010: 1–2)*

What Fromm perfectly describes here is a typical trickster act: the loss of Paradise is a transition from a non-human to human state; it is an act of rebellion; it is painful because it reveals the existence of evil – yet, far from being wicked and sinful, it is also an act that gives human beings the power to choose who they are. It is a moment of freedom. Fromm mentions another myth about breaking free from the bond of nature: the Greek myth of Prometheus. By stealing the fire from the gods, Prometheus heroically 'lays the foundation for the evolution of man' and proudly declares: 'I would rather be chained to this rock than be the obedient servant of the gods' (2010: 3).

Fromm, of course, implies that the womb of nature is a 'system' from which man escapes (through the tricksterish act of disobedience) by attaining consciousness. Nature is the first system in the world – preceding parental figures, family, culture, political and social giants as well as the gods of religion and economy. To make a break with nature, to cut off the umbilical cord, requires an almost inhuman force, a powerful impulse. This is exactly what the trickster principle does. It is an impetus, a thrust; it forces one to make a choice, to form an opinion, to make a decision, to take a stand against authority. It symbolises the ability to survive, to get up and move on. Probably, the closest phenomenon to this is motivation. And it is the trickster impulse that promotes independence and makes us human because it teaches us to say 'no' to systemic abuses and systemic excesses. As Fromm rightly points out,

> only if a person has emerged from his mother's lap and his father's commands as a fully developed individual and thus has acquired the capacity to think and feel for himself, only then can he have the courage to say 'no' to power; to disobey.
>
> *(2010: 9)*

According to Jacoby, shame is a unique emotional reaction because it does not necessarily stem from unethical behaviour. Rather, it is about wanting to be understood and accepted. Shame emerges when one feels different from the rest of the social group, or stands apart from the rest of one's surroundings; when one is too exposed, too different, too visible. Jacoby writes:

> Membership in a certain race or family, for instance, can also provoke a sense of inferiority. Thus shame results from the manner in which my entire being of self is valued – or, more precisely, devalued – not only by others but by myself.
>
> *(1996: 2)*

The world of 'reality', the world of consciousness, is a far cry from the psychological unity of the collective unconscious. Being born means being detached from the other objects. Individuals are separated from each other by a range of boundaries – physical, social, temporal emotional, psychological and mental. The trickster's enemy, boundaries, are the defining element of a system. They contain and protect psychological contents and keep the personality intact. They define the shape and contents of one's identity.

Kenneth Wright argues that 'feeling in touch with other people is integral to the sense of being alive. We usually take it for granted and it only becomes an issue when we start to feel disconnected' (Wright, 2009: 15). Thus shame is relieved when we 'connect' to others – the process which has its origin in two early childhood interaction experiences – *mirroring* and *attunement*. They include a range of verbal and non-verbal cues by which the mother confirms, clarifies and holds the baby's subjective experiences. She 'mirrors' the baby's behaviour (for instance, by smiling back), thus providing the baby with a rudimentary sense of identity. In fact, this first, incubator identity, filtered through the primary object, forms the base of all our adult experiences (2009: 22–25). When surrounded by like-minded people, we feel safe, understood, cared for. We feel empowered and in charge of things. Mario Jacoby quotes the detective writer George Simenon talking about the correlation between shame and mirroring:

> Everyone has a shadow side of which he is more or less ashamed. But when I see someone who resembles me, who shares the same symptoms, the same shame, the same inner battles, then I say to myself, so I am not alone in this, I am no monster.
>
> *(Jacoby, 1996: xi)*

Unlike guilt – which implies the feeling of being in control, albeit negatively – shame is a deeper feeling associated with being out of control, being helpless – disarmed as an agent. Jacoby writes:

> It may be less painful to search for what caused the relationship to break up than to imagine that one simply was not attractive or sexy enough. If a person does not simply escape the pain by blaming the other, he may prefer to think of the times that he was guilty of hurting, abandoning, and treating his lovers insensitively. Confessions of guilt also hold out the hope that mistakes will be rectified, all will be forgiven. But the feeling that one is personally unworthy of love cuts much deeper.
>
> *(1996: 2)*

The issue of control, which starts on the level of individual actions and events, and continues into social and political aspects of society, is of paramount importance for our discussion of the relationship between the pro-individualist trickster-force and the 'civilising' social machine. Control is also an important part of our analysis of modern contexts as avenues in which the trickster impulse reigns. In *Modernity and Self-identity*, Anthony Giddens argues that the overriding emphasis of modernity is on control, which primarily manifests itself in human mastery over nature, 'the subordination of the world to human dominance' (Giddens, 2012: 144).

To sum up, shame and control arrive to supersede the trickster paradise. Shame comes to establish the boundaries and 'tame' the child's sense of omnipotence while control re-establishes the lost connection with the world. Compared to the previous uroboric state, this connection is mediated and unreliable, and therefore has to be constantly maintained and laboured on. This is how the agent is born – limited by shame on the one hand, and feeling the acute need to influence the world on the other. The trickster, as we remember from mythology and folklore, knows neither shame nor control, and does not seek confirmation of its existence via approval, acceptance or admiration. By contrast, shame and control are the two main ingredients in the individual's residual narcissism.

Shame and mirroring

Human beings are wired to connect and share. It can be said that people are programmed to seek the original state of unity with the object – the mythical Paradise that can never be achieved. We are compelled to break boundaries in order to make others share our language – or to borrow theirs. This feeling becomes particularly unbearable during the moments of imminent failure or consistent absence of acknowledgement and praise – at times when mirroring is scarce. This pain of internal loneliness and sense of loss can be eased by establishing mirroring connections with others – by seeking and giving attention; by sharing emotional experiences. However, an unresolved, suppressed, uncontrollable sense of shame may transform human relationships into a curious – and sometimes tragic – cut-and-paste exercise entailing superficial sharing of part-objects, projecting one's own pain and problems onto others without working through them. Alternatively, one can use the trickster as an example of successfully dealing with shame – which entails revealing and uncovering the shameful contents, recognising and accepting one's shame, dragging it out to the conscious surface, and sublimating or transforming it into humour.

When mirroring does not happen naturally, control is the second effective way of making oneself feel 'in charge'. This last method often goes awry as it is all too easily confused with true affection and true relatedness. The lost 'trickster state' is alluring precisely because one remembers being loved without any efforts to manage, direct and mould the situation. It was the time when 'love' just happened – one did not have to work for it, fight for it, or manipulate someone into giving you attention and affection.

As Jacoby puts it, 'susceptibility to shame is very common on the level of the "subjective sense of self"', with its need for mutuality' (1996: 50). Moreover, 'a basic sense of being unloved in all spheres causes an underlying feeling of being utterly rejected, and this condition is accompanied by intense susceptibility to shame' (1996: 50). Thus, feelings of shame can be alleviated by mirroring and attunement – i.e. by positive attention. Growing out of the paradisiacal state of omnipotence, the child begins to feel insecure and 'separate' from the world. These states of insecurity, anxiety and helplessness, triggered by the feeling of being out of control, are mitigated when the primary carer 'reflects' or mirrors the infant in all its positive and negative emotional states. By reflecting and precipitating the baby's reactions, and by closely interacting with it, the mother ensures that the baby feels secure and protected – both physically and emotionally.

Mirroring, as the English paediatrician and psychoanalyst Donald Winnicott notes, goes beyond physical holding and touching – it is also a framework of communication (Wright, 2009: 33). The mother (with her responsive face) becomes a 'transitional object' guiding the child through the phase of uncertainty – brought about by the loss of omnipotence – and through to acceptance of separateness and the limitations of control over the outside world. This transitional stage, Wright notes, cushions the infant against the sudden onset of crude reality, and allows 'the passage into objectivity to be smoothly negotiated' (2009: 33). When conducted successfully, this stage becomes 'an imperceptible phase in the progress towards independence' (2009: 33).

However, this stage does not mean that the 'mirror' in which the infant sees himself crying, playing and having needs, has to be perfect. The dialogue between the two objects should not be a form of passive reflection, but an active interaction in which both the sides take equal part and receive attention. It is about participation, not passive acceptance. Enid Balint writes that the feedback process, 'which starts in the child and acts as a stimulus on the mother, who must accept and recognise that something has happened', presupposes 'an interaction between two active partners', which 'differentiates it from projection and introjection in which one of them is only a passive object' (Balint, 1993: 51).

Mirroring is the background of all human development. The nascent self does not emerge out of nowhere – it is born out of and shaped by human contact. It is only by linking to and separating from 'the other', from the object that is not 'you', that human beings can gain a better understanding of who they are. It can even be metaphorically seen as a creative process during which a new personality is born out of raw psychological matter. To quote Kenneth Wright once more:

> It is central to Winnicott's theory of development that the self has only latent or potential existence until subjectively realized within the responses of another person. Only when self-experience is reflected does the baby adult feel fully alive. His understanding of creativity is bound up with this view: only a subject who is alive in this way can be creative, but equally, being creative enhances the feeling of being alive. It is thus implicit adult creativity involves something analogous to early maternal mirroring, as though the creative person, in the act of creation, performs for himself the activities which the adaptive mother once provided.
>
> *(Wright, 2009: 62)*

The child's personality is thus created by mirroring and adjacent transitional objects – but it is also created by the dynamic between absence and presence of these objects. As he grows up, the child not only gradually learns that he is not omnipotent, and that people in his immediate environment and in the world at large are not objects whose sole duty is to keep him happy and perfectly mirrored – but also that he has a separate personality that is not reliant on mirroring, and that can survive psychologically and physically regardless of the presence of other people in the vicinity.

The mother's task is to successfully guide the baby through the process of separation from 'the universe'. Ideally, this should result in the baby's 'maximal psychological maturation' (Winnicott, 1992: 111). The good-enough mother, from Winnicott's view, should astutely sense how to take away the infant's omnipotence without overwhelming it with a feeling of helplessness and despair. Meanwhile, using the mother as a transitional object, the child should be allowed to retain an illusion of control – for the time being: 'The mother's eventual task is gradually to disillusion the infant, but she has no hope of success unless at first she has been able to give sufficient opportunity for illusion' (1992: 11). This view is echoed by Heinz Kohut who argues that optimal frustration is important for the eventual establishment of boundaries and an acceptance of reality and its limits (Kohut, 2009: 123ff.). Thus, shame should not jump at the infant in a form of a mighty tsunami crashing everything on its way, but instead should be introduced to him gradually.

Jacoby rounds up his theory of the origins of shame by combining the ideas of two psychologists – Solomon Tomkins and Rene Spitz. He argues that shame is an innate affect that emerges together with the infant's ability to distinguish between familiar faces and those of strangers:

> Infants normally take great interest and joy in exploring their mothers' faces. If a child turns to its mother in the expectation of meeting the 'gleam in her eye' (Kohut), but meets instead with a strange face, its curious, expectant engagement is abruptly broken. The infant's reaction has all the characteristics of shame that we know from the experience of adults.
>
> *(1996: 47)*

Shame is thus born out of the moment of misrecognition – out of the realisation that the person you see in the mirror is not you.

Speaking metaphorically, the mother's task is to guide the child out of the trickster state, on the one hand, without leaving the trickster at large, unlimited by anything; and on the other, without burying the trickster under a heavy load of shame. The child should both have access to the trickster's mad creative powers and be able to frame and organise these powers correctly. Jacoby notes that forceful introduction of the concept of shame to the child, quite far from teaching him about boundaries and showing him the effective ways of 'framing the trickster', often result in killing the trickster altogether – and killing the nascent personality:

> The socialization of a child involves setting limits on the 'naked truth' of its fantasies and needs, and especially curbing its impulses to immediately act out such needs. Limits are necessary if we want to live in human society. Yet they may also have a stunting effect, furthering neurotic inhibition and suppressing vital, spontaneous expression.
>
> *(Jacoby, 1996: 54)*

The result is an adult who is terrified of overstepping the boundaries (and, as such, he is the system's dream subject): 'One runs the risk of appearing obtrusive and of being rejected whenever one asks for attention or claims space for oneself. And if one suffers from a lack of self-esteem, even the smallest hint of rejection causes hurt and pain' (1996: 54). This is when 'being like everyone else' (suppressing the trickster) instead of being an agent (releasing the trickster) is the safer option.

Framing the self

Following Winnicott's ideas, it can be argued that the initial stages of communication between the infant and the 'object' determine the child's personality as well as his future ability to be an agent. The infant's rudimental self is formed through the initial stages of communication, through the first attempts to establish a meaningful emotional connection with the object as 'mirroring confirms the infant's sense of being and agency' (Winnicott, 1992: 33). Successful parenting produces wholesome personalities: people who know who they are and what they want. They have a genuine personality core, a stable identity base, which Winnicott terms 'the True Self'. However, the failure of the transitional stage may result in the formation of the False Self – a structure protecting the (often undeveloped) True Self. Winnicott writes in *The Maturational Process and the Facilitating Environment* (1965):

> The good-enough mother meets the omnipotence of the infant, and a True Self begins to have life, through the strength given to the infant's weak ego by the mother's implementation of the infant's omnipotent expressions.
>
> The mother who is not good enough is not able to implement the infant's omnipotence, and so she repeatedly fails to meet the infant gesture; instead, she substitutes her own gesture which is to be given sense by the compliance of the infant. This compliance on the part of the infant is the earliest stage of the False Self, and belongs to the mother's inability to sense her infant's needs.
>
> *(1965: 145)*

Using our trickster paradigm, the True Self can be regarded as a balanced structure, which has retained a healthy connection with the trickster, and in which the spontaneous expression is not blocked by a wall of shame. The True Self is the healthy aspect of the ego – the genuine character core. From the True Self 'come the spontaneous gesture and the personal idea. The spontaneous gesture is the True Self in action. Only the True Self can be creative and only the True Self can be real' (1965: 148). Meanwhile, the False Self, according to Winnicott, is a form of ego-distortion that corresponds to social compliance and social masks. The False Self can be healthy (a polite and mannered social attitude) or unhealthy (a set of superficial social masks concealing profound fragility) (1965: 143). When we react from the False Self, we are restricted to the limited expressive capacity of our masks (Jacoby, 1996: 78).

The Winnicottian True Self is born out of the realisation that one cannot possibly control every moment of human interaction, or every moment of one's interaction with the world at large. 'Independence' in this context means the creation of the new individual – the creature whose cravings of omnipotence and desire to control the world are balanced out by an objective assessment of himself and the objects outside of himself. By contrast, the False Self appears to be heavily dependent on social approval and other forms of mirroring and identity merger. Its actions towards the world are programmed by the desire to be in charge of every situation, which automatically means being in charge of the object(s). Failure to establish control over the object results in the feelings of shame and helplessness.

The dead trickster buried under the pile of shame on top of which a mask is placed is also discussed in Jungian psychology. The Winnicottian False Self is conceptually similar to what Jung called the persona – a

> functional complex which has come into existence for reasons of adaptation and/or necessary convenience, but by no means is identical with the individuality. [. . .] [It is] a compromise between the demands of the environment and the inner structural necessity of the individual.
>
> *(Jacobi, 1973: 27–28)*

In a well-adjusted individual, the persona is a 'subtle protective coating that makes for easy, natural relations with the outside world' (1973: 28). This 'official' mask comprises two features: 'the ego-ideal', or the image of perfection on which the individual 'would like his nature and behaviour to be modelled', and the traits approved by the external collectivity (1973: 28).

Whenever the persona weakens or falls off, the sense of shame at being 'unprotected', powerless and too exposed may emerge. Persona protect human beings like a shield when their personality is not strong enough to deal with lack of object control or not wise enough to accept things 'as they are'. In this sense, persona and shame are interrelated. Jung postulates:

> It is, as its name implies, only a mask of the collective psyche, a mask that feigns individuality, making others and oneself believe that one is individual, whereas one is simply acting a role through which the collective psyche speaks. When we analyse the persona we strip off the mask, and discover that what seemed to be individual is at bottom collective; in other words, that the persona was only a mask of the collective psyche. Fundamentally the persona is nothing real: it is a compromise between individual and society as to what a man should appear to be. He takes a name, earns a title, exercises a function, he is this or that. In a certain sense all this is real, yet in relation to the essential individuality of the person concerned it is only a secondary reality, a compromise formation, in making which others often have a greater share than he.
>
> *(CW7: para. 245f.)*

The trickster does not have a persona and does not feel shame at the exposure of his non-existence as a human being, as a separate personality. He does not have to conceal his weaknesses because he does not yet see them as such – his weaknesses are his strength. Moreover, he does not yet have a core personality that has to be protected. Jacoby writes: 'Shame stands in close relationship to the persona. When the persona has holes in it, letting what is beneath "show through", there is a feeling of nakedness, and thus a reaction of shame' (Jacoby, 1996: 56). At the same time, the persona is important as the compromise between individual and society, as a set of definitions of one's functions; as a framing device. When not used by the frameworkers to stifle individual identity (and true identity can only be alive when it has a functioning trickster impulse), the persona helps one deal with everyday reality, with everyday roles and responsibilities. As such, it is an important part of the individual's cultural belonging. It is only when it outgrows the core personality and detaches itself from it that serious narcissistic issues arise.

The American psychoanalyst Heinz Kohut was also interested in the shame/control axis of identity and identification. His attempts at defining a 'personality core' resulted in the concept of selfobject – a person or object that helps the self regulate affect and feel whole and competent, but causes frustration if not there when needed (Fromm, 2010: 201). The self in Kohut's psychology is self-representation rather than the totality of the psyche. Self-representation is the way in which 'I-as-a-person am represented in my own mind – in contrast to representations of persons and things that are not myself – i.e., objects' (Jacoby, 2010: 59). In this sense, the concept of the self as self-representation is also close to the Jungian ego – its subjective and introspective experience (2010: 59).

Like Winnicott, Kohut regarded the self as being split into true and false parts. Jacoby notes that the concepts of the split self – its false and true parts – correspond to Jung's concepts of persona and the personal ego/transpersonal self structure (Jacoby, 2010: 59). The false self is an external and largely artificial structure (very much like the persona) that 'behaves' in a way that brings social benefits. In narcissistic disturbances, when the true self is damaged, the false self is particularly well-developed as its overgrowth serves to protect the fragile personality core.

The child starts by using its parent as a selfobject and gradually grows into an independent human being. By contrast, people with narcissistic disturbances whose sense of self is weak, feel 'empty' and keep relying on other people to provide them with a sense of identity even in adulthood. The genesis of the disorder, Kohut argues, can be insufficient mirroring of the child's self by the mother. As a result, the child's self cannot

> establish itself securely (the child does not build up an inner sense of self-confidence; it continues to need external affirmation). [...] But ... we do not see merely fixation on a small child's need for mirroring – the traumatic frustration of the normal need intensifies and distorts the need: the child becomes insatiably hungry for mirroring, affirmation, and praise. It is this intensified, distorted need which the child cannot tolerate and which it therefore either represses (and may hide behind pseudoindependence and emotional coldness) or distorts and splits off. [...]
>
> In the narcissistic transference, the infantile need for selfobject is remobilized.
> *(Kohut, 2009: 558)*

Kohut's selfobject (or Winnicott's transitional object) is the meeting point of the subject and the object. It is through selfobject that the baby gains self-confirmation and self-esteem, which are reinforced and nurtured through careful maintenance and gradual development of boundaries between the subject and the object. The mother's ability to deal with the baby's perceived omnipotence is crucial for the regulation of the shame/control axis. The sense of separateness – and the accompanying sense of shame – creep up at the start of the adaptation process when the infant, to use Winnicott's phrase, starts to 'develop a capacity to experience a relationship to external reality, or even to form a conception of external reality' (Winnicott, 1992: 14). The new unique identity is weak at first, and its control over the immediate environment, as well as its attention supply, are usually achieved by means of manipulation.

A stable, secure identity – such as the one weaned by the Winnicottian 'good-enough' mother – is capable of dealing with 'reality' without extreme reactions caused by fragmentation and shame. In other words, it is able to pull itself together and overcome a feeling of powerlessness, disillusionment and being un-mirrored. It does it by being reflective and proactive; it has an in-built trickster. It also keeps alive the basic trust in the positive outcome of things – the basic sense of security, faith in the rational foundations of the world. The 'securely held' and 'optimally frustrated' infant learns that communication process should not be one way, and that it is a mutual process that leads to a consensus. By contrast, a fragmented self – a broken, unstable identity, an incomplete knowledge of who one is and what one wants at every given moment – is the result of an unstable early relationship. A fragmented self is prone to shame because it 'remembers' that asserting oneself can be followed by demeaning and unpredictable actions of those with authority. Jean Knox writes:

> To feel hated by a parent is intolerable and the fear, humiliation and sense of helplessness are likely to produce profound narcissistic damage, unless this can be modified by a degree of omnipotent fantasy. For example, a child who is subject to random and unpredictable violence from a parent will feel not only pain and terror but also a sense of complete helplessness, with no power to influence the parent's behaviour or to have any control over the situation. In addition, without any cause for the parent's cruelty, the child has to face the intolerable fact that the parent is at that moment hostile, malevolent and sadistic towards the child.
>
> *(Knox, 2010: 122)*

The parental other is thus the first structure in the baby's life – and the relationship with it already proves to be complex and uneven. It also prepares the future human being for encounters (and conflicts) with all future structures and systems. Crucially, it prepares the individual to deal with boundaries, frameworks and shame. A psychologically healthy individual is able to see the difference between himself and others as well as between himself and the system. The individual with stable relational patterns is capable of resisting the tenets of false mirroring, including its dangerous collective forms (the Jungian 'collective shadow', which will be discussed further in this chapter). In other words, the infant learns to trust the system and to deal with its demands in ways that are not damaging to his budding individuality. Meanwhile, any serious mistakes in the process of transforming the primary (paradisiacal) omnipotence into healthy adult confidence and self-respect may result in a distorted vision of the self. This is when the trickster may die or transmogrify into a narcissistic monster, laden with shame, self-hatred and envy towards the outside world.

The trickster and the shadow

The trickster's antithesis – that very shame-laden creature who already knows about boundaries and restrictions, but still feels that they should only apply to others, is best described by the Jungian concept of *the shadow.*

Jung defined the shadow as primarily 'a moral problem that challenges the whole ego-personality, for no one can become conscious of the shadow without considerable moral effort. To become conscious of it involves recognising the dark aspects of the personality as present and real' (CW9/II: para. 14). According to Jung, the shadow is the dark brother in whom all the negative aspects of human nature are stored. The shadow is home to greed, aggression, envy, jealousy, fear and hatred.

Human relationship with the shadow has always been one of the key leitmotifs of art and literature. Human struggle with it is brilliantly described, for instance, in Stevenson's *The Strange Case of Dr. Jekyll and Mr. Hyde* (1886) and Oscar Wilde's *The Picture of Dorian Gray* (1890). Morality and civilisation fight with the shadow, and human beings usually try to forget about its existence because its qualities are shameful and unacceptable in a civilised society. These qualities are not conducive to peaceful human interaction and coexistence, and certainly go against the Kantian categorical imperative. Jung uses colourful metaphors to describe the shadow: it is 'an invisible saurian tail that man still drags behind him' as well as 'a tight passage, a narrow door, whose painful constriction no one is spared who goes down to the deep well' (CW9/I: paras. 45, 98). The shadow is the mirror of our 'good selves', and, as such, it is always inside us:

> Whoever looks into the mirror of the water will see first of all his own face. Whoever goes to himself risks a confrontation with himself. The mirror does not flatter, it faithfully shows whatever looks into it; namely, the face we never show to the world because we cover it with the persona, the mask of the actor. But the mirror lies behind the mask and shows the true face.
>
> *(CW9/I: para. 43)*

The shadow, Jung theorised, comes in two versions: the personal and the collective. The collective version is particularly terrifying because it emerges when personal negative feelings become multiplied and transform into collective negative feelings; when hatred, envy and rage express themselves on a mass scale. This is why it is important to recognise and deal with one's own personal shadow lest it becomes seduced by the power of the mass:

It is a frightening thought that man also has a shadow side to him, consisting not just of little weaknesses and foibles, but of a positively demonic dynamism. The individual seldom knows anything of this; to him, as an individual, it is incredible that he should ever in any circumstances go beyond himself. But let these harmless creatures form a mass, and there emerges a raging monster; and each individual is only one tiny cell in the monster's body, so that for better or worse he must accompany it on its bloody rampages and even assist it to the utmost. Having a dark suspicion of these grim possibilities, man turns a blind eye to the shadow-side of human nature. Blindly he strives against the salutary dogma of original sin, which is yet so prodigiously true. Yes, he even hesitates to admit the conflict of which he is so painfully aware.

(CW7: para. 35)

One cannot get rid of the shadow entirely, but one can learn to manage it. As such, shadow is an important part of the individuation process. As Christopher Hauke notes in *Jung and the Postmodern*, for Jung, individuation means integrating neglected parts of the psyche in the hope to become 'fully oneself'. Individuation is:

[. . .] nothing more or less than being fully oneself. This means including parts of oneself that have been lost or neglected not only due to circumstances or personal history – parents, upbringing and so on – but have also been lost or neglected due to the collective conditions of the era and culture [. . .] However, the personal and the collective, as well as the past and the present, are difficult to differentiate and separate in any final way.

(Hauke, 2000: 109).

The issue of the shadow is certainly related to the social on the one hand, and to shame on the other. The shadow lies at the heart of all shameful feelings. Its mother is shame and its father is civilisation. It emerges out of the need to belong to society, to be part of the habitus, to be supported by the framework. The shadow is the former trickster – it is the trickster tamed, repressed or resolved. Whereas the trickster is pre-shame and pre-civilisation, the shadow is the civilised, socialised person's 'dark corner' where all the selfish, greedy, immature tendencies are stored. Most 'decent' people, Jung notes, would prefer to forget about the existence of such a corner in their psyche, for the tendencies it harbours are shameful and unacceptable if one wants to be taken seriously and regarded as a decent human being. These tendencies certainly need to be restrained:

In reality, the acceptance of the shadow-side of human nature verges on the impossible. Consider for a moment what it means to grant the right of existence to what is unreasonable, senseless and evil! Yet it is just this that the modern man insists upon. He wants to live with every side of himself – to know what he is. This is why he casts history aside. He wants to break with the tradition so that he can experiment with his life and determine what value and meaning things have in themselves, apart from traditional presuppositions.

(CW11: 528)

Interestingly enough, Jung uses the metaphor of water and mirror in his description of the psychological qualities of the shadow. In fact, the shadow archetype's qualities largely correspond to the Freudian concept of narcissism.

Freud first formulated this concept in the essay called 'On Narcissism: an Introduction' (1914), in which he conducted the basic analysis of this psychological phenomenon and outlined the main aspects of narcissism. They included self-reliance, self-obsession, protection of self-esteem and deflection of interest in the outside world. Importantly, Freud also mentioned that there exist different 'levels' of narcissism and that in limited quantities it is an important part of the mechanism of self-preservation, and, as such, can be 'justifiably attributed to every living creature' (Freud, 2001b: 73–74). Narcissism is also related to the mechanism of emotional exchange between human beings because each individual has limited emotional resources. A narcissistically wounded person is not prepared to 'depend' on others emotionally because it is a position of vulnerability. It is safer to be emotionally self-reliant:

> The effect of dependence upon the loved object is to lower that feeling [of self-regard]. A person in love is humble. A person who loves has, so to speak, forfeited a part of his narcissism, and can only be replaced by his being loved.
>
> *(Freud, 2001b: 73–74)*

As Mario Jacoby notes, although Jung was not particularly interested in narcissism and narcissistic disorders, he inadvertently contributed to Freud's essay on narcissism, and thus exerted an influence on the concept: 'Among other things, Freud's essay comes to grips with Jung's revised view of libido as quantitatively neutral psychic energy and with his idea of the introversion of libido' (Jacoby, 2010: 5–6). This is pertinent for our concept of narcissistic exchange (discussed in Chapter 3), which describes various types of relating in post-industrial societies. Jacoby also briefly links narcissistic rage to the shadow:

> From the Jungian point of view, narcissistic rage, with the vindictiveness and the envy it implies, is to be imputed to the 'shadow'. [...] For Jung, the shadow contains all those characteristics and tendencies that are incompatible with the person's self-image. The person will thus experience great difficulty in accepting those shadow aspects as being part of oneself. [...] It will be fairly obvious to the outside observer that people possessed by narcissistic rage are not capable of self-critical reflection; they will not realize the disproportionately dark-shadow aspect of their rage, nor its implacability.
>
> *(2010: 174)*

I will argue that the shadow possesses more than just *some* narcissistic qualities – it entirely consists of them. The shadow's desire to own the world and to turn it into a reflection of itself is limited by systemic boundaries and rules. The shadow is the shadow of that primary narcissism; the memory of primary narcissism. It is the blocked, shamed and humbled trickster. The shadow in human beings is that element that consciously seeks mirroring because, without mirroring, it feels out of control. By contrast, the trickster is the impulse that is pre-shame, pre-control and pre-civilisation. It exists prior to the system whereas the shadow is an integral part of the system, fully reflecting its structure (since it looks for mirroring). The trickster impulse reflects the power of uniqueness and individuality. Both are important aspects of the system's internal dynamic.

The trickster and the shadow are thus two developmental stages of the same phenomenon – the drive to be an individual, to be a personality, to leave one's mark on the world. Individuals need ways of influencing the world in order to deal with their shameful 'smallness'. They can choose to control the world creatively – by transforming it. Alternatively, they may attempt to change it by force or to alleviate shame by being manipulative and expecting attention and love without giving anything back. Others turn communication into a narcissistic contract (further discussed in Chapter 3).

One's personality is seen and measured by the degree of the outside world's response to its ideas and activities. Being responded to – positively or negatively – makes one feel in control. Only validation by others can make the person feel alive. The individual's realisation of his weakness and fragility is what makes him seek success; it is what motivates him. However, when this feeling is too powerful, or when the individual fails to deal with it in an adequate way or to make it conscious, the trickster becomes the shadow, and the feeling of shame becomes overwhelming.

Table 1.1 outlines the basic differences between the trickster and the shadow.

Table 1.1 Basic differences between the trickster and the shadow

The trickster	*The shadow*
Freedom	Repression
Pre-civilised	Crossed the threshold of civilisation
Individualising force	Collective norms
Spontaneity	Safe decisions
Change	Stability
Out of control	Control
Creativity	Prescribed norms
Originality	Uniformity
Shapelessness	Clear boundaries
Shape-shifting	Rigidity
Ecstasy of power	Fantasy/memory of power
Omnipotence	Will to power
'Living out'	Remembering the 'loss'

'Personal' control of the 'world'	Control possible via collectivity
Sense of being 'at one' with the world	Separation, loneliness and longing for the collective
Not controlling the body	Controlling the body
Pre-shame	Sense of shame
Making rules and worlds	Living in the real world and following pre-established rules
Perfectly imperfect	Desire for perfection
Assured of the world's love	Hunger for love
Unconscious	Consciousness
Energy comes out freely	Restricted exit
Anti-structure	Structure
Pre-Oedipal	Oedipal

The social aspect of shame

Shame has traditionally been linked by theorists to the Oedipal dynamic because its arrival and gradual introduction coincides with socialisation and transition into the 'civilised society'. Shame-inducing devices in various shapes and forms (legal, psychological, anthropological, social) serve to protect the fragility of culture and civilisation from the destructive instinctual forces. They are used by the habitus to protect itself from internal or external change. Taboos and boundaries are employed by the 'frameworkers' to protect the existing rules and to keep the subject's life in check.

Shame frames and shapes the social part of the individual's behaviour by making him feel less whole and by chipping off bits of his experience. The first victims of shame are bodily functions; later on it spreads its influence onto social interaction. Finally, shame is often used by systems to shape the individual's values and views. This means direct encroachment onto that part of the personality that is meant to remain private and independent.

In *Childhood and Society* (1950) Erik Erikson argues that the child's introduction to the feeling of shame coincides with its first steps. This is when the child realises its exposed position. This is also the first step towards autonomy. At this stage, Erikson points out, the child also notices that it has a 'backside', and that it is exposed and not always predictable. This 'backside' is dangerous precisely because its behaviour can have social consequences:

> The 'behind' is . . . an area of the body which can be magically dominated and effectively invaded by those who would attack one's power of autonomy and who would designate as evil those products of the bowels which were felt to be all right when they were being passed.
>
> *(Erikson, 1995: 253)*

Moreover – this is the prime example of how the feeling of shame can be balanced out by being in control over one's body and immediate environment:

> The anal zone lends itself more than any other to the display of stubborn adherence to contradictory impulses because, for one thing, it is the modal zone for two conflicting modes of approach, *retention* and *elimination*. Furthermore, the sphincters are only part of the muscle system with its general duality of rigidity and relaxation, of flexion and extension. The development of the muscle system gives the child a much greater power over the environment in the ability to reach out and hold on, to throw and to push away, to appropriate things and to keep them at a distance.
>
> *(1995: 71)*

The 'dirty' and inappropriate bodily functions are subject to social approval and correct methods of dealing with them. Compare this to the mythological and folkloric tricksters' preoccupation with scatology and everything else related to 'the backside', which usually has a mind of its own and does not render itself easily to human control. Moreover, the trickster is often amused by his 'independent' backside and gives it complete free reign without feeling ashamed of the consequences. This is also why tricksters (for instance, Uncle Tompa who presented his master with 'celestial shit') solve social conflicts using scatological or sexual insults. Bodily functions are universally subject to shame, systemic control and social approval. Breaking these basic rules is akin to showing the middle finger to the whole concept of a civilised society.

Shame influences all aspects of human existence. It can also cripple the individual's ability to be an agent, to be proactive, to transform the world. Shame is capable of blocking human creativity. The trickster's sense of agency is boundless precisely because it is not crushed by shame, while human beings are framed by systemic influences and prohibitions. Being part of society automatically means having parts of one's agency sacrificed to the structure or structures. This is because we are programmed to belong, to comply and to relate to our environment.

Mario Jacoby writes that people who move upwards socially or who move from the country to the city often suffer from the discrepancy between subjective experience and the new reality:

> Insecurity about the expectations of a given environment often produces a shame-anxiety of behaving out of line. In general, social inhibition hides a fear that initiative and spontaneity might seem out of place and cause embarrassment. [...] Pastors, professors, or politicians exposed to the public eye really may not be able to afford certain 'human weaknesses' unless they are carried out secretly.
>
> *(Jacoby, 1996: 57)*

Moreover, how can one feel creative and 'whole' when one has bits of one's body–soul experience chipped off by shame? How does one know what is 'appropriate' in terms of self-expression and what is not, for every shame-inducing regulation tends to be culturally specific. For instance, one can wear camouflage clothing as a fashion statement in the UK, but in Barbados it is exclusively reserved for the military, and unwitting tourists are not exempt from this law. Being fined or arrested in a foreign country for something that one had never viewed as illegal before is a shameful and terrifying situation. It is psychologically close to Erikson's description of the child's discovery of his backside – one never knows when the 'normal' might become 'the illegal'. Jacoby writes:

> [A]nxiety is always at work when we anticipate potential shame-producing situations. This is the case with examination-anxiety, stage-fright, fear of meetings with important persons, or certain forms of sexual anxiety. It is the anxiety associated with the prospect of getting into shameful situations in the near or distant future. [. . .]
>
> Discussion group leaders, givers of toasts, actors, musicians, lecturers all subject themselves to the expectations that they have something to offer that is worth the public's hearing or seeing. When they fail, their disgrace is compounded by the embarrassment of having their high opinion of themselves revealed for all to see.
>
> *(1996: 5)*

The 'sense of autonomy' described by Erikson and Jacoby is a source of misery and unhappiness since it puts the individual into the position of physical exposure and psychological vulnerability. Being an individual presupposes assembling oneself from psychological fragments over and over again, for the state of 'true indivisibility' had been left at the trickster stage. There is an alternative path – another effective method of mitigating the sense of shame that comes with feeling small and insignificant. This psychological phenomenon was termed by Jung *participation mystique* (the term, in fact, belongs to Lucien Lévy-Bruhl) – a form of collective identification. According to Jung, *participation mystique* occurs naturally whenever the individual finds himself in a group and is forced to mould with it in order to feel safe or to survive. Jung describes it as an unconscious and automatic process:

> Identification with a group is a simple and easy path to follow, but the group experience goes no deeper than the level of one's own mind in that state. [. . .] But as soon as you are removed from the crowd, you are a different person again and unable to reproduce the previous state of mind. The mass is swayed by *participation mystique*, which is nothing other than an unconscious identity. Supposing, for example, you go to the theatre: glance meets glance, everybody observes everybody else, so that all those who are present are caught up in an invisible web of mutual unconscious relationship. If this condition increases, one literally feels borne along by the universal identity with others.
>
> *(CW9/I: paras. 226–267)*

In the essay titled 'The Relations between the Ego and the Unconscious' Jung discusses the dangers of projection: although it may start on the personal level, it quickly spreads out and may transmogrify into an aggressive and blind mass movement. This happens because the individual – despite looking independent – is still the same as he had been before the arrival of modernity. He is possessed by the same demons (CW10: para. 431). Human beings are still terrified of standing out, of looking small and helpless; they are scared of the consequences of being different or expressing their views openly. They cannot deal with systemic shame. It is easier to 'imitate' the mass, or imitate the existing system. Jung is pessimistic about the enlightenment dream of an independent, rational and balanced individual. It is much safer to copy someone else's behaviour (which is further analysed in subsequent chapters) or to merge with the system:

> [W]e see every day how people use, or rather, abuse the mechanism of imitation for the purpose of personal differentiation: they are content to ape some eminent personality, some striking characteristic or mode of behaviour, thereby achieving an outward distinction from the circle in which they move. We could almost say that as a punishment for this the uniformity of their minds with those of their neighbours, already real enough, is intensified into an unconscious, compulsive bondage to the environment.
>
> *(CW7: para. 242)*

Compared to the mighty structure, the individual is, indeed, small. Meanwhile, projection is a powerful tool that can supply terrified, unimportant human beings with artificial 'understanding' and 'affection' – with mirroring. When this happens on a mass level, the individual feels ecstatic and empowered. Mirroring someone and identifying with someone is an easy path to shame elimination and to gaining control over the environment. Often insecure individuals – and individuals unsure of their identity – subconsciously seek identification with a structure because it makes them feel powerful and gives their life a certain meaning. The structure is capable of artificially inflating egos of power-hungry people who otherwise feel helpless, insignificant and lack a sense of belonging. As a result, they 'borrow' the 'personality' of the system, which mainly consists of a rigid set of rules and prescriptions. The structure is a mask; it makes them feel powerful on the one hand, and rids them of responsibility for their actions on the other because the rules they follow, endorse and use to abuse others have been invented by someone else. They are pre-made and pre-existent. These people – the frameworkers – are only executers of these regulations, and therefore are not to blame for any bad decisions or excessive use of force. When many shame-ridden people come together and merge their anger and embarrassment into one, the collective shadow is born. And when this happens, the individual gets caught in a mass movement, and 'all human control comes to an end', as Jung puts it (CW10: para. 395).

In *Politics on the Couch*, Andrew Samuels astutely notes that it is not the wild and predictable trickster that poses danger for the individual, but those parts of the system that follow the regulations without questioning them. It is not the trickster that is dangerous, but the personal shadow that joins the system in the hope of acquiring more power, and eventually transmogrifies into its collective version. It is those people who are quiet, who do not welcome change and who appear to be 'normal' that need to be watched because of their propensity to merge into the collective shadow:

> Never forget that it is the solid folk, well placed in the hierarchy, nary a Trickster among them, the ones who follow the orders and know the ropes, who often do the cruel and nasty things in organizations, playing the power games, performing the backstabbing, carrying out the exclusions and executions. It is the mature, rounded, realistic people who sometimes hold the whole thing back, and deal out the nasty stuff. But they are not really mature if they have no vision. It is the apparently harmless visionaries, leaders who may not know too well who they are as people or even that they are actually leaders, who, every now and again, get results.
>
> *(Samuels, 2001: 94)*

Shame is both a personal and a collective experience. It is personal because it involves a sense of personal failure, weakness, inadequacy – in other words, the ultimate sense of powerlessness. It reduces human beings to the state of being a child, to the state of not having an identity with formed views and preferences. People feel powerless and guilty about their instincts, bodily functions and sexuality. They feel guilty and scared when they do not fully fit into their social group, when they break social norms or ignore established rules of behaviour. And they are *made* to feel guilty by political ideologies when they refuse to 'follow the party line'. Shame is a powerful tool of manipulation in all areas of life.

In the film *The Truman Show*, Truman's 'owner' Christof explains his success in controlling the protagonist: 'We accept the reality of the world with which we are presented. It is as simple as that.' The best reaction to this claim is reviving the inner trickster – unearthing him from the pile of dead instructions and protocoled behaviour. The only answer to this is: 'I have my own reality. I do not need yours.' Or even simply: 'I don't care.'

The Truman Show (1998)

The Truman Show (1998) is a film about the struggle of the individual against a system and about the survival skills of the trickster impulse. A common man, an ordinary insurance salesman Truman Burbank (Jim Carrey) is living on an island called Seahaven. He is pleased with his job, and is happy in his personal life. He has a house, a wife who works as a nurse, and a best friend who stacks shelves in a local shop. Truman's life is so wonderfully ordinary that, as people around him constantly remind him, he will never need anything else as he already lives in 'paradise'. Truman does not believe them. His biggest dream is to visit Fiji, but circumstances always prevent him from going there.

Little does he suspect that Seahaven is one big film set, and that he was chosen out of five babies to be the star of his own reality program, *The Truman Show*. The script-writer Andrew Niccol's idea was certainly prophetic as, back in 1998, reality shows had not yet dominated Western television. Truman's friends, his neighbours, his wife, his relatives, his job, his hobby, his biography – everything in his life is fake. He is owned by the corporation, and his day-to-day movements are controlled, directed and decided by a team of scriptwriters and the show's executive producer aptly named Christof (Ed Harris). The cameras film every second of Truman's life, including eating and sleeping. The protagonist does not control a single bit of his own existence.

Even the 'love' he receives from both the characters in his show, and the audience, is artificial, controlled and contrived. This kind of love is fake mirroring – the actors 'love' him because the script tells them to, and the audience watches his life because he is a 'celebrity' (the issue of 'celebrity' as a selfobject will be further discussed in Chapter 4). Truman ('true man') has an illusion of control, but in reality he is completely powerless. The corporation, consisting of a number of abstract systems, to use Giddens's terminology, has his life pre-written and pre-determined. Meanwhile, Christof thought up a convenient way of making the protagonist stay on the island: he conditioned him to be afraid of water by 'drowning' his dad (also an actor) when Truman was a child. The event traumatised the boy so much that he developed a fear of the 'sea' separating the island-set from the mainland. The sea became the natural boundary keeping Truman's trickster qualities – love of freedom, independent decision-making – in check. His inner trickster is subdued and managed by the corporation. Eventually, Truman realises that something is wrong with his life, and stages a revolt, which ends with him escaping across the sea in a boat and arriving at the wall of the dome surrounding the set. This is the end of Christof's show and the beginning of Truman's real life.

The television show as a metaphor of life that is entirely fake is precise in its description of the systemic control characteristic of modern contexts. This type of control is based on abstract systems' recommendations, and it is these recommendations that Christof parodies and fakes when he stuffs the show with product placements, advertising slogans and 'health and safety' discussions. In fact, the film's director Peter Weir has anti-systemic views himself. He says in an interview with *The Independent*'s Sheila Johnston:

> It's not a polemic; I don't think there's an attack, because there's no war. I'm not part of the liberation movement. I just try to poke a stick in the eye of the beast. Just to laugh. It's a dark laugh. But as long as you laugh, they ain't got you. When I read the script, I had an intellectual appreciation of its theme, but I was also looking for an emotional connection. And what stuck with me was the risk Truman took when he realised his situation. The desperate desire for freedom that was so deep he was prepared to risk his life and, in doing so, to overcome his greatest fear. I remember someone saying to me, 'This is a very bizarre movie', though its story is very old. But the setting is new and it reflects our times.
>
> *(Johnston, 1998)*

It is interesting that Weir wants to 'laugh' at the system in order to disarm or weaken it – because laughter is a typical tricksterish, creative-spontaneous reaction to a controlling structure. Laughter deflates systemic control; it diminishes the significance of the *habitus* with its set rules and regulations; it is therapeutic. Laughter rebuilds the self because it shows that the oppressive regime is nothing but a pile of ideological rubble. As such, laughter is a powerful tool against any self-obsessed structure.

However, laughter is not the only possible way of challenging the system. Powerful structures can be challenged by a range of methods, including resistance and chance. Altogether, they make for an effective liminal concoction and gradually erode the framework's confidence and its ability to reproduce itself by putting pressure on its human elements, and by moulding them into one-dimensional beings incapable of thinking for themselves.

The corporation does everything to limit Truman's aspirations and make him as 'ordinary' as possible. Everyone on the set keeps programming him on staying the way he is, on not developing the desire to escape the small box in which he is locked. Christof uses different ways of discouraging Truman to take risks: emotional, physical and intellectual. Truman's trickster is tightly controlled. This kind of obsessive control of the object is Christof's mistake, because this is what eventually brings the corporation down.

Meanwhile, the key word in Truman's vocabulary is 'out'. He feels stifled by the people who surround him, and he feels stifled by the circumstances limiting his physical movements and controlling his thoughts. As he explains to his friend Marlon (Noah Emmerich), he wants to get out of his job, 'out of this city' and 'off this island'. He wants to explore the unexplored world because there are islands in Fiji where 'human being has never set foot'. To this Marlon replies that there is nothing wrong with his job, and that he is very lucky to have a desk job at all. He should try stocking vending machines for a living!

Parallel to this, Truman's wife Meryl (Laura Linney) keeps reminding him that they are going to try for a baby, and therefore his trip to Fiji is financially unviable. Having a baby, Meryl tells him, is going to be 'an adventure' in itself. Besides, they have mortgage payments, car payments and other financial obligations. Meryl accuses Truman of behaving like a teenager and having unrealistic dreams. She reprimands him for wandering stupidly on the beach, getting wet in the process. The 'maternal' part of the system is shown when she treats him like a child, telling him that he will soon grow out of his childish explorer ambition because 'we all think like this now and again'. She then helps him out of wet clothes, and commands him to go to bed.

Interestingly enough, the two frameworkers Marlon and Meryl use abstract systems to scare and control Truman: a steady job, health and safety, and financial obligations feature prominently in their discourses. This fear is aimed at behavioural modification. In addition, abstract systems – surveillance, the insurance business and advertisements reminding about the dangers of travelling – inform Truman that staying at home and obeying the corporation is the best option for him. Surveillance (to which we will return in the next chapter) is the most powerful of all the abstract systems that regulate and control the protagonist's inner trickster, and prevent him from becoming a trickster himself.

Under the watchful eye of the camera, Truman is both 'loved' and very lonely: 1.7 billion viewers watched his birth; 220 countries tuned in for his first step; his life is recorded on a network of concealed cameras twenty-four hours a day, and broadcast live and unedited around the globe. It is a safe and 'truly blessed' life (as Meryl puts it) for which the protagonist should be really grateful to the system. The protagonist needs no trickster, the system reminds him, in order to be happy. He should be happy having the regularity of daily rituals – post-industrial rituals – instead of the uncertainty of the wild world of adventure and discovery.

Apart from the maternal, mild reinforcement, of Marlon, Meryl and Truman's mother, the corporation employs elements of negative reinforcement embodied by his job. At work, Truman daydreams and looks at the picture of Lauren – the girl he fell in love with some time ago, but she was whisked away by members of the team since Christof had already decided that Truman would marry someone else. Since then, Lauren (her real name is Sylvia) became his guiding star. Meanwhile, Lauren/Sylvia joined the movement to free Truman from his prison. When an office neighbour catches Truman not doing his job properly, he (just like Marlon) reminds him that he might lose it, and that there are going to be 'cutbacks' at the end of the month: 'You're going to lose a lot more than your teeth, Truman.' The protagonist is constantly reminded by the frameworkers representing various abstract systems that he should be grateful for having a 'clean', middle-class job, but that he is perfectly replaceable within the organic solidarity (to use Emile Durkheim's term) of the capitalist system. It is this basic replaceability of human elements within the powerful structure that frames Truman's behaviour. The financial and emotional 'security' (a job and a family), offered by the corporation, is used to keep the trickster at bay. The uncertainty that comes with thinking independently and making your own choices is worse than the little stability granted to the individual by the patronising framework.

Even Christof's language when he describes his methods of observing and conditioning Truman's behaviour is full of management jargon. Truman's life is framed by abstract systems, described using economic terminology, and measured in the amount of 'revenue' it generates. As the show's creator explains to the audience in an interview outlining the background of the show, he had to 'manufacture' ways of stifling Truman's creative instinct and keeping him on the island. Christof's early attempts to destroy the protagonist's ambition were only relatively successful – for instance, when teachers at school told the boy that 'there is nothing left to explore' in the world. Eventually the director came with the idea of 'drowning' Truman's father Kirk, thus negatively conditioning the boy to stay in Seahaven. Moreover, Truman was chosen 'in competition with five other unwanted pregnancies' to live under surveillance and be constantly filmed by 5,000 cameras. The show generated 'enormous revenues' equivalent to the 'gross natural product of a small country'.

Even though he is constantly reminded of the dangers of thinking for yourself, Truman does not want to be swallowed by the narcissism of the system. In the film, the efforts of the structure are undermined by random events, chance, resistance and defiance. The corporation does not collapse in a day – it takes Truman time to erode it before it falls down on itself. It all starts with a stage light falling from the sky, and nearly hitting Truman. It is explained to him that it is part of an aircraft that had recently had an accident. One day, while driving to work, he accidentally overhears an exchange on his car radio between the crew members discussing the protagonist's route. He gradually begins to notice other weird 'regularities' in his life, and realises that he lives within a regime established by someone 'from the above': the same people greet him in the morning, and the same people appear in the same places on his way to work every day; his wife Meryl advertises products looking at the hidden camera; and eventually one of the actors accidentally calls him by the name.

Truman's prison begins to rot because any system that does not respect the trickster cannot survive for a long period of time. The structure that is obsessed only with its own regimes becomes so sure of itself that it loses the ability to deal with random events. Wise systems have the liminal integrated into them, and thus are aware of the unpredictable aspects of life. In this sense, Christof's corporation is a typical stale structure that is unprepared for sudden change, and, as a result, it starts breaking up. After spotting the tricksterish 'glitches' on the set, Truman takes up the job of the trickster and becomes proactive – he becomes random and unpredictable from the point of view of the system. He attempts to escape his prison and gain some meaning in his life, because only a life with the trickster integrated in it can be regarded as meaningful.

The individual, as one of the building bricks of the habitus, cannot be genuine within a stagnating social order, for one is treated by it merely as an object. Truman wants his life to be real, to be genuine – he wants to experience true emotion; he is searching for his true self. His dream about visiting Fiji is a metaphor for indi-viduating, for becoming oneself. He wants to be more than just a 'normal' person, with an ordinary job, ordinary life, ordinary house, ordinary wife and ordinary kids. He wants to have a choice in his life, but the conglomeration of abstract systems, united under the auspices of 'the corporation' and Christof, make all the choices for him. This is Nolan and Weir's criticism of post-industrial settings – the film argues that the freedom of choice in contemporary society is only illusory, and that in reality (just as Durkheim argued) the individual is as unfree as he had been before the advent of industrialisation. In the film, the artificiality of the lifestyle orchestrated by the abstract systems (TV and media, the insurance industry) becomes the symbol of oppression and control. Marlon oxymoronically describes this kind of lifestyle as 'real but fake': 'It's all true. It's all real. Nothing here is fake. Nothing you see on this show is fake. It's merely controlled.'

Truman's hunger for control is not narcissistic, but tricksterish. By contrast, Christof is a narcissist who thinks that he 'creates' something new by controlling someone else like a puppet and taking away their freedom. He enjoys manipulating his hapless object and attempts to limit his trickster-ambition. In fact, Truman is used by Christof as a selfobject for emotional regulation – and this is how he is also sold to the audience who see in him their own mirror. Interestingly enough, Weir links the film's narrative to celebrity hysteria and the contemporary mass voyeurism, which replaces the authentic genuine life with the stale shadow of passively watching someone else do interesting (or even ordinary and boring) things. All the audience in the film wants is a mirror that reflects their own mediocrity.

The film is full of cut-ins of 'audience reactions': spectators in bars and at home watch Truman fight for the right to 'be someone' and to overcome his destiny. Meanwhile, Marlon kindly explains to Truman at the height of his friend's crisis that 'dreams like this' might be just 'wishful thinking', and that everyone now and then imagines himself being a celebrity and giving interviews on 'Seahaven Tonight'. 'Who hasn't wanted to be somebody?' – Marlon asks him in a false-therapeutic voice.

Weir says in the interview to *The Independent* (Johnston, 1998):

> In the middle of editing *The Truman Show*, Princess Diana died. 'It was hard not to make comparisons. If there had been cameras trained on her that last night, people would have gone on watching. The romantic tryst at the hotel . . . she's coming out of the Ritz . . . and then – oh, my God! – she's going to die. It was fascinating to me, the agony the audience was feeling – I call them the audience. Yet the paparazzi were working for them. We are complicit in creating the monster.'

Weir has no difficulty in finding contemporary counterparts to Truman: he mentions the Internet site which transmits video images of a young woman taken in her bedroom at two-minute intervals, and a notorious suicide on the Los Angeles freeway:

> 'A guy set fire to his truck and shot himself. The whole question was whether to zoom in. And most of the channels did. It was the cartoon hour on television and a lot of children saw it. A friend asked me if I had, and I replied: "No, and I'm glad I didn't". You have to say to yourself, quite frequently, "I don't have to carry that image in my head". There is no dictator forcing us to live in a certain way.'

Meanwhile, Christof typifies the mass media that creates new objects and feeds them to the audience as replacement identities. In this production cycle there is no space for true creativity, there is no space for the trickster. When Truman decides to escape, his owner gets very nervous – but not because he is concerned about the star's welfare when he is trying to cross the 'sea'. On the contrary, the jealous author orders his crew to 'create' a storm and drown Truman, for he dared to aspire to become genuine in the world of fakes.

Now that Christof's ownership of the object is disputed, the protagonist might as well die in a storm. The stand-off between the author and the hero is, in fact, the fight between the shadow and the trickster; between fake, man-made and mass-produced identity formulae, and a genuine human being; between the possessive narcissism of the tyrannical system and a freedom-seeking rebel. The system is prepared to destroy the unruly object as the object has lost its 'functional value'. At the same time, the tyrant is angry and jealous, and – although he is not going to show it to the object – he is in pain because he is out of control. The system's claim to total control has been successfully challenged by the trickster impulse.

This kind of jealous attitude towards collected and owned objects, Jean Baudrillard argues, is typical for a capitalist economy. He writes in *The System of Objects* (1968):

> At the terminal point of its regressive movement, the passion for objects ends up as pure jealousy. The joy of possession in its most profound form now derives from the value that objects can have for others and from the fact of depriving them thereof.
>
> *(Baudrillard, 2005: 105)*

Meanwhile, the sequestered object (i.e. the object whose trickster impulse is repressed or voided) is only valuable as long as it remains quiet and silent:

> What does the sequestered object represent? (Its objective value is secondary, of course – its attraction lies in the very fact of its confinement). If you do not lend your car, your fountain pen or your wife to anyone, that is because these objects, according to the logic of jealousy, are narcissistic equivalents of the ego: to lose them, or for them to be damaged, means castration.
>
> *(2005: 105–6)*

Baudrillard also notes that collecting behaviour is systemic and systematic – the owner is the little tyrant presiding over his silent and obedient objects. As such, this kind of behaviour is regressive, immature and neurotic – whenever it occurs, it flags up the fact that the obsessive owner is delusional as the world he creates is separated from the outside world; it is a closed, uroboric system that imagines itself to be omnipotent. It is not surprising, then, that Truman discovers it working in a loop – it is not built on live creativity but is stale and repetitive. It only generates and perpetuates itself by avoiding any challenge, whether internal or external:

> Obviously, this jealous pleasure occurs in a context of absolute disillusionment, because systematic regression can never completely eradicate consciousness of the real world or of the futility of such behaviour. The same goes for collecting, whose sway is fragile at best, for the sway of the real world lies ever just behind it, and is continually threatening it.
>
> *(2005: 106)*

The owner, Baudrillard emphasises, does not care a bit about the 'real identity' of the object but only about the identity and value projected upon it by the owner's ego. By manipulating it, the collector/owner lives through the object. Confining the object and locking up its trickster is the key action in ensuring its collectibility:

> What the jealous owner sequesters and cleaves to is his own libido, in the shape of an object, which he is striving to exorcise by means of a system of confinement – the same system, in fact, by virtue of which collecting dispels anxiety about death. [. . .] For one is always jealous of oneself. It is oneself that one locks up and guards so closely. And it is from oneself that one obtains gratification.
>
> *(2005: 106)*

Truman is the only thing that keeps the self-obsessed, self-perpetuating structure alive because he remains true to himself despite all the efforts of the corporation to kill his desire to develop as a human being. After several unsuccessful attempts to escape his confinement, which are blocked by the TV crew, Truman decides to overcome his fear of big water and cross the sea. He is no longer afraid of crossing the boundaries of 'proper' behaviour as well as the geographical boundaries. He is also prepared to defend his right to be different despite the fact that his owners programmed him to react with shame and fear to any 'exposure' and to any deviation from the norm. After surviving the storm, Truman's boat drifts in the 'sea' until its prow pierces the wall of the dome surrounding the giant film set. Metaphorically, this means that the trickster impulse has successfully escaped its prison and finally reclaimed freedom for the protagonist.

The birth of the trickster is the death of shame.

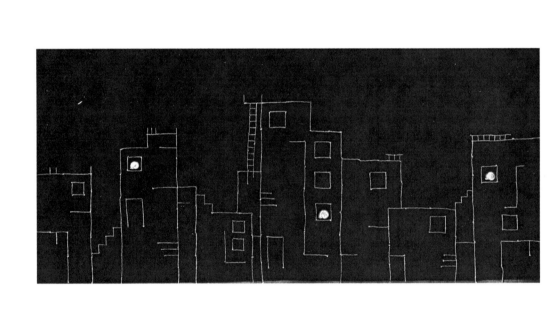

2

THE ARRIVAL OF RAGNARÖK

Modern Western societies have always intrigued me because their operating principles seem to be based on two opposing forces: individualism on the one hand, and a set of stringent, precise structures on the other. From the point of view of the 'trickster theory' this means that the trickster is framed in such a way that the system does not prevent it from expressing itself. Or does it mean that Western social, economic and political structures simply learned to exploit the trickster, and that its freedom of expression (as well as individual freedom) is only illusory? In the pages that follow I explore the relationship between the individual and society, and between the trickster and authority, after the arrival of Ragnarök – the onset of industrial modernity in the West. Shame, control and autonomy form the psycho-anthropological basis of this relationship.

The ideal individual: the civilised trickster

Capitalist philosophy is founded on the oxymoronic ideal created by Renaissance Humanism and Enlightenment thinking. This ideal envisaged a free human being who unrestrainedly created himself out of a range of choices available. As Colin Morris argues in *The Discovery of the Individual 1050–1200*, the concept of identity began to emerge in the West during the High Middle Ages when rapid population growth began to influence the economic and political balance in society:

> The Asiatic and Eastern tradition of thought has set much less store by the individual than the West has done. Belief in reincarnation virtually excludes individuality in the Western sense, for each person is but a manifestation of the life within him, which will be reborn, after his apparent death, in another form. Western individualism is therefore far from expressing the common

experience of humanity. Taking a world view, one might almost regard it as an eccentricity among cultures.

(Morris, 2004: 2)

This ideal is already visible in Renaissance literature, and particularly in François Rabelais's grand opus *Gargantua and Pantagruel* (1532–1564). Rabelais was a humanist and rebel who went through most systems available in sixteenth-century France: monastic life, university training, medical profession – and even politics. Therefore, he had first-hand knowledge of the complex relationship between the system and the trickster – and not just *any system* – but a medieval system – stale, stagnant and hostile to any planned or unplanned change. Rabelais's giants and other creatures eat, drink and make merry, celebrating the lower stratum of the body with its lowly needs and shameless desires. Rabelais's idea in *Gargantua and Pantagruel* was to show that all systems – including human mind with its propensity to oppressively over-civilise the body – are not conducive to human creativity. His aim was also to show that the human mind cannot be creative when the body is repressed, or when freedom of expression is limited by an external structure. The book itself is purposely gross, offensive, tasteless – in other words, it is the true reflection of the trickster in all its glory. And yet, in all its physicality and 'literalness' it is but an allegory of the freedom of human spirit.

Today this text, with its wild phantasmagorical images, disregard for the notions of decency and total lack of boundaries, looks recklessly brave both against the social rigidity of the Middle Ages and the behavioural code of modernity – the bourgeois morality. It is trickster personified – totally shameless and announcing its shamelessness with stories of scatological, sexual and gluttonous adventures. In these stories, pregnant women eat rotten tripes and then have to be administered anti-diarrhoea potions, baby giants demand alcoholic drinks the moment they are born, and are capable of drowning a crowd in a flood of urine. There is also a hidden class element in all this turbulent carnival of imagery: Gargantua's mother during her long labour is so angry with the baby's father, Lord Grangousier, that she threatens to castrate him. Gargantua's 'individuation' takes place against the background of aristocratic property disputes and scholastic arguments about the true nature of Christianity.

Renaissance literature was particularly sensitive to the questions of individualism and refusal to obey the authority – Shakespeare's *Hamlet* probably best exemplifies this. In the second scene of Act 2 Hamlet mocks Rosencrantz and Guildenstern for their lack of ability to think for themselves, and says that he, too, 'could be bounded in a nut shell' and count himself 'a king of infinite space' had it not been for 'bad dreams' (Shakespeare, 2007: 1095). Morris notes that Shakespeare plays down the notions of destiny and fate, emphasising the concept of agency instead – even when agency leads to unpredictable and tragic consequences. Control is transferred from an authority (in any form) onto the individual. There is, thus, a serious trickster at work in Shakespeare's plays:

There is also much truth in the view that the Greek tragedy is a drama of circumstance, whereas the Western tragedy is essentially a drama of character. The personal character of Oedipus is really irrelevant to his misfortunes, which were decreed by fate irrespective of his own desires. Conversely, the tragedies of Shakespeare turn on the flaw in the hero's own character. [. . .] Even where there is a prophesy of doom spoken at the beginning of the play, as in *Macbeth*, we still feel that Macbeth and Lady Macbeth are the authors of their own destruction. 'The fault, dear Brutus, is not in our stars, but in ourselves, that we are underlings'. [. . .] There has also been in Western literature a strong element of self-discovery, expressed in highly personal lyric poetry or in the stress of personal experience in religion. This 'inwardness' or acute self-awareness has been a distinctive feature of Western man.

(Morris, 2004: 4)

In his seminal work, *Rabelais and His World* (1965), Mikhail Bakhtin outlines the birth of modern consciousness – and the humble beginnings of 'the civilised trickster'. He writes about the rebellious stance of Renaissance authors who, in defiance of the medieval norms of profound religiosity and social immobility, sought their inspiration in popular culture and the anarchic spirit of folk humour. Rabelais's imagery and stories, Bakhtin argues, 'are completely at home within the thousand-year-old development of popular culture', a grand world of humorous forms and narratives that defied 'the official and serious tone of medieval ecclesiastical and feudal culture' (Bakhtin, 1984: 3–4). This means that the medieval world was two-fold: its surface was rigid, but deep down, in the depths of folk culture and wisdom, it was carnivalesque, mad and anarchic:

Carnival festivities and the comic spectacles and ritual connected with them had an important place in the life of medieval man. Besides carnivals proper, with their long and complex pageants and processions, there was the 'feast of fools' (*festa stultorum*) and the 'feast of the ass'; there was a special free 'Easter laughter' (*risus paschalis*), consecrated by tradition. Moreover, nearly every Church feast had its comic folk aspect, which was also traditionally recognized. Such, for instance, were the parish feasts, usually marked by fairs and varied open-air amusements, with the participation of giants, dwarfs, monsters, and trained animals. A carnival atmosphere reigned on days when mysteries and *soties* were produced. This atmosphere also pervaded such agricultural feasts as the harvesting of grapes (*vendange*) which was celebrated also in the city. Civil and social ceremonies and rituals took on a comic aspect as clowns and fools, constant participants in these festivals, mimicked serious rituals such as the tribute rendered to the victors at tournaments, the transfer of feudal rights, or the initiation of a knight.

(1984: 5)

Bakhtin notes that authors such as Rabelais, Cervantes and Shakespeare were re-assessing and re-building medieval folk traditions, integrating the 'low' into the 'high', while preparing the path for new authors, characters and literatures of modernity. The carnival moments of anarchy, Bakhtin argues, were

> sharply distinct from the serious official, ecclesiastical, feudal, and political cult forms and ceremonials. They offered a completely different, nonofficial, extraecclesiastical and extrapolitical aspect of the world, of man and of human relations; they built a second world and a second life outside official-dom, a world in which all medieval people participated more or less, in which they lived during a given time of the year.
>
> *(1984: 5–6)*

In other words, they sought change without challenging either the system or the economic circumstances. This change, of course, was make-believe because the world was still immobile, and the opportunities for the individual to develop or to alter his 'fate' were minimal. 'Party-time' allowed a liminal distance, which temporarily distanced the official vision of the world, but failed to trigger real change. The mad power of the carnivalesque spirit compensated for the rigidity of the system. During the carnival, equality was a form of role-play, a make-believe never destined to become a reality:

> Rank was especially evident during official feasts; everyone was expected to appear in the full regalia of his calling . . . and to take the place corresponding to his position. It was a consecration of inequality. On the contrary, all were considered equal during carnival. Here, in the town square, a special form of free and familiar contact reigned among people who were usually divided by the barriers of caste, property, profession, and age. The hierarchical background and the extreme corporative and caste divisions of the medieval social order were exceptionally strong. Therefore such free, familiar contacts were deeply felt and formed an essential element of the carnival spirit. People were, so to speak, reborn for new, purely human relations. These truly human relations were not only a fruit of imagination or abstract thought; they were experienced. The utopian ideal and the realistic merged in this carnival experience, unique of its kind.
>
> *(1984: 10)*

The individuation process itself is an inherent part of the post-medieval world, and all subsequent literature continued to foreground the importance of the trickster – the importance of the individual and his struggle for the independence from mass thinking or obedient behaviour. Bakhtin writes that, under Cervantes's pen,

> bodies and objects begin to acquire a private, individual nature, they are rendered petty and homely and become immovable parts of private life, the goal of egotistic lust and possession. This is no longer the positive, regenerating and renewing lower stratum, but a blunt and deathly obstacle to ideal

aspirations. In the private sphere of isolated individuals the images of the bodily lower stratum preserve the element of negation while losing almost entirely their positive regenerating force. Their link with life and with the cosmos is broken, they are narrowed down to naturalistic erotic images. In Don Quixote, however, this process is only in its initial stage.

(1984: 23)

Similarly (but also differently) Enlightenment thinkers and liberal philosophers re-examined the relationship between the individual and authority (which was particularly important in the new emerging world), and placed the individual at the centre of the social universe. Some of them – such as Wilhelm Von Humboldt – tried to determine the precise limits of the system in the new type of society, in which the practical power of the small community was replaced by the bureaucratic might of the nation state. His book *The Limits of State Action* is all about the interaction between human freedom and the unwieldly government structure. Humboldt places the trickster's rights above the rights of the state – yet also argues in favour of a balanced relationship between the two. Moreover, he links the trickster to logic and reason: it is only logical for individuals to live at peace with their inner (and outer) tricksters; this is the only way to live creatively. Reason and the trickster (contra the traditional Christian view) are inseparable as they support each other and ensure each other's full realisation and survival. The monotony of 'reasonable behaviour' and logical routine is diluted with creative spontaneity:

> The true end of Man, or that which is prescribed by the eternal and immu-table dictates of reason, and not suggested by vague and transient desires, is the highest and most harmonious development of his powers to a complete and consistent whole. Freedom is the first and indispensable condition which the possibility of such a development presupposes; but there is besides another essential – intimately connected with freedom, it is true – a variety of situations. Even the most free and self-reliant of men is hindered in his development, when set in a monotonous situation.
>
> *(Humboldt, 1993: 10)*

To live creatively, Humboldt implies, is to be aware of yourself and to treat others with respect. Our trickster is what makes us alive and what makes us 'enjoy the most absolute freedom of developing ourselves by our free energies' (1993: 15). Amazingly, the philosopher places the energy – the impulse, the trickster, the feel-ing of being alive – at the heart of being happy and being human: 'Energy appears to me the first and unique virtue of mankind. Whatever raises his energies to a higher pitch is worth more than what merely puts materials into our hands for its exercise' (1993: 72). This energy resides in the very nature of things, and is capable of bringing down oppressive structures that limit human freedom. Most impor-tantly, this basic, primitive energy gives birth to all things high and refined. A genuinely happy, friendly and understanding society is perpetuated by the products of creative activities of its citizens:

> For the ever-active, restless energy inherent in the very nature of things struggles against every pernicious institution, and actively promotes everything beneficial; so that it is in the highest sense true, that the most active evil influence can never equal the good which is everywhere and at all times being spontaneously produced.
>
> *(1993: 32)*

Thus, the citizen is a paradoxical combination of jubilant trickster energies and self-restraint, or, rather, a combination of the trickster and respectful attitude towards one's surroundings. At the same time, Humboldt is well aware of the emotional difficulties that come with being an individual, and of the propensity of people to rely on structures and to seek support from them. It is much better to 'enjoy' one's free creative energies than depend on the giant 'parent' in the form of the state machine. He warns against such dependence because it inevitably kills the trickster – the precious capacity for spontaneous action:

> The man who is often led easily becomes disposed willingly to sacrifice what remains of his capacity for spontaneous action. He fancies himself released from an anxiety which he sees transferred to other hands, and seems to himself to do enough when he looks to their leadership and follows it.
>
> *(1993: 20)*

To be an individual thus means, according to Humboldt, keeping the trickster (in the form of creative personal initiative) alive and not letting the state replace it with rules and recommendations, for the state is, in fact, faceless. It is a dead nothing: 'As each individual abandons himself to the solicitous aid of the state, so, and still more, he abandons himself to the fate of his fellow-citizens' (1993: 21). When a system has respect for the trickster, everyone benefits:

> I could depict a state in which energy would keep pace with refinement and richness of character, and in which, from the endlessly ramified interconnection between all nations and quarters of the globe, the basic elements of human nature themselves would seem more numerous.
>
> *(1993: 32)*

Meanwhile, the 'true end of the state' is to regulate the trickster energies of its citizens without stifling or killing them. All power should be carefully balanced:

> The state must wholly refrain from every attempt to operate directly or indirectly on the morals and character of the nation, except in so far as such a policy may become inevitable as a natural consequence of its other

absolutely necessary measures; and that everything calculated to promote such a design, and particularly all special supervision of education, religion, sumptuary laws, etc., lies wholly outside the limits of its legitimate activity.

(1993: 81)

The view that the citizen is capable of managing his trickster without the help or the intervention of the state is upheld by other political philosophers belonging to the liberal tradition. This view places trust in the individual's ability to self-regulate and to determine the limits of one's freedom using rational means. In his famous essay 'On Liberty' (first published in 1859) John Stuart Mill effectively argues that human beings should be free to do as they wish unless they harm others:

> The sole end for which mankind are warranted, individually or collectively, in interfering with the liberty of action of any of their number, is self-protection. That the only purpose for which power can be rightfully exercised over any member of a civilized community, against his will, is to prevent harm to others. His own good, either physical or moral, is not sufficient warrant. He cannot rightfully be compelled to do or forbear because it will be better for him to do so, because it will make him happier, because, in the opinion of others, to do so would be wise, or even right … The only part of the conduct of anyone, for which he is amenable to society, is that which concerns others. In the part which merely concerns him, his independence is, of right, absolute. Over himself, over his own body and mind, the individual is sovereign.
>
> *(Cited in Morgan, 2001: 905)*

Mill outlines several key 'trickster qualities' without which the individual cannot exist psychologically: choice, individuality, freedom of emotional expression, restricted power of the social order (including any traditions), plurality, difference and spontaneity. Like Humboldt, he links trickster energies to human ability to act rationally and to arrive at the optimal decision when faced with a range of options. Paradoxically, there is no rationality without the creative and unsettling influence of plurality:

> [T]he human faculties of perception, judgement, discriminative feeling, mental activity, and even moral preference, are exercised only in making a choice. He who does anything because it is the custom, makes no choice. He gains no practice either in discerning or in desiring what is best.
>
> *(Mill cited in Morgan, 2001: 904–905)*

Mill's defence of individuality is reinforced by his criticism of 'imitation' – the innate human desire to be 'part of the system' and to alleviate the anxiety that comes with making a choice by following a trodden path. In our 'trickster vocabulary' imitation leads to the emergence of the collective shadow and its subsequent destruction of difference and individual identity. Mill writes: 'He who lets the world, or his own portion of it, choose his plan of life for him, has no need of any other faculty than ape-like one of imitation' (2001: 905).

Mill is a great believer in the 'civilised trickster' – a passionate person who can nevertheless control his impulses and knows right from wrong. He acts with conviction and has a point of view that is different from the one offered by authorities and accepted by the dumb mass. Such an individual does not need an external structure to manage his energy – he is strong and intelligent enough to do it himself. He can 'frame' and guide his spring-like creativity towards exceptional accomplishments. In so doing, he rejects the complete 'despotism of Custom' (2001: 911). This person has 'great energies guided by vigorous reason, and strong feelings strongly controlled by conscientious will' instead of being an average citizen with 'weak feelings and weak energies' and 'without any strength either of will or reason' (2001: 910). Mill implies that every human being is unique and we should 'cultivate' this uniqueness in order to fight 'uniformity' – but only 'within the limits imposed by the rights and interests of others' (2001: 907). In other words, a society consisting of 'civilised tricksters' is both passionate and careful not to harm others; paradoxically, such citizens are both free and limited in expressing their needs and desires.

At the same time, Mill is less optimistic than Humboldt about the ability of human beings to balance out their inner tricksters with reason, to manage them correctly or to find fruitful ways of letting them out. Most people, Mill laments in 'On Liberty', lack both the strong creative impulse and the will to tame it. Human beings tend to look for pseudo-parental systems that would organise their lives and thoughts:

> The general average of mankind are not only moderate in intellect, but also moderate in inclinations: they have no tastes or wishes strong enough to incline them to do anything unusual, and they consequently do not understand those who have, and class all such with the wild and intemperate whom they are accustomed to look down upon.
>
> *(2001: 910)*

Collectivity is alluring precisely because it reduces the sense of shame that comes with being small and powerless: 'individually small, we only appear capable of anything great by our habit of combining; and with this our moral and religious philanthropists are perfectly contented' (2001: 911). Thus, despite painting pictures of ideal passionate individuals, Mill does not trust the 'average' man, who can be easily enslaved by the state and turned into a small element of the big machine. With the might of the system behind him, the small individual would feel invincible and tempted to abuse his newly-found power. Mill paints a sad world in which everyone is the same thanks to mediocre universal education and mass communications aimed at, well, the 'mass man':

> The circumstances which surround different classes and individuals, and shape their characters, are daily becoming more assimilated. Formerly, different ranks, different neighbourhoods, different trades and professions, lived in

what might be called different worlds; at present, to a great degree in the same. Comparatively speaking, they now read the same things, listen to the same things, see the same things, go to the same places, have their hopes and fears directed to the same objects, have the same rights and liberties, and the same means of asserting them. Great as are the differences of position which remain, they are nothing to those which have ceased. And the assimilation is still proceeding. All the political changes of the age promote it, since they all tend to raise the low and to lower the high. Every extension of education promotes it, because education brings people under common influences, and gives them access to the general stock of facts and sentiments. Improvements in the means of communication promote it, by bringing the inhabitants of distant places into personal contact, and keeping up a rapid flow of changes of residence between one place and another. The increase of commerce and manufactures promotes it, by diffusing more widely the advantages of easy circumstances, and opening all objects of ambition, even the highest, to general competition, whereby the desire of rising becomes no longer the character of a particular class, but of all classes. A more powerful agency than even all these, in bringing about a general similarity among mankind, is the complete establishment, in this and other free countries, of the ascendancy of public opinion in the State.

(2001: 912)

Thus, Enlightenment thinkers and liberal philosophers tried to solve the practical paradoxes that come with the dual duty of being a creative individual and a good citizen. They envisaged a human being with a paradoxical combination of abilities: on the one hand, such an individual openly expresses his creativity and individuality; yet, on the other, he is sensitive to the needs of others and respects the rules of decent conduct. In other words, he is honourable, able to self-reflect, modify his behaviour and – most importantly – is able of going outside the narrow cage of his subjectivity. He understands what it means to be someone else. He is capable of putting *himself* in the *other person's shoes*.

The postmodern trickster

The individual who utilises his trickster fully, yet in ways that are not socially harmful (unless it is absolutely necessary for them to be socially harmful), is an idealistic construct. The problem with becoming such an individual, and particularly creating a society consisting of such individuals, is that it requires someone prepared to make choices in the absence of immortal 'gods' with their eternal laws. And yet this is exactly what is expected of the post-Ragnarök (or, as we call him today – postmodern) individual. Supposedly autonomous and seemingly independent, he faces a barrage of lifestyle choices at every stage of his existence. Apparently, his trickster is so emancipated that the abundance of choice threatens to drown the individual in confusion and psychological fragmentation. The trickster stands and fights for choice – but with choice comes responsibility and the possible failure to adopt and select the right option. Separated from the innocent safety of Mother Nature, the new individual feels ashamed of his own 'nakedness' in the face of the powerful, multiple and complex world. Instinct does not presuppose a choice of action, but consciousness and free will do. As Mario Jacoby notes: 'Openness to the world and free will imply a certain loss of instinctive confidence. [...] No wonder we experience consciousness as a double-edged sword, even as "original sin"' (Jacoby, 1996: 17).

It is not surprising that with the trickster at large and the concept of authority in decline, the quest for the self in post-industrial societies has become the main philosophical problem. The ethic of autonomous self is the only stable moral currency left in the West today, while everything else seems to be impermanent and unstable. The sociologist Nikolas Rose argues that this fascination with the self 'seems to trace out something quite fundamental in the ways in which modern men and women have come to understand, experience, and evaluate themselves, their actions, and their lives' (Rose, 1998: 1). Moreover, the self – in the absence of any other universal faith – became that unifying force that keeps together individuals in the morally fluid and emotionally turbulent society:

> If there is one value that seems beyond reproach, in our current confused ethical climate, it is that of the self and the terms that cluster around it – autonomy, identity, individuality, liberty, choice, fulfillment. It is in terms of our autonomous selves that we understand our passions and desires, shape our life-styles, choose our partners, marriage, even parenthood. It is in the name of the kinds of persons that we really are that we consume commodities, act out our tastes, fashion our bodies, display our distinctiveness. Our politics loudly proclaims its commitment to respect for the rights and powers of the citizen as an individual.
>
> *(1998: 1)*

Our contemporary perception of Ragnarök as a metaphor for value-pluralism and the end of normative authority was born in 1889, with Nietzsche's publication of *The Twilight of the Idols: How to Philosophise with a Hammer (Götzen-Dämmerung, oder, Wie Man mit dem Hammer Philosophiert)*. This is a pun on the title of Wagner's opera, *The Twilight of the Gods (Götterdämmerung*, the German translation of Ragnarök; premiered in 1876).

In his book Nietzsche (at the time gradually descending into madness), indeed, nonchalantly challenges the idols of ethics and philosophy including Socrates and Plato, while praising Napoleon and the Sophists for being strong and resilient. In the opening paragraph he defines his messenger's task as that of a trickster spirit – to destroy the false idols that have dominated Western morality for a long time. Nietzsche describes himself as a sort of trickster-philosopher with a hammer: 'Nothing succeeds if prankishness has no part in it.' His task, he adds, is 'gloomy', difficult and dangerous, yet important, for he intends to bring down the stale idols and change the way we see ethics and morality. Nietzsche is Loki at war with the gods:

Maintaining cheerfulness in the midst of a gloomy task, fraught with immeasurable responsibility, is no small feat; and yet what is needed more than cheerfulness? Nothing succeeds if prankishness has no part in it. Excess strength alone is the proof of strength.

A revaluation of all values: this question mark, so black, so huge that it casts a shadow over the man who puts it down — such a destiny of a task compels one to run into the sunlight at every opportunity to shake off a heavy, all-too-heavy seriousness. Every means is proper to do this; every 'case' is a case of luck. Especially, war. War has always been the great wisdom of all spirits who have become too introspective, too profound; even in a wound there is the power to heal. A maxim, the origin of which I withhold from scholarly curiosity, has long been my motto:

Increscunt animi, virescit volnere virtus.

['The spirits increase, vigour grows through a wound.']

(Nietzsche, 2012: 10)

Nietzsche explains his decision to challenge the idols in a series of mischievous metaphors: society has too many useless gods, therefore the author intends to test the stupid statues by 'posing his questions with a hammer'. Their entrails will produce a hollow sound, delighting the trickster's 'evil ears'. This book, Nietzsche announces, is his way of casting his 'evil eye' upon this world (2012: 10). He also declares himself

an old psychologist and pied piper before whom just that which would remain silent must finally speak out. [. . .]

And are new idols sounded out? This little essay is a great declaration of war; and regarding the sounding out of idols, this time they are not just idols of the age, but eternal idols, which are here touched with a hammer as with a tuning fork: there are no idols that are older, more assured, more puffed-up – and none more hollow. That does not prevent them from being those in which people have the most faith; nor does one ever say 'idol', especially not in the most distinguished instance.

(2012: 10)

Then he proclaims one of his most famous maxims: 'what does not destroy me, makes me stronger' – the war-cry of the trickster, who, having announced his lack of respect for the empty gods, grabbed a hammer and cheerfully started to bash away at anything that remotely looked like an intellectual structure (2012: 13). Another maxim, number thirty-eight, not surprisingly, concerns identity, its solidity and authenticity: 'Are you genuine? Or merely an actor? A representative? Or that which is represented? In the end, perhaps you are merely a copy of an actor. Second question of conscience' (2012: 13).

To this day Nietzsche is used as the mascot of Western Ragnarök – a condition that has been variably termed 'modern', 'postmodern', 'post-industrial', etc. It is characterised by the increased and increasing tension between authority and the individual both on the personal and social levels. In other words, at the core of this condition lies the trickster force – the force of change, challenge or even destruction if one is not careful enough with it. The destruction or diminishment of authority inevitably triggers identity problems, for the trickster will not supply you with lifestyle instructions or existence-organising rituals after significantly weakening authority as a concept. The order has a meaning-making function, even if this meaning is subjective, narrow and suffocating. Despite its limiting and oppressive effects, the order stabilises and solidifies identity while the trickster challenges the very concept of a stable or structured, well, anything.

With the arrival of modernity, the local, narrow and stabilising character of culture gradually begins to change. When the idols are tested with a hammer, the predictable world – 'the good-enough mother' – starts to crumble. All kinds of tricksters escape their caves, rocks and bottles, and begin to haunt cultural landscapes. Ragnarök has arrived – and fluidisation of the self is one of its primary manifestations. Industrialisation drives the individuals out of the socio-cultural milieu in which their predecessors had spent centuries living a well-ordered and unchanging lifestyle. Torn from his roots, the individual loses awareness of both himself and his surroundings. With the stabilising influence of the social milieu no longer available, human beings start to look for alternative forms of self-identification – and for alternative and effective ways of stabilising the internal trickster that is the self.

The individual living in post-industrial society is bombarded with impressions, feelings, events; he is drowned in sensory overload. Too many things happen around the inhabitant of the modern metropolis. The world is seething with trickster qualities: change, variety, choice, movement. Political, social and technological change makes his life inconstant and unpredictable, and his experience of the environment fragmenting and unsettling. Just because the individual is born into this kind of lifestyle, it does not mean that it has no consequences for the psyche. Human ability to withstand high sensory intensity has been the topic of discussion amongst mental health specialists, sociologists, philosophers and anthropologists for at least 200 years. For instance, the German sociologist Georg Simmel writes in his essay 'The Metropolis and Mental Life' (1903):

> The psychological foundation, upon which the metropolitan individuality is erected, is the intensification of emotional life due to the swift and continuous shift of external and internal stimuli . . . To the extent that the metropolis creates these psychological conditions – with every crossing of the street, with the tempo and multiplicity of economic, occupational and social life – it creates the sensory foundations of mental life, and in the degree of awareness necessitated by our organization as creatures dependent on differences, a deep contrast with the slower, more habitual, more

smoothly flowing rhythm of the sensory-mental phase of small town and rural existence.

(Cited in Schwartz and Przyblyski, 2004: 54)

External reality in late modernity is essentially confusing and superficial; it is trickster personified. Contemporary types of authority – mainly because they are no longer allowed to generate universal truths – fail to provide human beings with firm answers as to what to do and how to live one's life. As a result, the trickster keeps taunting the individual with unrealised opportunities and unlived lives and lifestyles. Without the stability and safety of systemic control, without the regulating influence of tradition, without the regularity of rituals and meaning-making symbolism, the individual, Fredric Jameson argues, feels like a schizophrenic patient. In post-modernity, according to Jameson,

> the experience of the present becomes powerfully, overwhelmingly vivid and 'material': the world comes before the schizophrenic with heightened intensity, bearing a mysterious and oppressive charge of affect, glowing with hallucinatory energy. But what might for us seem a desirable experience – an increase in our perceptions, a libidinal or hallucinogenic intensification of our normally humdrum and familiar surroundings – is here felt as a loss, as 'unreality'.
>
> *(Cited in Malpas, 2001: 34)*

It is amidst these deeply unsettling experiences that the individual comes face-to-face with the trickster – and with the task of forging a self-identity. However, the weakening of the concept of authority does not automatically produce the new breed of people – independent individuals and civilised tricksters – with a clear vision of who they are, and embracing the plurality of the intolerably intense world without the universal truth. While the notion of choice looks appealing in theory, human beings are not always psychologically ready to embrace it in all its complexity. Anxiety (pointed out by Humboldt and Mill) that is part of society with opportunities and choices comes into play when the ideas of uniformity and 'imitation' lose their status. It can be difficult to embrace the trickster because this would entail looking after it yourself instead of re-directing this task to the relevant authority. Anthony Giddens calls the modern individual's obsession with genuine identity 'the reflexive project of the self' and notes that

> the reflexive project of self-identity is inherently fragile. The task of forging a distinct identity may be able to deliver distinct psychological gains, but it is clearly also a burden. A self-identity has to be continually reordered against the backdrop of shifting experiences of day-to-day life and fragmenting tendencies of modern institutions.
>
> *(Giddens, 2012: 185–186)*

Jung believed that finding an identity outside one's community is a difficult task, and that one can only truly fulfil one's potential only in connection with others. He called this process 'individuation' – 'the fulfilment of [the individual's] own nature as it is related to the whole' (cited in Jacobi, 1973: 107). Thus, individuation does not mean some kind of narcissistic loneliness, but always presupposes involvement with one's fellow human beings (CW7: para. 267). Jung writes in 'Psychological Types':

> In general [individuation] is the process by which individual beings are formed and differentiated; in particular, it is the development of the psychological *individual* as a being distinct from the general, collective psychology. Individuation, therefore, is a process of *differentiation*, having for its goal the development of the individual personality.
>
> *(CW6: para. 757)*

In a way, Jung's idea is similar to Humboldt and Mill's 'civilised trickster' because it involves a balance between realising your own potential and appreciating others. Individuating in modern settings is a difficult task because the very concepts of communal duty and ritual have almost dissolved. The individual is instinctively bound to seek communal settings to complete his individuation, and to feel 'whole' rather than lonely and fragmented.

The sociologist Zygmunt Bauman paints an even darker picture of the individual who lost control of his trickster, and consequently feels anxious and lost, unable to choose the right path in life. Post-industrial societies require the individual to make almost heroic efforts 'to be a personality' and to 'think for himself', which had not been required of him in communal settings. Bauman almost mourns the decline of community and subsequent dissolution of 'human bonds' characteristic of urban settings:

> This kind of uncertainty, of dark premonitions and fears of the future that haunt men and women in the fluid, perpetually changing social environment in which the rules of the game change in the middle of the game without warning or legible pattern, does not unite the sufferers: it splits them and sets them apart. The pains it causes to the individuals do not add up, do not accumulate, do not condense into a kind of 'common cause' which could be pursued more effectively by joining forces and acting in unison. The decline of the community is in this sense self-perpetuating; once it takes off, there are fewer and fewer stimuli to stem the disintegration of human bonds and seek ways to tie again which has been torn apart.
>
> *(Bauman, 2001: 48)*

Interestingly enough, Victor Turner argues that human beings cannot be criticised for lack of independent thinking amidst the sensory overload and the burden of ontological problems. Yes, such a citizen is no 'civilised trickster', but it would be unfair to criticise him for failing to find original and creative frameworks for his life and experiences. It is only unfair to call him 'average' and 'common' if all he does is look for advice from community-like structures. Turner notes that the pressure to find 'personal and individual salvation' often leads people to seek old-style meaning-producing structures providing a 'transcendental source of support' (yoga springs to mind):

> As societies diversify economically and socially and as particularistic multiplex ties of locality and kinship yield place to a wide range of single-interest relationships between members of functional groups over ever wider geographical areas, individual option and voluntarism thrive at the expense of predetermined corporate obligations. Even obligations are chosen; they result from entering into contractual relations. The individual replaces the group as the crucial ethical point. [. . .] And, as Max Weber has pointed out, the individual extruded from previous corporate, mainly kin-based matrices becomes obsessed with the problem of personal and individual salvation. The need to choose between alternative lines of action in an ever more complex social field, the increasing weight, as he matures, of responsibility for his own individual decisions and their outcomes, prove too much for the individual to endure on his own, and he seeks some transcendental source of support and legitimacy to relieve him from anxieties about his immediate and ultimate fate as a self-conscious entity.
>
> *(Turner, 1975: 200).*

The search for identity is often supported by psychotherapy and other therapeutic abstract systems, including spiritual movements and self-help guides. The expansion and development of various therapies in the twentieth century proved that the metropolitan individual needs help in dealing with his disorganised and unpredictable existence. With so many things happening to him in one day, and with so many professional, cultural and personal choices and possibilities on offer, people simply lose the ability to act according to 'common sense' in their day-to-day operations. The father of cognitive therapy, Aaron T. Beck, writes:

> When we consider the complexities and pressures of everyday life, we can only marvel that our fellow man is able to function as well as he does. He not only adapts to helter-skelter changes in his environment and difficult confrontations with other people, but also manages to negotiate numerous compromises between his own wishes, hopes, and expectations, on the one hand, and external demands and constraints, on the other. Disappointments, frustrations and criticisms are absorbed without lasting damage.
>
> Modern man if often forced to make extremely rapid life-and-death decisions (as when driving a car). He makes even more difficult judgements in distinguishing circumstances that are actually dangerous from those that simply *seem* dangerous . . . .

> If it were not for the man's ability to filter and attach appropriate labels to the blizzard of external stimuli so efficiently, his world would be chaotic and he would be bounced from one crisis to another. Moreover, if he were not able to monitor his highly developed imagination, he would be floating in and out of twilight zone unable to distinguish between the reality of a situation and the images and personal meanings it triggers.
>
> *(Beck, 1991: 10–11)*

Thus, the individual drowns in the sea of fragmenting trickster experiences, from sensory stimuli to complex interpersonal situations, relying mostly on himself to structure these tasks and experiences. In fact, cognitive therapy is one of the many 'abstract systems' able to perform the framing, experience-organising and meaning-making functions previously performed by ritual and tradition. Anthony Giddens notes that the lifespan of the 'modern man' is structured around 'open experience thresholds' rather than ritualised passages and is freed from 'externalities associated with pre-established ties to other individuals and groups' (Giddens, 2012: 147–148). The relative absence of ritual in modern contexts removes an important psychological prop to the individual's capacity to cope with major transitions of life: birth, adolescence, marriage and death (2012: 148). And when the reflexive project of the self is expected to be achieved in a technically competent but morally arid environment, Giddens concludes, even the most thoroughgoing process of life-planning is bound to be plagued by 'the looming threat of personal meaninglessness' (2012: 201).

The trickster does not 'make meaning' and neither does he respect ritual or tradition. It is notable that the Winnebago cycle about Wakdjunkaga's adventures starts with the rogue breaking all possible warpath rituals. He transforms into a chief who announces to the village that he is going on the warpath. He then organises a feast, abandons his guests in order to have sex with a woman, wakes up the next morning and goes on the warpath alone. From the Winnebago perspective, this story is hilarious: a Winnebago tribal chief cannot under any circumstances go on the warpath, the giver of the feast should be the last one to leave the party, and any sexual activity before military operations is strictly forbidden (Radin, 1972: 92). The psychological meaning of this tribal tale is: it is useless to expect structure and meaning from the impulse that is responsible for providing challenge to the uniformity of any organised existence. Its very shapeshifting, chaotic nature cannot bear the functionality of the ritual and the symmetry of tradition. Similarly, it is not fair to expect the same from the trickster impulse in modern contexts. The individualising, progressive trickster force brings little reassurance to the individual in the long term because it destabilises existing patterns of living without actually offering a replacement. Its aim is to show the plurality of systems and plurality of options, not to reassure the individual that here exist a limited number of options, all of which are safe, reliable and valid. The trickster is not exactly an insurance broker.

The British stand-up comedian Jack Dee provides an interesting insight into the mind of the individual longing for ritual, meaning and direction in life. In a newspaper interview, he admits that he spent the first twenty-five years of his life not knowing what he wanted to do in life, and this ended in depression and alcohol addiction (Dee, 2009). This led him to 'seek out spiritual answers, believing that maybe the sense of permanent restlessness I felt was a sign of some kind of metaphysical calling'. At the time Dee had an average job, which he did not see as his true vocation, but what his real calling in life was he did not exactly know. He tried conventional religion but somehow this approach to finding an identity did not work:

> I would go to bookshops and 'research' Christianity. My amateur theology extended to attending one or two talks at the same church, as well as occasional services. The Church of England for me had always been like an elderly relative that I felt I should visit from time to time. I took religion much too seriously, however, and its overall effect was depressing. I would have really liked to discard it, but somehow I couldn't.

Meanwhile, his depression worsened because his life lacked authority (which he expected to arrive in the form of 'signs from above') and meaning:

> I found it harder and harder to lighten up and enjoy life. I would suddenly break off relationships for no good reason, and neglect friends for weeks on end.

> I would fall into a silent inertia that would only temporarily be resolved by an AA meeting. It was a despondency that wouldn't leave and could make me feel very panicky.

> I had a longing for ritual, something I could cling to, a routine to make me feel well and contented. I hoped that reading Bible commentaries and theological critiques would nudge me closer to some kind of absolute that I could hold up as a torch to light my way.

> *(Dee, 2009)*

Seeking meaningful ways of connecting with others when one feels lost in the transient, mercurial world is a laudable thing. However, there are different ways of doing it and there are dangers involved. One of these dangers – the collective shadow – poses a threat to individuality precisely because it promises to relieve the anxiety and shameful feelings of powerlessness by means of 'imitation' and bland uniformity. This could lead to the death of individuality – and automatically to the death of the trickster.

Authority today

Regardless of the fact that the trickster is a powerful force in modern settings, it would be incorrect to assume that the concept of authority has been erased from Western societies. This section outlines the new types of authority that emerged in place of the 'old truths' shaken off their pedestals by Ragnarök. They have been reincarnated in the form of the state and what Anthony Giddens calls 'abstract systems' – codified systems of expert knowledge (health and safety, management strategy, psychotherapy – the list is endless), oriented towards continual internal improvement or effectiveness (Giddens, 2012: 31).

The emergence of these professional structures in place of old, communal forms of environment organisation and control is logical. Trickster energy can only be productive when it is shaped by culture. Without the framework, the trickster force is just pure energy, pure havoc, pure uncontrolled change. The framework is necessary for its successful utilisation. In his essay 'On Psychic Energy', Jung argues that without the 'framing devices' provided by culture and civilisation, people are left helpless in the face of the vague and powerful trickster impulse:

> When Nature is left to herself, energy is transformed along the line of its natural 'gradient'. In this way natural phenomena are produces, but not 'work'. So also man when left to himself lives as a natural phenomenon, and, in the proper meaning of the word, produces no work. It is culture that provides the machine whereby the natural gradient is exploited for the performance of work. That man should ever have invented this machine must be due to something rooted deep in his nature, indeed in the nature of the living organism as such. For living matter is itself a transformer of energy, and in some way as yet unknown life participates in the transformation process. Life proceeds, as it were, by making use of natural physical and chemical conditions as a means to its own existence.
>
> *(CW8: para. 80)*

Similarly, the anthropologist Clifford Geertz argues that control as a 'civilising' instrument is profitable not only for the system (which performs the difficult task of taming animal tendencies in human beings), but also primarily for individuals themselves. Without systematisation of his emotions and mental abilities, the growing individual would feel fragmented, empty and completely at a loss. Humans' very mental abilities depend on and are kept alive by their propensity to learn, retain and transmit knowledge. People are nothing without their culture because 'the human brain is thoroughly dependent upon cultural resources for its very operation' (Geertz, 1973: 76). Even when it is narrow-minded, constrictive or oppressive, culture still provides a framework for self-definition and for the functioning of mental and psychological processes:

> [H]uman intellections in the specific sense of directive reasoning, depends upon the manipulation of the certain kinds of cultural resources in such a manner as to produce (discover, select) environmental stimuli needed – for whatever purpose – by the organism; it is a search for information. And this search is the more pressing because of the high degree of generality of the information intrinsically available to the organism from genetic sources. The lower an animal, the less it needs to find out in detail from the environment

prior to behavioural performance; birds need not build wind tunnels to test aerodynamic principles before learning to fly – those they already 'know'. The 'uniqueness' of man has often been expressed in terms of how much and how many different sorts of things he is capable of learning.

(1973: 79)

Moreover, relationships – emotional and intellectual encounters, mirroring con- nections – can only happen within an already existing social system. People have difficulty giving themselves definitions. The language of social definitions unites human beings who would otherwise drown in diversity. Choice in relation to self- definition and social relations can be as confusing – if not more confusing – as in every other part of human activity. However, even with the help of behavioural etiquette, protocol rules and other framing devices, the clarity of communication is not guaranteed because of inter-subjective differences. Beyond maternal mirror- ing, human beings feel socially insecure. Thus, culture has a stabilising influence on the emerging human being – just like the proverbial Winnicottian 'good-enough mother' would. Like Jung, Geertz argues that we become individuals *only* within our cultures, and that there is no such thing as a human nature independent of culture (1973: 49):

> [Relationships] are grasped only through the agency of cultural formulations of them. And, being culturally formulated, their precise character differs from society to society as the inventory of available cultural patterns differs; from situation to situation within a single society as different patterns among the plurality of those which are available are deemed appropriate for application; and from actor to actor within similar situations as idiosyncratic habits, pref- erences, and interpretations come into play. There are, at least, beyond infancy, no neat social expectations of any importance in human life. Every- thing is tinged with imposed significance, and fellowmen, like social groups, moral obligations, political institutions, or ecological conditions are appre- hended only through a screen of significant symbols which are the vehicles of their objectification, a screen which is therefore very far from being neutral with respect to their 'real' nature. Consociates, contemporaries, pre- decessors, and successors are as much made as born.
>
> *(1973: 367)*

The commonplace argument (and one of the self-advertising slogans of Western civilisation) is that modernity 'freed' individuals from the caging effect of a specific culture by allowing them to travel, by giving them opportunities to pick lifestyles and identities, and by cancelling the unnecessary rituals. Now people in industrialised society can 'build themselves' out of a wide range of choices available. Children in democratic societies grow up to be creative, free individu- als, and they have at their disposable an infinite number of means for self-expression.

At the same time, the humanistic branch of contemporary philosophy has traditionally maintained that the much-praised individual freedom in the West is only illusory. In his essay 'Prophets and Priests' (1967), the psychologist and philosopher Erich Fromm points out that late modern society requires not an independent individual but 'an organisation man' – mediocre, unhappy and moulded by universal education into an obedient mass creature. Far from being 'the civilised trickster', he has 'opinions, but no convictions; he amuses himself, but is unhappy; he is even willing to sacrifice his life and that of his children in voluntary obedience to impersonal and anonymous powers' (2010: 23). Such a man, Fromm continues, is exploited by the state and other organised bureaucracies, which do not need anyone too creative, too unpredictable or – God forbid – too original, lest he ruins the smooth operation of the machine:

> This century is the century of the hierarchically organised bureaucracies in government, business and labour unions. These bureaucracies administer things *and* men as one; they follow certain principles, especially the economic principle of the balance sheet, quantification, maximal efficiency, and profit, and they function essentially as would an electronic computer that has been programmed with these principles. The individual becomes a number, transforms himself into a thing. But just because there is no overt authority, because he is not 'forced' to obey, the individual is under the illusion that he acts voluntarily, that he follows the rational authority.
>
> *(2010: 22–23)*

A similar thought is echoed by Bertrand Russell. In *Authority and the Individual* (1949) he notes that Western modern world is self-contradictory – despite proclaiming itself democratic, it is terrified of 'civilised tricksters' because they are a threat to its stability. The 'civilised trickster' is no more than an oxymoronic fantasy: 'The inferiority of our age . . . is an inevitable result of the fact that society is centralised and organised to such a degree that individual initiative is reduced to a minimum' (Russell, 2010: 36). Interestingly enough, Russell argues that, when the man was attached to his community, he had better access to liminal forces as well better ways of self-expression. He had the kind of spontaneity in his life that is not approved in the world overregulated by systems and governed by faceless structures:

> The modern man lives a very different life. If he sings in the street he will be thought to be drunk, and if he dances a policeman will reprove him for impeding the traffic. His working day, unless he is exceptionally fortunate, is occupied in a completely monotonous manner in producing something which is valued, not like the shield of Achilles, as a beautiful piece of work, but mainly for its utility.
>
> *(2010: 37–38)*

In other words, the individual makes mass-produced things, and his own creativity is stifled. Contemporary society, which relies on the smoothness and regularity of its systems, cannot afford to use such pernicious trickster qualities as spontaneity and creativity for fear that they disturb the flow of tightly organised regimes.

Fromm's and Russell's scepticism is echoed by Jung. All three authors wrote out of their experiences of the bureaucratised, programmable 'collective man' taking over whole countries and destroying millions of lives. Jung was not particularly interested in shame on the personal level, and neither did he analyse the narcissistic aspects of the shame/control axis, but he was deeply concerned about human propensity to join systems in order to feel better, more important, more adequate or even to acquire some meaning in life. In 'Psychology and Religion' (1938) Jung warns that 'individualism' is a fragile idea, and that, deep down, human beings are plagued by impersonal forces, which, during difficult political moments, threaten to engulf and destroy any trickster's efforts to create a man capable of thinking and acting differently from the crowd:

> There is indeed reason enough for man to be afraid of the impersonal forces lurking in [the individual's] unconscious. We are blissfully unconscious of these forces because they never, or almost never, appear in our personal relations or under ordinary circumstances. But if people crowd together and form a mob, then the dynamisms of the collective man are let loose – beasts or demons that lie dormant in every person until he is part of a mob. Man in the mass sinks . . . to an inferior moral and intellectual level, to that level which is always there, below the threshold of consciousness, ready to break forth as soon as it is activated by the formation of a mass.
>
> *(CW11: para. 23)*

Meanwhile, the state, Jung observes, has been transformed in the minds of its subjects into a kind of idol: it is invoked, made responsible, grumbled at, and perceived as 'the inexhaustible giver of all good' (CW10: para. 554). Society is elevated to the rank of a supreme ethical principle (CW10: para. 554).

True, under the pressure to develop 'an identity' or under the burden of shame, individuals can be tempted to swap their precious trickster for the faceless narcissism of the collective shadow. However, trickster-control can also be achieved in less troublesome ways, including using the services of abstract systems, which 'give external form to narratives of self-identity' (Giddens, 2012: 62). Abstract systems – including self-help programmes, diet books, lifestyle magazines, psychotherapy, etc. – create what Giddens calls 'regimes' (which, essentially, are anti-trickster weapons) – ways of organising one's life amidst the endless sea of choice (Giddens, 2012: 7).

Abstract systems are effectively in charge of external reality. They emulate the systems of the past and traditional settings whose task was to control change and chance – including individual behaviour and societal development. To use Winnicottian language, they guarantee the stability of the framework within which the individual feels safe and psychologically secure. They are the guarantors of basic trust – the adult version of the child's basic trust in the world. In other words, abstract systems play the role of the mother who mediates the relationship between human beings and the outside world. In this, they replaced traditional settings and community rules that used to organise the individual's life before the arrival of abstract systems. The structure – whether in the form of tradition or 'expert knowledge' – is a substitute parent that is the source of mirroring and psychological safety. Abstract systems, like tradition before them, protect human beings from the fragmenting influence of the trickster.

New forms of control

Much of the success and day-to-day survival of Western societies depends on the smooth operation of systems. In some of them, such as banking, healthcare or entrepreneurship, the margin for error is supposedly minimal (although, in practice, it is not); while in others, for instance, the aviation industry, it is close to zero. The modern world is founded on the assumption that the trickster should be captured and tamed; that the creative impulse is also the force that has the dangerous ability to mess things up, and spoil the organisations' operational capacities.

There is a wide range of tricksters to control: nature with its unpredictability; accidents and emergencies; human behaviour, which should be moulded in ways beneficial for society; human emotions and instincts, which, left unframed, may disturb the structure in many ways. Whole new narratives have been devised to tame the tricksters: occupational health speak; management speak; therapy speak. Emotions are controlled with boundaries, human relationships are professionalised and restricted to easily predictable and governable patterns, the sexual instinct is relegated to the private sphere, and incidental happenings are managed with the help of well-planned abstract systems (such as, for instance, vehicle traffic regulations). They ensure the uniform safety of various mechanisms. As Anthony Giddens argues: 'With the maturation of modernity, abstract systems play an increasingly pervasive role coordinating the various contexts of day-to-day life. External disturbances to such reflexively organised systems become minimised' (2012: 149).

As a result, the liminal is left unexpressed and brooding under the smooth external layer of culture. This makes modern contexts paradoxical: on the one hand, modernity is based on human control over natural and artificial environments; on the other hand, underneath all this, at its base, in fact, lies the psychological brokenness characteristic of uprooted, fluid, 'trickster' societies. Even when natural, turbulent trickster phenomena, such as emotions, look tamed and controlled, they never truly are. Hidden under the veneer of civilisation, lie dangerous things – mass hysterias and mass obsessions, all fuelled by the very human desire for bonding and 'imitation'.

According to Giddens, control is the key ingredient of modern society, and it has been becoming increasingly accentuated, particularly with the radicalisation and globalisation of modern institutions:

> The expansion of surveillance capabilities is the main medium of the control of social activity by social means. Surveillance gives rise to particular asymmetries

of power, and in varying degree consolidates the rule of some groups or classes over others. [...] Much more fundamental is the intensifying of administrative control more generally, a phenomenon not wholly directed by anyone precisely because it affects everyone's activities. Surveillance always operates in conjunction with institutional reflexivity, even in pre-modern systems. It is the condition of institutional reflexivity and at the same time also in some part its product, and thus expresses in a specific institutional form that recursiveness characteristic of all social reproduction.

(2012: 149)

Both surveillance and reflexivity are forms of control, either actual or possible. If something goes wrong, one can sit down, think about it, discuss it with other 'members of the group', with the boss, with the therapist or even with oneself – and thus next time the mistake will be avoided. Both these activities have as their aim avoidance of any trickster activity. As Giddens astutely notes, surveillance plus reflexivity 'means a "smoothing of the rough edges" of such behaviour which is not integrated into a system – that is, not knowledgeably built into mechanisms of system reproduction. Such behaviour becomes alien and discreet' (2012: 150). It is this repressed, burdened with shame 'alien and discreet' behaviour that tends to grow into narcissistic monsters – either personal or collective. Giddens also points out that systemic control characteristic of modern contexts increases a sense of shame and powerlessness in the individual – and not least because it challenges self-identity:

> [S]hame is more directly and pervasively related to basic trust than is guilt, because guilt concerns specific forms of behaviour or cognition rather than threatening the integrity of the self as such. Unlike guilt, shame directly corrodes a sense of security in both self and surrounding social milieux. The more self-identity becomes internally referential, the more shame comes to play a fundamental role in the adult personality. The individual no longer lives primarily by extrinsic moral precepts but *by means of the reflexive organisation of the self.*
>
> *(2012: 153; italic added)*

Moreover, since the arrival of modernity, the system has been perfecting ways of 'correcting' trickster behaviours and phenomena such as crime, vagabondage and madness (2012: 153). Any behaviour different from the range approved by the system is punished or referred for correction. In fact, with the weakening of the ritual, which used to contain and give meaning to liminal moments, places and systems of correction – such as the prison and the asylum (and now, I should add, psychotherapy), gained prominence as geographical and temporal pockets for controlling the trickster.

The new systems of trickster-control far exceed the possibilities of traditional structures because the latter were only local whereas the former are global, and therefore more powerful. They are also more prone to attack by the trickster precisely because they are too bulky and unwieldy. Nobody can entirely control what happens in the smallest pockets of such systems. All the while, the individuals are dependent on them and trust them because without abstract systems – even though they offer little moral satisfaction – there is still chaos and emptiness:

> Various forms of dependency – or, to put the matter less provocatively, trust – are fostered by the reconstruction of day-to-day life via abstract systems. Some such systems, in their global extensions, have created social influences which no one wholly controls and whose outcomes are in some part specifically unpredictable. Yet in many respects the expansion of expert systems provides possibilities of reappropriation well beyond those available in traditional cultures.
>
> *(Giddens, 2012: 176)*

Colonisation of nature is the ultimate claim to mastery over the external world. The desire to predict nature also originates in the feeling of shame. Thus, the personal feeling of shame as well as the feeling of being dwarfed by the environment with its disasters, temperature extremes and majestic landscapes is ameliorated when several centuries of instrumental rationality result in accurate weather prediction, air travel and effective safety measures:

> One thing control means is the subordination of nature to human purposes, organised via the colonising of the future. This process looks at first sight like an extension of 'instrumental reason': the application of humanly organised principles of science and technology to the mastery of the natural world. Looked at more closely, however, what we see is the emergence of *an internally referential system of knowledge and power*. It is in these terms that we should understand the phrase 'the end of nature'. There has taken place a marked acceleration and deepening of human control over nature, directly involved with the globalisation of social and economic activity. 'The end of nature' means that the natural world has become in large part 'a created environment', consisting of humanly structured systems whose motive power and dynamic derive from socially organised knowledge-claims rather than from influences exogenous to human activity.
>
> *(Giddens, 2012: 144)*

In this case, the feeling of shame, if not completely erased, is at least dealt with because the source of shame is 'subdued' and 'conquered'. Nature is the king of all tricksters, the most dangerous and capable of destroying civilisation to which it gave birth. Its might triggers awe in human beings – but also feelings of embarrassment and powerlessness at not being able to control it completely.

The new kind of shame

Where the trickster sleeps, the shadow is wide awake. Mirroring lulls us to cognitive sleep as we feel in control, free of shame and being understood and accepted. This can be achieved by establishing a range of projective–introjective relationships – making people mirror us, copying other people's traits, or simply by joining a pre-existent powerful set of rules and beliefs.

By contrast, being an individual is psychologically hard. Maintaining a view that is different can only be sustained by a psyche that is mature enough to tolerate anxiety and frustration – i.e. mature enough to deal with shame. A stable personality core that does not fade easily into the background and that cannot be shamed into compliance and insignificance is capable of seeing through projections – deliberate or unconscious; ideological or personal; dangerous or innocuous. Such a personality would be able to say 'no' to anyone attempting to destroy its boundaries and contaminate it with contents that are alien to it.

The fragmenting aspect of modern life leads the individual to seek solace in the reassuring paternal embrace of instrumental rationality. Meanwhile, the genuine, spontaneous and creative elements of existence are being controlled, and their scope of influence is limited. The trickster is pushed back into the unconscious, suppressed, hidden from view, where it broods and grows, drowned in shame and guilt. Besides, a creative, wholesome individual with the trickster integrated into his psychic structure is not needed in a modern state because his thinking would be too independent, and his vision of things too hostile to the uniformity of systemic thinking. He would be ungovernable both politically and economically. Such a man would be able to think for himself. As Bertrand Russell observes, such a man would possess qualities not needed by either the state or the capitalist enterprise, for large, impersonal structures do not need 'energy and personal initiative, independence of mind and imaginative vision' but seek 'steadiness and reliability' instead (Russell, 2010: 53). Creativity and independence of mind are individualistic qualities, and they can be a double-edged sword in that they are not always easy to manage or predict:

> A man who possesses these qualities is capable of doing much good, or of doing great harm, and if mankind is not to sink into dullness such exceptional men must find scope, though one could wish the scope they find should be for the benefit of mankind. There may be less difference than is sometimes thought between the temperament of a great criminal and a great statesman.
>
> *(2010: 53)*

In modern contexts new avenues of trickster control have emerged. One of them is the individual's behaviour – particularly because in contemporary Western society there exists a clear boundary separating the private from the public. The boundary is guarded by shame, and whenever it is damaged, narcissistic, self-protecting inhabitants of the psyche are damaged too: the social mask (the persona), self-esteem, and dreams of perfection about the 'ideal' self. This is a particularly rich playground for the trickster as he enjoys crossing this boundary at most inappropriate moments, and exposing the 'private' and the 'hidden'. Because the boundary is very definite, and because it holds a number of qualities highly inconvenient in a civilised society – sexuality, greed, emotions – it becomes the main area of tension between the trickster and the shadow. When there is no natural integration between the two spheres, the trickster 'integrates' them by force – by simply exposing anything carefully hidden behind the mask.

Due to the fact that modern spaces (train stations, airports, the tube, cafes and supermarkets) are impersonal and complex, public life is tightly controlled and consists of prescriptive protocols. Large numbers of strangers come into brief contact with each other every day, and their encounter should be as frictionless as possible. One cannot be 'fully yourself', 'be genuine' or 'openly express their emotions' in public settings. Public life should be bland and uniform, governed by protocol and carefully staged. The self, terrified of fragmentation yet constantly on the verge of it, is trying to keep the trickster (choice, emotion, instinct, etc.) in check using the therapeutic resources offered to it. However, the strength and effectiveness of these resources are nowhere near the effectiveness of those given by, say, a traditional culture or a stringent political framework.

The sociologists Christopher Lasch and Richard Sennett associate the public sphere of modern existence with the rise of narcissism in capitalist countries. Their argument is that the separation of the social from the personal has led to unhealthy preoccupation with self-image. Self-limiting and cautious, protecting their inner core, contemporary individuals establish emotional 'exchanges' with others instead of giving (and giving out) themselves wholeheartedly. They use boundaries (such as professional conduct) to keep the trickster at bay, and to keep control over their emotional and physical lives. Such behaviour, Sennett argues, is narcissistic by nature – not pathologically or clinically so, but fuelled by the fear of 'losing one's face in public', of exposing one's fragile core (Sennett, 1978: 22). The common mirroring background has been withdrawn, and nothing can glue the individual internally, or link community members with each other.

The public arena stops being a communal avenue, and becomes a place where personal qualities are displayed, and where individual actions and identity are more important than the actions of a group. As the individual is compelled to 'authenticate himself as a social actor', the public sphere inevitably becomes dominated by narcissistic issues (1978: 22). One has to wear one's best mask in public:

> Narcissistic feelings often focus themselves on obsessive questions of whether I am good enough, whether I am adequate, and the like. When a society mobilises these feelings, when it deflates the objective character of action and inflates the importance of subjective states of feeling of the actors, these questions of self-justification in action, via a 'symbolic act, will come systematically to the fore.
> *(1978: 11–12)*

Moreover – Sennett argues – since the public domain is 'abandoned and empty' (1978: 12) and all the genuine human qualities are buried under the mask, the human ability to play is also stunted. Lack of integration between the two spheres leads to the repression of trickster qualities: spontaneity, action and independent thinking. When men stop thinking socially, they lose their ability to play:

> To lose the ability to play is to lose the sense that worldly conditions are plastic. This ability to play with social life depends on the existence of a dimension of society which stands apart from, at a distance from, intimate desire, need, and identity. [. . .]
>
> Under these conditions, everything returns to motive: Is this what I really feel? Do I really mean it? Am I being genuine? The self of motivations intervenes in an intimate society to block people from feeling free to play with the presentations of feelings as objective, formed signs. Expression is made contingent upon authentic feeling, but one is always plunged into the narcissistic problem of never being able to crystallize what is authentic in one's feelings.
>
> *(1978: 267)*

This view is echoed by Christopher Lasch in his book *The Culture of Narcissism: American Life in an Age of Diminishing Expectations* (1979). Lasch states the Western person's incessant self-promotion and preoccupation with self-image, his lack of concern for community and his, essentially meaningless and lonely, quest to find the 'authentic' self result in a sense of emptiness and loss of touch with reality: 'The weakening of social ties, which originates in the prevailing state of social warfare, at the same time reflects a narcissistic defence against dependence' (Lasch, 1991: 51). Meanwhile, 'the ideology of personal growth, superficially optimistic, radiates a profound despair and resignation. It is the faith of those without faith' (1991: 51).

Thus, in modern contexts, control (self-control and control of the environment) becomes one of the most sought after skills. Being in control equals being a magician who can mould the world according to his likeness. At the same time, the desirable degree of control over the environment is usually difficult to achieve, and the gap between fantasy (and fantasy of the ideal self) and reality sooner or later manifests itself. A new kind of shame arises – the shame of losing face in public, of being emotional, of being seen as weak, bad, inadequate or 'strange' – in other words, of being out of control. To use our trickster language, a society of strangers, in which the wall between the public and the private is thick, is plagued by the fear of the trickster. This is the fear of being 'discovered', and the fear of oneself – because the contemporary individual never stops to suspect that, underneath all the masks and the civilised veneer, he lacks a genuine personality (which can only develop, as Jung argued, in interaction with society, and in genuine exchanges with the community). Such an individual is far from being the 'civilised trickster' of liberal philosophy. Instead, he is torn between the feeling of being average and wanting to be a celebrity; between the feelings of inadequacy and secretly wanting to be the best; he does not know 'who he is' and despairs at not having achieved enough. He is obsessed with self-control and his behaviour is largely governed by shame.

Aaron T. Beck gives a good description of such 'trickster phobia' – the fear of not being able to control one's own mind and body, particularly in public settings.

This is the phobia of being suddenly engulfed by everything that civilisation – and particularly contemporary civilisation – prescribes to tightly control: emotions, instincts, bodily functions. This is also the fear of 'being genuine' or behaving naturally in settings in which any manifestations of the trickster are highly inappropriate, such as exams, public talks, conferences or office environments. The trickster's habit of slipping out unexpectedly, thus transgressing the wall between the public and the private, is seen as catastrophic, as the worst nightmare possible.

In *Cognitive Therapy and Emotional Disorders* Beck describes a range of 'trickster' scenarios most feared by his patients: a man is terrified of losing his role as authority in a particular area; a student is anxious before an exam because he wants a high grade; a usually self-confident woman does not know what to wear before an important meeting; a man has nightmares on the eve of public presentations. Such reactions, Beck observes, are catastrophic because the individual who is anxious about a future has a fear of something that has not yet occurred; he is thinking about narcissistic risks and precipitating narcissistic injuries even before they actually happen. These injuries are invariably related to being 'exposed', to not doing your best, to not being 'perfect'. On this border between the 'natural' trickster and the socialised, narcissistic shadow all kinds of mental disturbances emerge, triggered by acute self-consciousness, including anxiety and panic attacks, paranoia, depression and all sorts of obsessions and compulsions (Beck, 1991: 78–89).

As Erik Erikson points out, the fear of being out of control first manifests itself in childhood, when the child gradually crosses the boundary between the 'pure', unconscious trickster and a civilised man. Bowel and bladder training, in Erikson's view, has become the most disturbing item in child training in the wide circles of Western society. This is because the most basic of trickster parts, 'the anus' is stubborn and not always predictable. Its unpredictability and unreliability, Erikson points out, does not fit into the Western ideal image of the mechanised body as well as contradicting the middle-class mores (Erikson, 1995: 71). Therefore, vigorous training ('taming of the trickster') is 'absolutely necessary to the development of orderliness and punctuality' (1995: 71). But even relatively tamed, 'the anus' keeps causing various psychological disturbances, from obsessive-compulsive disorders to anxiety and panic attacks. Erikson writes:

> [T]he neurotics of our time include the compulsive type, who has more mechanical orderliness, punctuality and thrift, and this in matters of affection as well as in faeces, than is good for him, and, in the long run, for his society.
> *(1995: 71)*

To this Jacoby adds that 'the backside' is often a psychological bedsit of nightmares in people prone to shame. Its stubbornness leads to 'shameful brooding over what one has "given away" of oneself to others in an uncontrolled way, or with doubts about what one has "left behind". Such doubts often lead to compulsively controlling behaviour' (Jacoby, 1996: 52).

It is not surprising that so many trickster tales are preoccupied with evacuation of waste and other inconvenient bodily functions. The trickster in these tales is not ashamed of the behaviour of his 'buttocks' or the actions of his penis. Neither is he embarrassed by his stupidity, his mistakes or his impulsiveness because he represents a creature who does not know shame – he is just on his way to becoming a decent human being. The civilising process involves the gradual 'framing' and shaping of the trickster's behaviour with the help of the most powerful psychological tool – shame. And yet, even tamed and suppressed, the trickster is never going to stay in his cage without putting up a fight. This is particularly true of post-industrial settings obsessed with control, orderliness, punctuality and other idealistic-narcissistic properties necessary for the smooth operation of the capitalist system. It is these properties that the trickster regularly attacks, and it is to these attacks that we, humans, respond with outbursts of neurotic behaviour. However hard man tries to establish control over nature – including human nature – the human body and human psyche are alive. The trickster demands to be celebrated, not over-controlled.

Exposing the hidden: 'I don't care what you think'

The counter-tendency to the fear of over-exposure, to the terror of being 'different' from the rest of the mass, and to the phobia of saying and doing something wrong in public is being provocative, publicly declaring scandalous things and being insensitive to, well, everyone's feelings. This is professional tricksterism in action, and the comedian Frankie Boyle is a good example of this daring vocation.

Boyle particularly likes to explore taboo and controversial subjects, from the royal family to disability and sexual abuse. His jokes are often deliberately offensive. For instance, his gig for the BBC 2013 Comic Relief contained a distasteful remark about the Queen's recent hospitalisation: 'I wish she'd died – because they wouldn't have been able to tell anyone. They would have had to hollow out her body and get that guy who plays Gollum to wear it' (Bull, 2013). In the same monologue he joked about another 'sacred' subject – the royal baby: 'I was amazed to hear Kate ever got pregnant. She told me she was on the f***ing pill.' Boyle also comments on Kate Middleton's appearance in relation to the scandal with revealing holiday photos: 'I don't know what the fuss was about the pictures of Kate's tits. Anyway, in my paper I have to flick past pictures of good tits to read about the shit ones' (Wyatt, 2013).

In addition, Boyle touched on a range of social taboos. Commenting on the Jimmy Savile scandal, he said: 'I think the BBC made Jimmy Savile wear that jewellery so children could hear him coming . . . I had thought the only way I'd end up back on the BBC would be if I started f***ing kids.' He also remarked about the current resignation of Pope Benedict XVI: 'the Pope must have done something that even the Catholic Church found unacceptable. My theory is that he f***ed an adult woman' (Bull, 2013).

The entire sketch was omitted from the broadcast, and it is likely that Boyle knew that this would happen. He might have deliberately courted confrontation. Besides, this is not the first time the comedian publicly discussed taboos or besmirched high status or venerated figures. Some of his previously criticised comments included a joke about children with Down syndrome (Walker, 2010), Princess Diana and Madeleine McCann ('Frankie Boyle's Top 10 Controversial Jokes', 2013).

Boyle seems to be conscious about his use of comedy as the proverbial Nietzschean 'hammer', being indiscriminately rude and very insensitive in the process of striking the idols and listening to the hollow sound of their 'entrails'. From his view, by taking on the giant and unwieldy structures such as the Catholic Church, the aristocracy and the BBC, he gives laughter back its social edge and political significance. All three systems mentioned above are regularly exposed in the news as places where different kinds of mistreatment occur, yet their very elitism and lack of transparency are powerful tools that allow this abuse to be covered up. As Boyle argues in his book, *Work! Consume! Die!* (2011), the comedian has an important social function: because he is the person who thinks differently from the rest of the community, he can provide unusual angles on common issues. The comedian's true aim is to be able to say something that other people would never say out loud for fear of punishment or social disapproval. The comedian's role is that of the trickster – a statusless, marginal creature – which is the opposite of the shaman or priest (as they may enjoy their status and be tempted to feed their egos). The trickster-comedian de-powers and de-symbolises the world, which tends to operate with systems reproducing and perpetuating themselves. He sets out to destroy and challenge them faster than they can regenerate:

> In man's original nomadic tribal state, the role of social critic would have been vital in deciding when to move on. Comedians are just the descendants of the guys and gals whose job it was to say, 'It's fucking shit here', and moan until everybody upped sticks and headed west, into an ambush prepared by a rival tribe, or a barren wasteland. [. . .]
>
> Shamans, priests are all people whose role is to power-up symbols. In our scientific reality tunnel a hallucination might be a manifestation of the unconscious mind. In a shamanic one it might be a fairie, in a religious one, an angel. The comedian is actually there to de-power the symbolic world. With Lenny Bruce, cancer goes from being this big demonic taboo to being, well, just cancer. The best comics are really trying to wake you up from symbolic world; they are desentimentalisers, pointing out that those First World War soldiers who had a truce to play football at Christmas probably killed each other the next day, and not even remorsefully but muttering, 'That was never offside, you cunt'.
>
> *(Boyle, 2011: 44)*

Seen in this light, the social trickster-comedian performs a dual task: he drags everything that is embarrassing, shameful, unpleasant or simply too painful to think about, from under the mask and onto the social surface. He exposes shame and displays it for everyone to see. During the process of this extreme de-shaming, he aims to damage the mask and deflate the structures that guard propriety and define behavioural norms. Being indiscriminate, he often damages the structures that should be left intact, and exposes contents that should not be exposed. However, being a trickster, he lacks respect for the sacred, and refuses to see the difference between the acceptable and the unacceptable.

Boyle explains in the introduction to *Work! Consume! Die!* that his art, as he sees it, consists of disturbing people and making them angry: 'I sincerely hope that you will be disappointed by this book. To disappoint, anger and dismay has always been my ideal' (2011: 1). Like his mythological colleagues, the contemporary social trickster refuses to understand the notion of taboo, thus aiming at the very heart of the concept of 'the perfect order'. The aim of such a trickster is not to destroy the structure – but to challenge it, to push it into the liminal zone, to make it question itself. The damage to his reputation (like the mythological tricksters' body parts falling off) is a normal aspect of the process. And if the social trickster's actions eventually result in the breach of the system's narcissistic armour, he has reached his oxymoronic purpose – which is 'to enlighten' humans out of their blind acceptance of the mesmerising structural element of civilisation. Largest structures tend to have the darkest corners, dirtiest secrets and cruellest intentions – which is perfect for any abuser laden with shame and burdened with inferiority complex. Only a genuine trickster, who does not see systems and organisations as eternal gods, can expose narcissistic intensions.

Trauma, emptiness and failure to relate in Steve McQueen's *Shame*

The opening scene of *Shame* (2011) is shocking in its colourlessness and stillness: the film's protagonist Brandon (Michael Fassbender), with his hand almost on his groin, is lying in bed looking rather dead. The shot's colour temperature is cold; the *mise-en-scène*'s minimalism – the still naked body against the background of blue-white sheets – evokes associations with hospital rooms and mortuaries. The bird's-eye shot lasts half a minute and looks almost like a freeze frame until Brandon blinks. That's when the viewer sighs with relief – the protagonist is alive and breathing.

However, Brandon's life is all an illusion. Although his body perfectly works, internally he feels like a corpse. Psychologically, he is just about able to function. Professionally successful, personally he is a failure – lonely, sad, repressed and unable to establish meaningful connections with others. He is a typical urban dweller, bland and unfeeling, and wearing a cold defensive mask. Brandon's family consists of dysfunctional sister Sissy (Carey Mulligan) whose psychological problems mirror his own. When not sleeping with prostitutes or masturbating, Brandon goes out drinking and clubbing with his silly boss David (James Badge Dale) in an attempt to pick up women.

His trickster, in the form of obsessive behaviour and repressed feelings, keeps him alive and disturbs him out of his slumber. There is nothing he can do about the powerful, insane obsession pulsing in him: Brandon is a sex-addict. He has sex with assorted prostitutes, is addicted to porn in all forms and sizes and masturbates compulsively and obsessively. His life is spent in sterile, grey, minimalist rooms – his flat, hotels, offices. His existence is framed, narrowed, sliced and fragmented by the angular urban architecture – by all this glass, steel, concrete. Brandon's surroundings perfectly reflect the fragmented state of his soul; they emphasise a terrifying internal emptiness that is occasionally flooded by powerful and overwhelming waves of shame. The only highlight of his life is the smiling and mysterious female stranger (Lucy Walters) whom he meets on subway train at the start of the film. He chases after her but she disappears in the crowd.

The whole film is focalised through Brandon's eyes (the cinematic equivalent of free indirect speech). We are shown the world through his colourless, lifeless narcissistic lens. His vision of the world is one extended projection. The viewer sees – and empathises with – Brandon's painful and compulsive search for an ideal prosthesis to fill the dark, painful void, to soothe the agony, to numb the pain of the internal wound. Brandon treats every woman as a potential replacement of his missing identity, and gets overwhelmed by a sense of helplessness and embarrassment when they refuse to be controlled. Every time he fails to establish mastery over the world, the terrible feeling of shame returns and throws him out of balance.

A perfect prosthetic object would be the exact mirror opposite of Brandon. It would be something that he denies and represses in himself. It would perfectly fit into the edges of his wound. In fact, he already has such an object in his life – his attention-seeking sister Sissy, a female trickster, who has a number of rather annoying incestuous habits including arriving, unannounced, at her brother's flat, storming into the bathroom when he is masturbating, cuddling up to him in bed or watching porn on his laptop. However hard Brandon tries to protect his bland, spiritless, self-sufficient, lonely existence, Sissy's persistent and unwelcome intrusions ruin his plans and fill his life with guilt, shame, incestuous desire, affect and conflict.

However, McQueen is keen to stress that Brandon's bloodless selfishness is not just a problem originating in troublesome childhood or a result of some personal trauma. It is a malaise, a virus (that's the metaphor McQueen uses) gradually colonising the entire body of the Western world. The film's protagonist is a just a cell in this body. The internal emptiness of the individual in post-industrial society is the result of the trauma of modernity. The individual, eternally trapped in this traumatised, immature state seeks his lost self in outer objects which he alternately sees as seductive and beautiful or aggressive and unmanageable. The tragedy of this kind of existence lies in the fact that these outer objects cannot be manipulated. Like a child unable to grasp the concept of the autonomy of others, and consequently unable to relate to the world in a mature way, he breaks down in fury and frustration.

Sissy and Brandon represent an ideal narcissist co-dependent couple. They obsessively seek to merge with each other despite the incest taboo. The brother and sister are locked in an emotionally violent yet indissoluble relationship. Sissy is everything that Brandon had long ago buried under the heap of false identities: emotional, creative, childish, dependent, demanding, lacking in self-sufficiency. She is his undeveloped true self – bleeding through the layers of artificial coldness and other means of psychological insulation. Being a trickster, she manages to break through Brandon's iron boundaries by forcing herself into his soul, and the might with which she does this is reflected in the rather repetitive song *I Want Your Love*, which is playing in a loop when Brandon finds her in his bathroom.

Sissy's existence in her brother's life reminds him of his own inability to control the world, his failure to manage and manipulate objects. She reduces him to a helpless child. Sissy is Brandon's shame – she makes him cry with her singing, she makes him shout, she terribly shocks him by attempting to commit suicide. She has sex with her brother's boss on her brother's bed. She makes him painfully, vulnerably, terrifyingly alive by reviving their shared childhood trauma. Her existence – and her forcible boundary-breaking – throws Brandon into cycles of obsessive jogging and compulsive trouble-seeking in an attempt to regain control over the world and its objects. Their relationship is a form of addiction, dependency, compulsive merger – it is not a mature connection.

In fact, mature relationships are missing from Brandon's life. Prostitutes, internet girls and pornographic images are all remnants of the magical world of uroboric omnipotence, of pre-individual existence. They maintain an illusion of perfect control over the object. Challenged – or rather, enraged – by Sissy, Brandon gathers and bins all of his porn magazines and the infected laptop. To make sure that they are gone, he empties his fridge into the bins as well. He attempts to bury his shame under platefuls of food. This does not help, however – he is still unable to have mature sex or have an equal relationship with a woman. The second date with his co-worker Marianne (Nicole Beharie) ends in a shameful sexual disaster.

Following Sissy's suicide attempt and the subsequent hospital visit, Brandon collapses in a heap on the river bank. This is a powerful scene because it shows the height of his helplessness – and his ultimate refusal (or inability) to grow up. The rain and the relentless grey urban landscape transform the successful city executive into a miserable tramp, they reveal his spiritual poverty, the tragic emptiness of his life. His only hope now is the subway stranger – the smiling woman wearing both a wedding ring and an engagement ring. She symbolises the protagonist's hope for wholeness, for regaining his identity, for bringing together the fragmented parts of his personality. She is the idealised picture of the Jungian self – distant yet possibly attainable.

However, McQueen does not allow the audience to become too optimistic about the outcome of Brandon's 'shock therapy'. The ending of the film is open. The last shot is the close-up of the protagonist's face looking at the woman. His revival – or survival – lies in the future, and we do not know whether it will take place at all. The cut to a black screen, although not entirely excluding hope for the protagonist's psychological survival, nevertheless hints that Brandon has a lot to work through before he regains his self – and before he is united with the mysterious stranger.

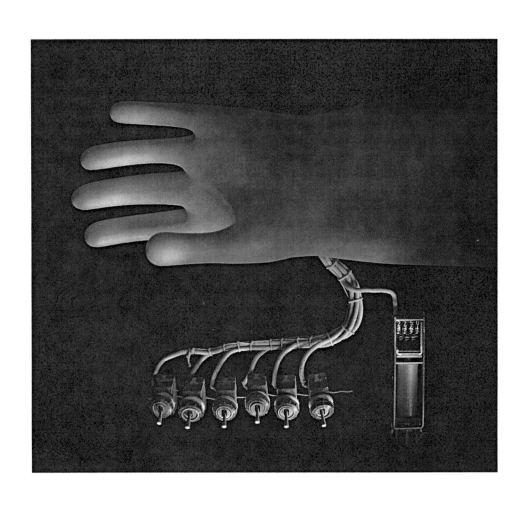

3

THE TRICKSTER AND THE CAPITALIST SYSTEM

Several times in this book I criticise the socialist system for failing to support the individual, and for oppressing the trickster in all spheres of human existence – from the personal level to the highest social and political strata. Socialism presupposes that the individual sacrifices his narcissistic impulses for the sake of community; that he gives up the desire to stand out, the impulse to be different from the crowd, in exchange for the feelings of safety and security. Regardless of their initial intentions, in the long run socialist ideologies do not discern between the trickster and the shadow; between the jubilant creativity of primary omnipotence and craving for power and control; between the impulse to become an individual and self-obsession laden with shame and guilt. These systems repress the impulse to individuate lest it becomes uncontrollable, too big or too ambitious. Moreover, they know that the individualist impulse is always going to challenge them, and therefore it should be controlled – preferably absorbed by the structure, and its energy used to further collective purposes (as opposed to personal ambitions). The impulse's impact should be neutralised before it has any chance to escape or seek self-expression. In fact, in a socialist society, the individual swaps his personal narcissism for the collective, impersonal narcissism – the narcissism of the system.

In the West, the situation is clearly different. The trickster permeates the fabric of Western societies. Their fluid structures rely on the presence of the trickster impulse in the social and political dynamic. These structures are not permanently fixed; they are not set in stone like the Soviet system of symbols or its self-limiting economy. In a porous capitalist society, there is always a margin for change, which means that the trickster is truly free and that individuals have maximum opportunities to individuate and self-express. Or do they?

Interestingly enough, the philosophy of capitalism is based on a paradox: on the one hand, the individual is supposed to be on an eternal personal quest for wholeness – for a unique identity and individuality, and to be an independent-thinking, rational member of society. On the other hand, this identity is constantly destabilised and challenged by the system, which has economic and ideological fluidity at its base. The capitalist system cannot afford to deal with individuals in possession of stable identities; deep down, it does not support the idea of 'the civilised trickster' who is confident and does not want to have more than he already has. Instead, it needs insecure human beings who can easily be influenced by systemic satellites, such as advertising, into purchasing new lifestyles. The capitalist ideology is heavily dependent on the narcissistic energies of each separate individual, generated by the eternal issues of shame, control and approval (or mirroring and attunement). In other words, the energy for its functioning is generated by the caged, worn-out trickster – by the artificially inflamed tension between the individual human being and the environment. Upon closer look, it becomes clear that the caged slave underneath its smooth surface is not the trickster at all – it is the narcissistic shadow.

As far as economic structures are concerned, the line between the innovativeness of the trickster energy and its narcissistic, degraded counterpart is often invisible. For instance, the operating principles of the market economy are based on the fluidity of human psychology as well as on the lack of social, financial and emotional stability characteristic of modern contexts. As Andrew Samuels argues in *The Political Psyche*:

> The tale of Hermes is, in many ways, the pattern of our particular socioeconomic epoch which, like him, is a shapeshifter with numerous names to match its myriad presentations: late capitalism, late-late capitalism, postcapitalism, post-Fordism, the information culture (Hermes as messenger), post-industrialism, post-modernism, late modernity and so forth.
>
> *(Samuels, 1993: 88)*

Samuels points out the dubious nature of the trickster – it is neither good nor bad, and the 'positive' or 'negative' aspects of its nature depend on how human beings handle them. After all, the Greek trickster Hermes is famous for his duality: on the one hand, he is the patron of orators and poets, invention and trade; on the other, he is a liar and a thief. This means that he possesses qualities viewed as 'shadowy' by a civilised society.

The trickster's light-hearted and playful nature, his euphoric 'primary' narcissism becomes the calculated, rational, mass-produced narcissism of the market economy. Samuels notes that the two sides of Hermes miraculously co-exist both in myth and in the capitalist system:

> In the myth, we hear of the deceit and lying of Hermes. This inspires associations to the ruthlessness of economic inequality, stock market fraud and insider trading. We also hear of the capacity of Hermes to bargain and negotiate in a compassionate and related style. That inspires associations to the need of any political culture to avoid oligarchic hegemony and gross injustice.
>
> *(1993: 89)*

Significantly, the capitalist energy is profoundly narcissistic, and this narcissism is no longer the playful babbling of a baby expecting to be fed, admired and looked after, but the dark, seething, rational narcissism of a dissatisfied grown-up. It is no longer the creative, pre-structural omnipotence of the trickster, but a relatively well-built structure driven by greed and selfishness. Samuels continues:

> Difficulties with images of the market economy are of central concern in both West and East as both struggle with their confused reactions to the market economy. In the rich countries of the West, we have to face that, in spite of growing disgust, we are still caught in a collective love affair with a rotten social order and an unfeeling culture. We made our commitment to this order of things a long time ago, and however much we may know intellectually that it does not work for us on the ethical level, however much we know about the psychodynamics of greed and envy, we cannot break our tie to our lover: economic inequality. It is a deep guilt over the undeniable fact of our love for economic inequality that takes us to the cheating heart of global capitalism, the partner we refuse to leave, having never really chosen, remaining locked in an enigmatic relationship whose tensions drive us crazy.
>
> *(1993: 89–90)*

Samuels also recalls Hermes's 'primary narcissistic' qualities when he analyses the tale in which Hermes steals Apollo's cattle, and drives them backward in order to confuse the rightful owner as to their whereabouts. In this myth Hermes is only a baby and does not need so much meat – he is physically incapable of eating all of it. What speaks in him is the unstoppable – yet playfully realised – narcissistic greed. The baby Hermes is not going to 'grow out' of his narcissism and into a 'healthy' version of it. He is going to remain voracious forever, and his appetite is not going to diminish. His hunger is a metaphorical representation of the internal emptiness characteristic of modern existence. His bottomless greed emphasises the oxymoronic combination of self-obsession and desire to relate, which afflicts the contemporary urban dweller:

> [T]he nagging and gnawing in Hermes's spiritual stomach, which our epoch surely can recognise, are settled only when, by acquisition, by takeover, by theft, he gets into a relation with another. Some might argue that tricksterism cannot constitute a type of relating. But it is clear that Hermes's magical introjection of food is more than just a phase or passage on the road to 'true' internalization.
>
> *(1993: 92)*

Moreover, Hermes enters the situation of interaction by force. He attracts attention of the other side using aggression, and leaves Apollo no choice but to respond. This demonstrates (to use Andrew Samuels's term) 'the economy of attention': 'Hermes gets Apollo's attention and this, too, is part of the psychology of economic inequality. Not only stirring up envy, but really being seen, and even mirrored' (1993: 92).

In his essay 'The Antinomies of Postmodernity', Fredric Jameson notes that although postmodern landscapes represent 'a gleaming science-fictional stasis in which appearances (simulacra) arise and decay ceaselessly, without the momentous spellbound totality of everything' (Jameson, 2009: 58–59), one should not be fooled by this superficial impermanence. One should not be duped into thinking that we live in 'the age of the trickster'. This kind of social organisation skilfully imitates archaic rhythms in new ways and forms. It is simultaneously stable and destabilised, its lack of security and constancy is largely self-inflicted, and does not damage its working core. And even though the floating images and fragments do not amount to any verifiable or final 'truth', they nevertheless do not fall apart and are firmly kept together by the principle of profit. In fact, profit becomes the only truth:

> Here, it is as if the logic of fashion had, accompanying the multifarious pene-tration of its omnipresent images, begun to bind and identify itself with the social and psychic fabric which tends to make it over into the very logic of our system as a whole. The experience and the value of perpetual change thereby comes to govern language and feelings, fully as much as the buildings and garments of this particular society [. . .]. What then dawns is the realization that no society has ever been so standardized as this one, and that the stream of human, social and historical temporality has never flowed quite so homog-enously. Even the great boredom or ennui of classical modernism required some vantage point or fantasy subject position outside the system; yet our seasons are of the post-natural and post-astronomical television or media vari-ety, triumphantly artificial by way of the power of their National Geographic or Weather Channel images: so that their great rotations – in sports, new model cars, fashion, television, the school year or *rentrée,* etc. – simulate formerly natural rhythms for commercial convenience and reinvent such archaic catego-ries as the week, the month, the year imperceptibly, without any of the fresh-ness and violence of, say, the innovations of the French revolutionary calendar.
> *(Jameson, 2009: 58–59)*

Deep down, Western societies are well-organised structures consisting, nesting-doll style, of a variety of abstract systems, all of which use the trickster for commercial purposes – sometimes as a scarecrow against which we need to purchase 'protec-tion' (insurance businesses) and sometimes as a driver of fake progress and superficial novelty (for instance, the fashion industry; mass media), which generates the need for goods and news. The trickster ends up playing the role for which it is not suited at all: constantly and needlessly undermining identity instead of ques-tioning and criticising the system. Underneath the smooth surface of the post-industrial society, the trickster-slave, repressed and overworked, worn out by repetitive chores, trapped in the dark box of the unconscious, is accumulating dark energy, which can erupt through the surface at any moment.

The shadow (and shame) of the metropolitan individual is as formidable and angry as any other. The problem is that he tends to deny its existence.

The middle classes: betwixt and between

The metropolitan dweller – the one whose trickster is forced under the surface of the bland, sterile, controlled, polite society – is predominantly middle class. He sees all things instinctual, including aggression, as something that should be swept under the carpet. He also conveniently forgets that the middle classes as a social phenomenon are the product of political and social trickster energies. Ignoring 'the beast', repressing it, using framing tools such as shame to tame it, or covering it up with masks and statuses, does not mean that it will willingly calm down or disappear. Like the antagonist Tyler Durden in Chuck Palahniuk's novel *Fight Club* (1996), it might eventually escape, launch 'Project Mayhem' and shake the giant, bland, faceless international-capitalist office to the core.

Being in the middle is a precarious position – the liminal position of being 'betwixt and between'. This existence between the low and the high, between inherited wealth and poverty, between the aristocracy on the one hand, and peasantry and the working classes on the other, has been shaping the psychology of the middle classes for nearly three centuries. The problem of self-definition for those in the economic middle has been particularly acute because this involves a whole complex of factors: money, status, property, professionalism, education, appearance and behavioural protocol. All these aspects of middle-class identity constitute a framework that keeps the trickster in check. In fact, psychologically, the middle classes exist mostly due to the perpetual process of definition and re-definition without which their social (and personal/psychological) base would fall apart.

The modern version of the middle classes was shaped by the need for the social and economic fluidity and mobility. As Colin Morris remarks, cities have always been places of unrest – even in the eleventh and twelfth centuries BC in Europe these hubs of economic activity were eroding the existing social order and undermining established forms of authority because the demands of the market were bigger than the opportunity-scarce, boundaried medieval society (Morris, 2004: 39–40).

Morris writes:

> The conventional account of the discovery of the individual attributes it to the Italian renaissance of the fifteenth century. Until that time, it is often supposed, a powerful hierarchy had enforced rigorously orthodox modes of thinking upon the peoples of the West, until a new freedom was achieved by the rediscovery of classical humanism.
>
> *(2004: 5)*

At the same time, the roots of individualism go deeper than Renaissance ideas and achievements. The origins of Western individualism are 'deeply rooted in the work of the preceding centuries' (2004: 5). Citing Walter Ullman's book, *The Individual and Society in the Middle Ages* (1966), Morris argues that, instead of the rapid rise of individualism beginning about 1450, 'we have a stead ascent beginning as far back as 1200' (2004: 6). The social layout of the European medieval society was also very limited, which meant that man had very little room for manoeuvre:

Between 900 and 1050 it is probable that one of the favourite relaxations of the aristocracy was to listen to epic poems, narrating the glories and tragedies of former heroes. From the limited idea we can form of these it is clear that aristocratic society was rigid in its ideals, and allowed little scope for individual initiative. A man had a few simple obligations prescribed by convention: to his lord, his kin, and his friend. Even friendship was not a matter of personal inclination, but was a formal obligation entered upon by oath to the comrade or *compainz*.

(2004: 33–34)

Richard Sennett describes the transition at the beginning of the eighteenth century from what he calls 'the ancient regime' (medieval/feudal) to the capitalist order. The newly-established bourgeoisie dwelling in large European capitals, London and Paris, largely lacked self-definition, which 'reinforced the sense of the stranger as unknown':

[S]ecure self-definitions were difficult given the economic formation of this class. It was a class into which people stepped, a new and expanding class; it was a matter of mobility rather than inheritance. It was a class far more blurred in outline than the older post-Renaissance mercantile classes, in that as trade in the city expanded, the nature of the urban market changed. In the early 18th Century this market moved from competition of trade to monopoly of trade in a given area or commodity. It was this change in the market which made middle-class identity unstable throughout the echelons of commerce.

(Sennett, 1978: 57)

Transitionality is ingrained into the social and psychological foundations of the middle classes. In the arts the trickster is traditionally presented as a low-life rogue, a tramp, servant, thief or conman, marginalised and sidelined by the moneyed social strata. However, he has more in common with the middle class than it seems. For instance, the lowly picaro of the early modern period (1500–1800), ultimately, is concerned with upward social mobility and transition. The mercurial picaro is laughing at the dumb, stale, immobile aristocracy and, ideally, would like to leave the ranks of prostitutes and servants, and join the emerging professional class. The picaro is a by-product of modernity; he is a city dweller, born with the end of feudalism. He never misses the opportunity to climb out of the social pit into which he was born. He is the future bourgeois (and the future bourgeois revolutionary).

There are numerous novelistic and comedic examples of trickster-picaros defying the rigid social structure and having a laugh at the expense of their much richer adversaries. The heroine of Defoe's *Moll Flanders* (1722) is a courtesan, thief and con woman who has extraordinary survivals skills: she manages to stay afloat by sleeping with all kinds of men of means, both married and unmarried. The daughter of a jailbird, Moll's flirtation with 'a decent life' is dubious and unstable. Having spent most of her life robbing, thieving and fooling honest people, she eventually ends up on a little farm in Maryland intent on leading a decent and quiet life.

The protagonist of Pierre-Augustin Beaumarchais's *Figaro* trilogy (1775–1792), which inspired Mozart's *Le Nozze di Figaro* (1786) and Rossini's *The Barber of Seville* (1816), is a cunning servant with social aspirations. He easily outwits his master even when the latter summons his (rapidly diminishing) feudal rights (i.e. attempts to apply the 'right of the first night' (*droit de seigneur*) to Figaro's bride). A writer, civil rights activist and revolutionary, Beaumarchais infused the *commedia dell'arte* structure of his picaresque comedies with a truly rebellious spirit. They became the literary satellites of the French bourgeois revolution. In the years before the revolution, Louis XVI made an attempt to have the play banned. The picaresque hero, according to Bakhtin, 'is faithful to nothing, he betrays everything – but he is nevertheless true to himself, to his *own* orientation, which scorns pathos and is full of scepticism' (1997: 408).

Being in the middle is a precarious position because any change of circumstances – any random trickster – can push one back into the abyss of non-existence, into the mass of voiceless people without an identity. The aristocracy has a stable social (if not always economic) position that affirms its confidence and sense of entitlement. By contrast, the middle class is mobile and opportunistic, and condemned to perpetual movement. It is always in fear of regressing, of becoming a 'loser'. Under the smooth decency of its lifestyle lies the memory of the gap, the memory of the cracked past; there exists 'another layer', which is very much alive. Throughout modernity, the expanding class embodied transition, movement and progress (personal and technological). In these circumstances, self-definitions are particularly important because they perform the function of 'wolf bane' guarding one against a variety of tricksters, from anger and aggression to professional failure.

This is made worse by the fact that business and good economic luck is never an object of entitlement. In the world of business, circumstances change very fast. This lack of permanence instils a sense of fear in a middle-class individual. A middle-class man, particularly a business man, is terrified of failure and geared for success because he believes that only perpetual movement, only perpetual work will save him from going back to the social abyss. He finds himself in the social purgatory, in the eternal liminal situation, perpetually having to defend and maintain the position he has carved for himself. He is stuck between the wild virility of the instincts and drives, and the dry, superficial rules of the social world in which he has to operate on a daily basis.

The horror! The horror!

In order to 'forget' about the existence of the trickster, which keeps rocking the precarious middle position, one needs to hide it below the surface of the social mask. This situation is particularly favourable for the emergence of the shadow, for the dignified superficiality of the 'middle way' can be at any moment overwhelmed by the turbulent waters of the unconscious.

The middle classes are sandwiched between the social strata characterised (from their point of view) by excess. These excesses can be behavioural, social or financial. Those who are not 'in the middle' lack restraint and moderation. The lower classes are too loud, too rough, too unrefined – too improper. Meanwhile, the aristocracy is too indulgent, too spoilt and too morally corrupt. Both of them, the lower classes and the aristocracy, are tainted by violence, only the first group displays it openly, and the second keeps it concealed.

The two towering characters of Gothic fiction, Frankenstein and Dracula, embody the middle classes' fears of social retribution and psychological engulfment. Frankenstein's raw rage, caused by his middle-class father's rejection of his ugliness, can be read as a metaphor of the lower classes' relationship with their social creators – the bourgeoisie. Published in 1818, Mary Shelley's *Frankenstein* was a timely piece as it reflected the fears and disturbances brought about by the French Revolution and its consequences, and the first wave of the industrial revolution in Britain. The arrival of the ugly mass, the mad mob, at large and seeking revenge on the ones who created and exploited them, is the social umbrella theme of Shelley's book. The monster, seeking education, his due rights and humane treatment, is the embodiment of the principal bourgeois nightmare of the nineteenth century: that the uneducated and excessive mass will escape its social prison and overflow the rational industrialised world.

Bram Stoker's *Dracula* (1897) represents the other side of the social sandwich. Echoing Gothic fiction of the end of the eighteenth century, Stoker's *fin de siècle* piece was concerned with the hidden excesses of the diminishing social strata. Classic Gothic fiction's preoccupation with aristocrats is explainable: the emerging 'middle' was assessing and establishing its position in the world, which was being rapidly changed by industrial developments. The darkness of medieval aristocracy in the form of brutal Manfred and his ilk, allowed the emerging middle stratum to define itself by negating all that was dark, brutal, deathly and excessive in aristocracy. Aristocracy, the first wave of Gothic fiction asserts, is a rotting class. In fact, this literary moment flagged up a highly handy moral and social position, and provided a foil against which the very middle-class virtues of moderation and balance were born.

Living in the shadows

In his book *White Collar: the American Middle Classes* (1951), the American sociologist Charles Wright Mills argues that the diverse world of the social middle neither includes a defined identity nor arrived at any secure social position in the process of its consistent repression of the trickster. Different from the nineteenth-century bourgeoisie (the one which, according to Jameson, still had residual hopes for wholeness in the form of the 'civilised trickster'), the white collar is a vapid, voiceless man who, although he is not gagged by a big ideology or other suchlike monster, gives up his voice voluntarily, in order to get a job and become part of the structure. He simply cannot afford to be a 'genuine person', because this would entail detaching himself from a system (or a set of systems). This is a venture impossible at worst, and expensive at best:

> The white collar people slipped quietly into modern society. Whatever history they have had is a history without events; whatever common interests they have do not lead to unity; whatever future they have will not be of their own making.

[...] Internally they are split, fragmented; externally, they are dependent on larger forces. Even if they gained the will to act, their actions, being unorganised, would be less a movement than a tangle of unconnected contests. As a group, they do not threaten anyone; as individuals, they do not practice an independent way of life. So before an adequate idea of them could be formed, they have been taken for grated as familiar actors of the urban mass.

(Mills, 1967: ix)

The white collar is expected by his society to fulfil what Emile Durkheim (1858–1917) calls 'a determinable function' – that is, your own unique role in the capitalist order (Durkheim, 1964: 43). Durkheim outlines the anthropological and social differences between pre-industrial and developed/capitalist communities in his seminal work *The Division of Labour in Society* (1893). He argues that the pre-industrial society is marked by a 'positive', 'mechanical' solidarity in that all members of the group resemble each other, are replaceable, and their individual differences are played down. None of them is supposed to have a sphere of action that is peculiar to him. In other words, members of a group held together by a positive solidarity are not in any way unique; and neither do they aspire to become 'personalities' (Durkheim, 1964: 131). Their tricksters' aspirations and actions are limited by the existing behavioural canons.

By contrast, each member of the 'organic' society is a recognisable personality, which does not at all mean that the liminal sphere of society in which they exist has more space for creativity and self-expression. Organic communities, Durkheim writes, are primarily characterised by the division of labour, and that is what is holding the different pieces of the system together – despite the undeniably fragmented character of the system. To be a successful member of this society everyone must acquire a profession, a role, and subsequently perfect themselves in this role while making their way up the professional ladder. 'The determinable function' becomes the most important postulate or, as Durkheim himself put it, 'the categorical imperative of the moral conscience' of the Western consciousness (Durkheim, 1964: 43).

Capitalist society is like a body consisting of various organs, each of them assigned its own unique function. The organs are different yet they cannot help but stay together because their survival depends on the health and effective functioning of the entire structure. Their narrow specialisation is important for the successful realisation and maintenance of the division of labour. Industries do not need workers who can perform every step of the production process – but do it very slowly; they need rows of people, each knowing his little operation to perfection. Durkheim postulates that the capitalist individual's 'natural milieu is no longer the natal milieu, but the occupational milieu. It is no longer real or fictitious consanguinity which marks the place of each one, but the function which he fills' (1964: 182). Compared to the stifling collectivity of the mechanical society, the capitalist individual is free and responsible for his personality and his decisions. To be a person, Durkheim proclaims, is 'to be an autonomous source of action' and not 'a simple incarnation of the genetic type of his race and his group' (1964: 403).

The question therefore arises: does the white-collar man want to be this 'autonomous source of action?' Does he want, instead of hiding in the great anonymous mass of people, to have a distinct point of view, which will put him in psychological (financial, social) danger? Is it worth releasing one's trickster and consequently risk being exposed, shamed or pushed to the margins? Is being genuine – trying to discover your real thoughts and opinions – worth losing the protection given by the structure? Being part of a system brings the white-collar security. In fact, he is terrified into seeking security within the system in the unpredictable 'trickster' world of modernity. The middle-class man agrees to trade up his tricksters – creativity, emotions, spontaneity – for measured and regulated existence within a system whose rules and functions effectively replaced the safety and relative facelessness of traditional living.

Mills is not optimistic about the white-collar man's ability to think independently, or to be creative. On the contrary – his littleness is even more conspicuous than that of the working-class man who is capable of organised action as he has 'nothing to lose but their chains' anyway (to use Marx's expression from the *Communist Manifesto* (1848)). The white collar is socially castrated because he 'is always somebody's man – the corporation's, the government's, the army's – and he is seen as a man who does not rebel' (Mills, 1951: xvi). Whereas the old-style bourgeoisie, being a relatively small group, had a mind of its own because it had to protect its property, the white collar is divorced from property and alienated from his own labour. The decline of the free entrepreneur and the rise of large corporations, Mills argues, 'has paralleled the decline of the independent individual and the rise of the little man in the American mind':

> In a world crowded with ugly forces, the white-collar man is readily assumed to possess all the supposed virtues of the small creature. He may be at the bottom of the social world, but he is, at the same time, gratifyingly middle-class. [...] Other social actors threaten to become big and aggressive, to act out of selfish interests and deal in politics. The big business man continues his big business-as-usual through the normal rhythm of slump and war and boom; the big labour man, lifting his shaggy eyebrows, holds up the nation until his demands are met; the big farmer cultivates the Senate to see that big farmers get theirs. But not the white-collar man. He is more often pitiful than tragic, as he is seen collectively, fighting impersonal inflation, living out in slow misery his yearning for the quick American climb. He is pushed by forces beyond his control, pulled into movements he does not understand; he gets into situations in which his is the most helpless position. The white-collar man is the hero as victim, a small creature who is acted upon but does not act, who works along unnoticed in somebody's office or store, never talking loud, never talking back, never making a stand.
>
> *(1967: xvi)*

The white collar lives in the shadows of big organisations – both corporate and governmental – and has no opportunity to express himself creatively. He receives little gratification from work (save for the regular and dependable salary) while demonstrating the 'morale of the cheerful robots' (1967: 233). His repetitive, emotionally draining, unsatisfying job means that he is not allowed to see 'the final product'. His vision of organisational processes is limited to the part he performs because 'free expression of self' is closely related to property ownership (1967: 225).

His trickster qualities – creativity and initiative – are relegated to the safe area of hobbies and interests, and remain largely outside his professional activity.

The white collar is forced by economic circumstances to belong to the 'organic solidarity' of his society and, ultimately, has limited control over his actions and decisions. His trickster is kept in check with a range of sanctions and penalties – both emotional and economic. The principal role in these trickster-controlling tools, not surprisingly, is played by shame.

Narcissistic capital and narcissistic exchange

One way of dealing with the 'shame of smallness', with the embarrassment of not being in control over one's environment, is to accumulate *narcissistic capital*. Narcissistic capital covers a range of qualities an individual can offer to other individuals and organisations, in the process of professional or personal interaction, and includes professional success, talents and abilities, appearance, gadgets, valuable character traits, etc. Women have an additional valuable quality, which is childbearing. In other words, narcissistic capital is tantamount to status. In fact, the qualities constituting narcissistic capital are the opposite of everything the trickster stands for: genuineness, spontaneity, lack of boundaries and disdain for social masks.

Narcissistic capital can inflate or deflate depending on the state of the (interaction) market, and the current value of particular qualities. In other words, when a person tells another: 'What can I give you?', it means that he is unsure of his narcissistic capital and will possibly try to inflate and/or over-emphasise certain qualities in order to appear more marketable. Exchange of the portions of narcissistic capital is *narcissistic exchange*.

The narcissistic economy is powered by shame as its participants keep measuring each other up not in terms of personality traits, but in terms of 'value for the self'. Any interaction – emotional, physical, intellectual, social or financial – becomes the matter of 'exchanging something for something else' – an exchange of energies. The self in this sense is regarded as a fragile construct always on the verge of falling apart, while its dealings with the outside world threaten to bleed the flimsy identity, barely held together by character threads, of its finite energy. One cannot give oneself to others 'for free' because this would require a high degree of confidence and authenticity. Yet, complete narcissistic detachment from the world is also impossible – and that is when exchange of capital comes into play. In fact, any relationships in the narcissistic economy evolve into an operation of measuring up the exact number of traits to be exchanged: knowledge for money, youth for wealth, connections for intelligence, fame for a peace of mind. In this kind of world, an expensive car is acquired to make up for a lack of attractive appearance, and fashionable clothes are thought to be replacing genuine personality. A man trying to impress a woman knows exactly his market value, which is a combination of looks, earning power, age, intelligence, personality, professional position and social status. Attention is also a currency – hence the process of its sharing and distribution is called 'paying attention'.

As a result, nearly all human interaction save, probably, for very close relatives (but not excluding them), become professionalised. Richard Sennett extends this obsession with exchange in personal and professional relations to privacy and self-disclosure. The narcissistic self of the contemporary individual can only enter a situation of intimacy provided he receives an equal degree of self-disclosure; otherwise it would feel fragile and exposed. As intimacy also becomes an exchange value, 'narcissism and the market exchange of self-revelations structure the conditions under which the expression of feeling in intimate circumstances becomes destructive' (Sennett, 1978: 10).

Paradoxically, narcissistic exchange precludes faith in the idealistic idea of 'being accepted as you are', of being loved for your genuine self – because it destroys the very idea of authenticity of self. The place of the paradisiacal state of psychological wholeness – the trickster state – is taken by shame, boundaries and the nagging feeling that one can only be loved if one possesses enough narcissistic capital. Any trickster qualities – such as spontaneity and impulse – are carefully removed from the process of narcissistic exchange because they can wreck havoc on the barely there, barely alive, fragmented, mostly self-reliant identity, hibernating in the darkness of the psyche because it is terrified of any exposure.

Advertising

John Berger argues in *Ways of Seeing* (adapted in 1972 from a television series commissioned by the BBC) that images in advertisements play on envy and anxiety. Advertising's main slogan seems to be: 'If you have nothing, you will be nothing' while 'those who have power become lovable' (Berger, 1977: 141). Mirroring does not necessarily have to be genuine – it can be purchased.

Both envy and anxiety are narcissistic issues flagging up the fear of self-dissolution. Advertising plays with narcissistic capital and with the panic of its disappearance. It offers the individual a psychological fig leaf to cover shame and thus regain control over his life. By purchasing certain identities or aspects of identities, and therefore enhancing his narcissistic capital, the individual feels more empowered. By filling the gaps in his sense of self, the consumer supposedly becomes 'whole'.

In fact, the cures suggested by the advertising industry are fake. The capitalist system uses shame to control the individual – it destabilises his identity by telling him that he is incomplete without a new product or service – and then offers solutions to deal with his impotence and shame. Like this, the system wounds the individual, and then heals this wound. It also assumes that there is no such a thing as a 'genuine' product, a genuine idea or a genuine feeling. Anything can be mass-produced and mass distributed – therefore the trickster does not exist. One should deal with shame and lack of narcissistic capital using prescribed and approved safe methods – shopping, primarily. In fact, the trickster still exists, and is only waiting for the right moment to come out. When he does come out, breaking through layers of shame and artificial decency, by the time he reaches the surface, he becomes the shadow.

Like mass media, advertising in post-industrial contexts serves as a provider of selfobjects – replacements of core personality elements. This is well illustrated by the nameless protagonist in Fincher's *Fight Club* who keeps wondering which IKEA piece of furniture 'completes him'. He ends up begging the trickster antagonist to deliver him from the dream of fake perfection and bogus completeness. This does not end well, however, because Tyler the trickster has already accumulated so much energy that he becomes an unstoppable dark force terrorising corporations and aiming to destroy the global financial heart. He has become a terrifying collective shadow. Instead of the 'bogus control' of the manipulated consumer, the protagonist gains control over his world via aggression, rebellion and terrorism.

Advertising operates under the presumption that Everyman wants to be guided and managed; that he is too lazy to make 'informed choices'; that he is a mass man and not a 'civilised trickster'; that he lacks genuine knowledge of himself, and therefore has very little idea of what he really wants, and how often he wants it. Deep down, the 'common man' still longs to be like everyone else, he longs to be part of the group. As Mario Jacoby writes: 'Do I fall too far outside of the "norm"?' is one of the most embarrassing questions (Jacoby, 1996: 60). The advertising industry is also aware of narcissistic fluctuations in consumers, and how these fluctuations can be manipulated in order to yield the desired results. Jean Baudrillard confirms this in *The System of Objects:*

> The abundance of products puts an end to *scarcity*; the abundance of advertising puts an end to *insecurity*. The worst thing possible is to be obliged to invent one's own motives for acting, for preferring, for buying. The individual in such circumstances is inevitably brought face to face with his own misapprehensions, his own lack of existence, his own bad faith and anxiety. Any object which fails to dispel such guilty feelings – is liable to be dubbed bad. If the object loves me, then I shall be saved. Advertising (and, more broadly, public relations as a whole) relieves psychological insecurity by deploying an enormous solicitude, to which we respond by internalizing the solicitous agency – namely, the whole immense enterprise, producing not just goods but also communicating warmth, which global consumer society actually is.
>
> *(Baudrillard, 2005: 186)*

Advertising can inflate the consumers' narcissistic capital by offering them extra qualities that can participate in exchange ('buy this and get slim fast', 'the Lynx effect'). From the point of view of the system, inflated narcissistic capital is even more effective than a 'fairly earned' one because the former gets deflated quickly, and the consumer is left dissatisfied, disillusioned and needing fresh identity elements in the form of mobile phones, fashionable clothes, cars and perfumes.

Not surprisingly, many advertising slogans refer directly to the act of gaining (inflating) one's narcissistic capital. The second-person singular pronoun, whether actual or implied, becomes the staple of many an advertising slogan: 'Make your mark', 'Because you're worth it', 'Have it your way', 'Just do it', 'We care about your success', 'Power to you', 'Take care' and 'Simply be'. The main promise of these slogans is shame reduction via control and empowerment. Whatever they say, the consumer hears: 'You are in control', 'We love you' and 'You are the best'. This control, however, does not include the trickster – the imperfect, the raw and the dirty. It is the 'perfect', narcissistic control over the perfect body and the mechanical, sleek world. It is the delusional control of the person using a mask to hide his psychological deficiency. As Guy Cook notes in *The Discourse of Advertising* (1992), the boundary between the 'you' of the receiver in ads and the 'I' of the sender is always blurred:

> The tendency to project the self into the 'I' and address somebody else as 'you' is hampered by the frequent absence of 'I' and the clear address of the receiver. The 'you' of ads has a *double exophora* involving reference to someone in the picture (salient because pictures dominate words) and to the receiver's own self (salient because everyone is interested in themselves). The characters of ads sometimes look out of the picture ..., making them both addressee and addresser. [...]

> This dual identity of 'you' is matched by the mysterious identity of 'I', which is not revealed. The visual presence of another person (the character) distracts from this absence, creating an illusion that the dialogue is between character and addressee.

> *(Cook, 1992: 156–157)*

As a result, the receiver acquires an omnipotent double identity, which, in fact, is the result of a narcissistic merger, a powerful idealistic projection between the addresser and the addressee. As the 'I' is invisible, it becomes the 'I' of God, a disembodied voice speaking directly to the consumer and commanding him to buy things in order to gain power. This 'godly' narcissistic merger creates an impression of regaining the long-lost exciting omnipotence, a false impression of being in control once more.

Moreover, these slogans act as transitional objects, as the promise to mitigate shame by 'taking care' of the consumer, by acting as a substitute mother, by reminding him of the lost (or non-existent) 'wholeness'. Likewise, following J. Williamson, Luke Hockley argues that advertisers create myths 'effective in concealing the capitalist power relations that exist between producer and consumer, and which delude the consumer into a false sense of control and autonomy' (Hockley, 2007: 78). In pre-industrial contexts the mass man was given 'meaning' (and manipulated) by the system with the help of meaning-making structures such as myth and ritual. The capitalist system (bearing in mind the same lack of independence in individuals as well as their unchanged influenceability) invents new myths, which, effectively, become tools of psychological and economic domination. Hockley writes that

> advertising uses a series of mythological and magical motifs to stimulate and spur consumers into life. Sometimes advertisers appear to deploy such imagery in a knowing manner, at other times it seems more intuitive. In either case the consumer is not supposed to reflect on the imagery. Instead the hope is that it should wash over them, it should appear natural, believable and desirable.

> *(2007: 85)*

The selfobjects thus acquired provide only temporary satisfaction because they are meant to replace genuine relationships sought by consumers. Therefore, the kind of individuation they provide is also unstable and illusory. To quote Hockley again:

> [I]n part, the imagery of advertising plays on [the need] to 'repair damage to the nuclear self' by offering the potential for self-improvement through the consumption of images and the purchasing of products. The potency of this need can be seen in the direct association that exists between narcissistic behaviour and the activities of consumers.
>
> *(2007: 87)*

Acquisition of objects is primarily aimed at the mitigation of shame, which can be dealt with in two ways. On the one hand, the energy is channelled into an entity that is governable and manageable, and therefore it is a 'shameless' relationship. On the other, because there is no actual involvement with a real person, the subject is not in a vulnerable position. The heart remains intact. To quote C.S. Lewis from *The Four Loves* (1958):

> Love anything and your heart will be wrung and possibly broken. If you want to make sure of keeping it intact you must give it to no one, not even an animal. Wrap it carefully round with hobbies and little luxuries; avoid all entanglements. Lock it up safe in the casket or coffin of your selfishness. But in that casket, safe, dark, motionless, airless, it will change. It will not be broken; it will become unbreakable, impenetrable, irredeemable.
>
> *(Lewis, 1988: 117)*

Paradoxically, the object is the most tragically imperfect replacement for the self or a part of the self. The illusion works as long as it does not encounter reality – and when it does, the myth gets shattered and the illusory wholeness is lost. As Baudrillard astutely notes, objects form the narcissistic mirror for the individual as well as provide him with tenacious mythology. The need for the 'truthful mirror' and a heroic, self-validating myth is so widespread that it constitutes contemporary neurosis. Consumer goods regulate anxiety, which is an intrinsic aspect of urban lifestyle. The individual purchases an oxymoronic 'neurotic equilibrium' and invests the objects with 'souls':

> The object . . . in the strictest sense of the word a mirror, for the images it reflects can only follow upon one another without ever contradicting one another. And indeed, as a mirror the object is perfect, precisely because it sends back not real images, but desired ones. In a word, it is a dog of which nothing remains but faithfulness. What is more, you can look at an object without it looking at you. *This is why everything that cannot be invested in human relationships is invested in objects.* [. . .] Objects undoubtedly serve in a regulatory capacity with regard to everyday life, dissipating many neuroses and providing an outlet for all kinds of tensions and for energies that are in

mourning. This is what gives them their 'soul', what makes them 'ours' – but it is also what turns them into the décor of a tenacious mythology, the ideal décor for an equilibrium that is itself neurotic.

(Baudrillard, 2005: 96)

Despite its carnivalesque atmosphere and magical playfulness, as an abstract system advertising sells the shadow because it consistently leaves the individual hungry and confused. Its actions and manipulations do not lead to the formation of a genuine personality. Ultimately, it fails to 'teach' the individual how to be oneself; and it also fails to provide the individual with a genuine insight into his personality. Abstract systems, which assume that 'the mass man' is lazy, lacks genuine passions and desires, and expects things to be decided for him, is immature and forever looking for a mother. They are convinced that the individual does not want to be a 'civilised trickster' because dealing with life choices is a fragmenting and painful experience.

Selling the trickster

Even rebellion can be packaged and sold as an element of narcissistic capital (and an identity element) – the famous iconic image of Che Guevara and the works of contemporary artists such as Tracey Emin and Damien Hirst come to mind. This, of course, renders the whole idea of the trickster useless. By drinking from a Che Guevara mug, or by discussing the artistic merits of Emin's Turner Prize-winning self-explanatory *My Bed* (1999) and Hirst's *The Physical Impossibility of Death in the Mind of Someone Living* (1991), which contains an actual preserved shark, one feels that he is partaking in a special event different from both the routine of everyday life and the bland, grey, sterile post-industrial spaces and rituals.

In contemporary Western societies, rebellion does not remain 'fresh' for long. Once it is captured and sold, a new consumable revolt is sought in the form, say, of a new art genre or edgy fashion. Genuine tricksters such as, for instance, the graffiti artist Banksy are very rare. As a system, capitalism is powered by change, and it has learned to survive trickster outbursts – all the shifts, explosions and turbulence that come with change and innovation – by filing off their rebellious edge and turning them into consumer products. It has used innovation and change to perpetuate itself. The processed, packaged and sold marginality (punk clothes, revolutionary symbols) is safe and controlled. 'Trickster products' have been inoculated and devoid of their authenticity by the very fact of being mass-produced and advertised. Art and creativity are particularly profitable 'tricksters slaves' because they set out as genuine impulses, but could be subdued and taken advantage of for profit. Yet, the memory, the whiff of 'something genuine' (and this is what the consumer ultimately buys) always remains inside them.

In his essay 'Postmodernism and Consumer Society' Jameson describes the clever way in which post-industrial societies absorb, package, sell and consume rebellion. This process, according to Jameson, began after the Second World War, with the onset of late capitalism and with the departure of old modernist aesthetics. In the early

1960s 'the position of high modernism and its dominant aesthetics become established in the academy and are henceforth felt to be academic by a whole new generation of poets, painters and musicians' (Jameson, 2009: 19). The old art had 'too much trickster in it' – it was still too shocking and too authentic. Jameson argues:

> The older or classical modernism was an oppositional art; it emerged within the business society of the gilded age as scandalous and offensive to the middle-class public – ugly, dissonant, bohemian, sexually shocking. [. . .]

> If we then suddenly return to the present day, we can measure the immensity of the cultural changes that have taken place. Not only are Joyce and Picasso no longer weird and repulsive, they have become classics and now look rather realistic to us. Meanwhile, there is very little in either the form or the content of contemporary art that contemporary society finds intolerable. The most offensive forms of this art – punk rock, say, or what is called sexually explicit material – are all taken in its stride by society, and they are commercially successful, unlike the productions of the older high modernism. But this means that even if contemporary art has all the same formal features as the older modernism, it has still shifted its position fundamentally within our culture. For one thing, commodity production and in particular our clothing, furniture, buildings and other artefacts are now intimately tied in with stylish changes which derive from artistic experimentation; our advertising, for example, is fed by modernism in all the arts and inconceivable without.
>
> *(2009: 18–19)*

The inoculated trickster is easy to sell because it gives one the illusion of control, empowerment and change. Meanwhile, by purchasing the fake trickster, consumers postpone the arrival of the real one. Fake rebellion can be used as a buffer against the jinni stored up in the calm and disciplined urban psyche.

Choice

Having no choice is a pre-shame, pre-independent, paradisiacal state when everything is decided for you by the parental figures. No wonder that many Russian citizens felt so disenchanted when the Soviet Union was dissolved and people were asked to be free and to learn to make choices. Soviet citizens had a large portion of their lives coordinated and decided for them: upon leaving the university, they had a guaranteed workplace waiting for them (although they could not choose it); they had cheap childcare organised by the state; a free apartment; and very affordable clothes and food. Many did not even mind the long queues to buy a car, many years of waiting to get a flat, and a very limited choice of consumer goods.

In addition, life was coordinated by party representatives and organised around rituals and symbols: twice a year, on the seventh of November and the first of May, people had to take part in mass parades, and walk from home to the main city square carrying slogans, symbols, balloons and flowers. In fact, what they were carrying was a dead trickster, the reminder of the rebellion that happened a long time ago and has since ceased to be a 'proper' communitas.

Soviet citizens' feelings at the loss of the big paternal structure are best rendered by seventy-two-year-old Natalia in an interview to the British *Vogue*. Natalia describes the necessity to make choices as something awkward and unfortunate. For many years she had been very happy without this burden. Choice is fragmenting and disorientating, and one is better off without it:

> If I think back to when I was twenty, I am amazed how my life has changed. I don't necessarily think today's world is better than it was when I was young. My life was completely regimented, and as such it was stable. I didn't suffer the sort of anxiety that girls [my granddaughter's] age go through. I think that was a blessing.
> *(Kalabin, 2013)*

Natalia did not mind that she could not get married in a long white wedding gown because 'it wasn't an option for any Soviet woman then, so I didn't mourn something I did not know'. In summer she rotated between a pair of printed cotton dresses and for winter she had one wool skirt. And even though every Soviet woman was supposed to have an elegant dress to wear for the theatre or for dinner, these dresses were impossible to buy (Kalabin, 2013).

The Soviet economy was a command economy, which means that the volumes of production, types of products and their prices were determined by the state. This type of economy assumes that humans have finite needs (not endless as advertising executives would think!), and they cannot possibly want to own more boots and coats than is needed to survive seasonal weather conditions and look proper in public. For this type of economy, the notion of change is alien and hostile. For it, any 'change' should be gradual, something that can only happen in a guided and well-planned situation such as a pre-industrial ritual. If a Soviet woman is allowed to buy a new evening gown every year, who knows what direction her expanding appetites will take next time! Change is a source of individualism, and individualism may lead to narcissism. The only narcissism that was allowed to thrive in the Soviet state was the narcissism of the state.

By contrast, change has become incorporated into the capitalist system as part of its driving force. Choice and rapid rotation of objects are also powered by the trickster impulse whose energy is harvested by the system. Although consumerism is an old phenomenon and certainly was not created by the industrial revolution, its modern form was shaped by the development of technology during the industrial revolution. Speedier, cheaper production methods triggered widespread consumption due to the accessibility of the products that had formerly been seen as luxuries. Besides, rigid hierarchies of pre-modern communities did not encourage individualism, particularly via acquisition of consumer goods. Consumption, by its very nature, is a process of self-making and self-definition. In pre-industrial Europe, as Peter N. Stearns notes, consumption was limited by a number of factors, including economic, social and religious ones. The upper classes, who could consume freely, limited this privilege to themselves to ensure lack of social transition and aspiration:

[U]pper-class people disapproved of any signs that elements of the lower classes, even if they had a bit of margin, displayed much individualism or propensity to cross social boundaries through consumer behaviours. And even in upper classes that did show periodic commitment to consumerism, there were recurrent hesitations and counterattacks that limited consistent consumerist interest. For all classes, other goals – devotion to the public good and/or religion – were meant to override much consumerism. In other words, cultural beliefs, and not just poverty, inhibited consumerism before modern times, and may continue to oppose it even today.

(Stearns, 2006: 1)

This kind of limitation was systemic, and aimed at controlling the possible gargantuan appetites of the individual; at limiting his 'primary omnipotence' (or, rather, the memory of it). The trickster was stagnating, locked in the social underworld and unable to escape the rigidities of the socio-economic circumstances, and it certainly benefited from the economic change brought about by the industrial revolution. Being an individual means knowing who you are and being able to choose aspects of your identity. It presupposes creating your own life from options, choices and alternatives. Today consumption and accessibility of goods have become the building blocks of personality, up to the point when some people can even say: 'I consume therefore I exist.' Stearns notes:

[M]any people formulate their goals in life partly through acquiring goods that they do not need for subsistence or for traditional display. They become enmeshed in the process of acquisition – shopping – and take some of their identity from the procession of new items that they buy and exhibit. In this society, a host of institutions both encourage and serve consumerism, from eager shopkeepers trying to lure customers into buying more than they need, to product designers employed to put new twists on established models, to advertisers seeking to create new needs.

(2006: vii)

On the surface of it, the abundance of choice is a positive thing. Both choice and self-reflection balance out the 'normalising' influence of the socio-cultural environment, the *habitus*. Both these notions are involved in the dynamic between the individual and society, which is prominent in the trickster conflict because they give the individual tools for self-evaluation and assist him in identity-building. They are the 'killers' of the *habitus*. The very idea of choice is tricksterish as it naturally unsettles patterns of everyday life on all levels, from personal to social and political. In an attempt to 'contain' the trickster, the liberal tradition has traditionally structured the process of choice-making. There exists an unspoken formula that rationalises and optimises choice-making. The main idea is that the individual

1   has a range of options in his life;
2   rationally considers these options;
3   makes choices in accordance with personal preferences – but also takes his environment into consideration.

Steps 2 and 3 presuppose that the choice-making individual is mature, rational and, ultimately, *knows himself*. His decisions will be biased towards individual interests yet they will still be within the law and basic moral principles. This is how the Western individual controls the trickster of choice – he breaks down the whole process into segments thus making it more transparent and de-emotionalising it.

However, the above would be true of a society consisting of 'civilised tricksters', of people possessing the ability to venture outside the narrow frame of their subjective perception and imagine themselves to be 'the other'. In reality, choice is manipulated, and the consumer is encouraged to develop a range of maladaptive behaviours, including poor impulse control and obsessive habits, as well as to lack a sense of stable identity. Fluid identities can easily be influenced by external cues (generated, for instance, by advertising). In this kind of 'narcissistic economy', the trickster is not completely ignored like it is in command economies, but its destabilising power is harnessed to artificially generate narcissistic qualities in consumers – lack of genuine self, delusional omnipotence, hunger and greed, obsessional behaviour and a permanent sense of self-dissatisfaction. In *The System of Objects* Jean Baudrillard points out the regressive aspects of such an economy because it results in objectification of the entire world, and loss of authentic human connection:

> Consumption is not a material practice, nor is it a phenomenology of 'affluence'. It is not defined by the nourishment we take in, nor by the clothes we clothe ourselves with, nor by the car we use, nor by the oral and visual matter of the images and messages we receive. It is defined, rather, by the organization of all these into a signifying fabric: consumption is *the virtual totality of all objects and messages ready-constituted as a more or less coherent discourse*. If it has any meaning at all, consumption means an activity consisting of the systematic manipulation of signs.
>
> *(Baudrillard, 2005: 218)*

Even though consumption may increase status, Baudrillard argues, this increase is nothing but a shallow inflation (of narcissistic capital), which is a sorry replacement for a genuine feeling of self-worth. Objects are personalised to act as prosthetic personality parts. Choice is a trap even though 'the system of manipulated personalization is experienced by the majority of consumers as freedom' (2005: 165). The trickster has become a robot producing conveyer-belt personalities for a society of narcissists. But what is really in demand, Baudrillard observes, is the relationship – idealised to the point when only 'a perfect connection' and 'a merger of souls' will do. Such a connection, of course, can only be possible with an object that one collects and loves – until he discovers a new silent partner:

So what is consummated and consumed is never an object but the relation-ship itself, signified yet absent, simultaneously included and excluded; it is the *idea of the relationship* that is consumed in the series of objects that display it. The relationship is no longer directly experienced: it has become abstract, been abolished, been transformed into a sign-object, and thus consumed.

This status of the relationship/object is governed at every level by the imperatives of production. The whole apparatus of advertising suggests that the living rela-tionship, with its contradictions, must not be allowed to disturb the 'rational' order of production, and that it should be consumed like everything else.

(2005: 219)

Another problem regarding the 'trickster of choice' is that the average consumer is not the oxymoronic passionate-rational creature of John Stuart Mill's dreams. Essentially, choice is chaos. Choice, as business psychologists are discovering, can be taxing on the human psyche. Today's variety of acceptable behaviours and possible 'life patterns' can be confusing for an ordinary person. Choosing one's 'external' identity is one thing; trying to discern stable patterns in one's emotional connec-tions and sexual attractions is another. How can a contemporary, post-Ragnarök individual psychologically survive, and build his life from scratch, from the myriad of choices available?

While limited choice makes sense, unlimited options disorientate humans to the point of refusal to finalise the choice process. Choice is not only anti-systemic, it is also pattern-breaking. This is the world in which unrestrained choice has pre-vailed over tradition and a 'given' pattern of behaviours is a hyperreality full of endless combinatorial possibilities that, however, do not necessarily result in a solid picture because the aim of the system is to keep the production-consumption process going. The trickster multiplies identities – but it also sells things. The system has learned how to employ chaos to sell mass-produced goods and services.

A consumer is anyone who makes identity-building decisions in the world without prescribed identities. Anyone who participates in the vortex of post-industrial society (or liquid modernity, or any other term) automatically becomes a chooser. Researchers in the theory of choice have emphasised the problem of the confused consumer surrounded by overflowing possibilities and opportunities, and struggling to understand what his 'true' identity is. As Sheena Iyengar rightly notes,

when the locus of power shifts to the choosing individual, the question of who that individual is – what his goals and motivations are – becomes very impor-tant. It necessitates self-scrutiny at a level that is confusing and, frankly, a bit scary. And, as our horizons widen, the number of possible selves also multiply. The block of marble surrounding our sculpture keeps getting bigger, with more and more to chip away before we can uncover the essential form within. In other words, the process of self-discovery becomes more challenging at the very moment it is most imperative. If no single path in life has a privileged

> claim to being right, there are no easy answers for any of us; it becomes expo-
> nentially more difficult to know ourselves, to be ourselves, to do our thing.
>
> *(Iyengar, 2010: 84–85)*

In her book *The Art of Choosing* (2010) she recalls a study in which people in a supermarket were offered to try different flavours of jam. It transpired that consumers who were offered a smaller number of flavours were more likely to purchase a jar of jam than if they had been given the full variety of options (2010: 178). She replicated the experiment in another supermarket, and the result was astonishingly similar. Ultimately, Iyengar argues in favour of what Giddens would call 'expert systems' (such as *Which?* magazines), which would guide baffled consumers, who are unable to make a decision and are wading through an endless sea of products, throughout this difficult process. Expert systems will help the consumer to 'simplify, prioritize and categorize elements and to recognize patterns' in order to 'create order in seeming chaos' (2010: 192). If anything, this is bad news for the trickster, for he is still seen as dangerous and impossible to handle – even when he is reduced to the role of the sweatshop worker, his area of influence limited and his voice unheard.

Trickster explosion: *Fight Club* (1999)

Christopher Lasch writes in *The Culture of Narcissism*:

> Twentieth century people have erected so many psychological barriers against strong emotion, and have invested those defences with so much of the energy derived from forbidden impulse, that they no longer remember what it feels like to be inundated by desire. [. . .] Outwardly bland, submissive, and sociable, they seethe with an inner anger for which a dense, overpopulated, bureaucratic society can devise few legitimate outlets.
>
> *(Lasch, 1991: 11)*

At the same time, urban individuals want to cure their inability to feel with extreme experiences; they try to 'beat sluggish flesh to life, attempt to revive jaded appetites' (1991: 11):

> Narcissism in the clinical sense diverges from the popular idea of love of one's beauty; more strictly, and as a character disorder, it is self-absorption which prevents one from understanding what belongs within the domain of the self and self-gratification and what belongs outside it. Thus narcissism is an obsession with 'what this person, that event means to me'. This question about the personal relevance of other people and outside acts is posed so repetitively that a clear perception of those persons and events in themselves is obscured. This absorption in self, oddly enough, prevents gratification of self needs; it makes the person at the moment of attaining an end of connecting with another person that 'this isn't what I wanted'. Narcissism thus

has the double quality of being a voracious absorption in self needs and the block to their fulfilment.

(1991: 8)

Lasch's description of the narcissistic urban psyche perfectly renders the problems of the main protagonist of David Fincher's iconic film *Fight Club*, based on the eponymous novel by Chuck Palahniuk (screenplay by Jim Uhls). True to the trickster genre, the protagonist (who is also the narrator) does not have a name. He is a faceless, bland white-collar worker who spends his life either in the sterile office environment or his IKEA-clad flat. With his average face and physique, Edward Norton is a good choice for the role because he emphasises the character's ordinariness. His job as a product recall specialist for a major car manufacturing company means that he has to separate his professional activity (assessing accident scenes) from his feelings about crash victims. As a result, he chooses not to have any feelings at all. The protagonist is a loner, collecting objects (because they are docile) and unable to form a connection with a fellow human (as this would be emotionally disturbing).

In the famous 'IKEA sequence', the furniture catalogue the protagonist is holding in his hands, comes to life and becomes his flat, complete with product descriptions and prices. Fincher's stylisation is meant to show that even though the narrator (whose true voice is separated from his physical screen presence) is hoping to find a piece of furniture that would 'define him as a person', he ends up with a simulacrum flat, stuffed with mass-produced objects and devoid of any authenticity. Even the products embodying the fake spirituality and fake morality – the yin–yang coffee table and the glasses with baubles crafted by the 'honest, hard-working, indigenous peoples of . . . wherever' do not make the narrator's life more meaningful, or more genuine. Surrounded by lifeless objects, he is still missing an identity.

The faceless protagonist is suffering from what Baudrillard calls the collector's malaise – a regressive state, the compulsion to collect things because they can be 'loved' without 'loving you back' (i.e. without being 'real' and dangerously proactive). When an object is alive and has genuine reactions, it threatens to destroy the subject's narcissistic mirror. This is when shame kicks in – the shame of seeing a stranger's face in the mirror, the shame that comes with the loss of perfection and 'ideal unity'; the shame at the realisation that you are separate from 'the other'.

A collector, Baudrillard notes, does not possess the actual physical items in his collection; he is not interested in their functionality, for he is at a stage when his basic needs are satisfied. What he possesses is '*an object distracted from its function and thus brought into relationship with the subject*' (Baudrillard, 2005: 91). The implied function of the collectable object is to serve as a mirror, to fill the void that cannot be filled with personality:

> In this context, all owned objects partake of the same *abstractness*, and refer to one another insomuch as they refer solely to the subject. Such objects together make up the system through which the subject strives to construct a world, a private entity.
>
> *(2005: 91–92)*

The collector is in search of an ideal relationship – and for the ideal 'self'. The world of objects becomes his very own, ideally controlled environment.

However, the emotionless world of objects fails to make the protagonist feel alive. With his chronic insomnia, which is the metaphor for his zombified state, he is 'never really asleep and never really awake'. He starts looking for ways to break the mirror which has become his trap, for ways to make himself feel something again, and eventually finds places where genuine feelings are available to observe and absorb. These oases of raw emotion in the sterile urban world are therapy groups for people with various physical and psychological ailments. Fincher gives us a range of hilarious yet uneasy sketches in which we see the protagonist crying as he buries his face in the giant breasts of a testicular cancer victim; gloating at the tragedy of a pale, skinny dying woman who nobody finds attractive; and participating in 'guided meditation' together with a group of real sufferers.

A self-absorbed narcissist, he is like a corpse, and can only access his emotions in extreme circumstances, via extreme sorrow or pain, on the verge of life and death. Nothing less than that can make him feel 'more whole' and help him regain his sleep. In the world of simulacra, he looks for situations he cannot control the way he controls his dead world of objects – he seeks dangerous, liminal, trickster situations, edgy events that go beyond the routine of his grey life. Only they can make him alive. Like a vampire, the protagonist devours the openness, the shame, the pain, the authenticity, the emotional rawness of the events, testimonies and conversations taking place in the therapy groups.

All the while, he is still a narcissistic fake, and this transpires when another 'tourist', a woman called Marla Singer (Helena Bonham-Carter) starts visiting the protagonist's favourite feeding places. Her presence reminds him that, despite his newly-found ability to cry, he is still dead because his relationships are not genuine. His new friends are still objects that he can switch on and off, and that he can use and abuse for his own purposes. He does not feel empathy towards the sufferers, but is addicted to their pain. The shame is not his; it is a sham. The narrator's trickster is unauthentic, and his self is still fragmented – or worse – non-existent.

Kohut considered his branch of psychoanalysis – self-psychology – to be a response to the problems of modernity and to the concomitant problems of the fragmenting self. The environment in which contemporary children grow up does not supply them with the necessary psychological building bricks. One of the problems Kohut quotes as being particularly pernicious for the budding self is emotional distance and emotional unavailability of parents brought about by the arrival of the nuclear family, and altered work and leisure patterns: 'The environment which used to be experienced as threateningly close, is now experienced more and more as threateningly distant; where children were formerly *overstimulated* by the emotional (including the erotic) life of their parents, they are now often *understimulated*' (Kohut, 2009: 275). Moreover, creative people from *fin de siècle* onwards have been able to express this fragmentedness of the self in their respective media. Their main subject has been the crumbling, decomposing, fragmenting, enfeebled self of the child, and, later, the fragile, vulnerable, empty self of the adult that the great artists of the day describe – through tone and word, on canvas and in stone – and that they try to heal. The musician of disordered sound, the poet of decomposed language, the painter and sculptor of the fragmented visual and tactile world: they all portray the breakup of the self and, through the reassemblage and rearrangement of the fragments, try to create new structures that possess wholeness, perfection, new meaning.

(2009: 286)

Kohut puts the solid self at the core of human happiness and human ability to function successfully as both an individual and a member of community. According to him, mental health is

not only freedom from the neurotic symptoms and inhibitions that interfere with the functions of a 'mental apparatus' involved in loving and working, but also as the capacity of a firm self to avail itself of the talents and skills at an individual's disposal, enabling him to love and work successfully.

(2009: 284)

The faceless protagonist, who still lacks the sense of self despite his attempts to excavate it with the help of support groups, eventually finds a more effective method of breaking though his own narcissistic armour. On board the plane he encounters, by his own admission, the most interesting 'single serving friend' he has ever met. The beginning of their friendship coincides with a gas explosion in the narrator's flat. As his flat is destroyed and he nowhere to go, the protagonist gives his new friend a call, and ends up at his place – a giant dilapidated house with a leaky roof, rotten furniture and crumbling walls. On the way to the house Tyler Durden (Brad Pitt) asks the narrator to hit him, and the two end up fighting in an empty street. This is how the formerly normal and boring protagonist is initiated into the 'fight club' – a secret organisation with strict rules ('you do not talk about fight club', 'only two guys to a fight', etc.), which has branches all over the world.

The narrative soon makes it apparent that Tyler is the protagonist's doppelganger who represents his repressed, split-off personality traits. Tyler is a social terrorist who expresses his disdain towards society freely, and who does everything the narrator does not dare to do: urinates in the soup at restaurants where he works as a waiter; makes soap out of liposuction fat and sells it to luxury perfumeries; destroys an Apple store; and has sex with Marla all night. As the film progresses, the doppelganger gets wilder, more brutal and more ambitious in his plans to destroy the global financial system while the feeble protagonist makes half-hearted attempts to control this runaway 'real self'. In this sense, the film has the traditional structure of a trickster narrative, in which the trickster serves as the action-driving element. It escapes at the start of the film, completely changes the life of the protagonist, plunges him into a pool of liminality, and then disappears while the protagonist is trying to reincorporate his experiences (to use Turner's term) into normal life.

With his many vocations, numerous talents, explosive might and destructive power, Tyler is the secret trickster of the urban individual – the trickster that had been kept in the cage for so long that, having broken through layers of shame, social masks and behavioural rules, he has transmogrified into the narcissist's angry, hungry, destructive shadow. Although Tyler still retains some playful qualities, his primary energy is not the playful energy of the trickster, but the dark and brooding might of the shadow, tainted with shame, and plotting to expand itself and eventually take a collective form. Tyler is a psychopomp, taking the protagonist back to the darkest corners of his psyche. He drags him out of his regimented way of life, out of his IKEA prison, and makes him face the physical basics of life, the primary enemies of all civilised systems: scatology, blood, violence, body and sex.

Meanwhile, to the traditional trickster list of system-shocking substances, Tyler, who calls himself a soap-maker, cheekily adds fat – the chief obsession of our time. In the fat-harvesting scene, Tyler and the protagonist steal plastic sacks, containing liposuction fat, from a waste bin, and one of them bursts upon hitting an iron fence. This deeply unsettling scene metaphorically stands for the trickster rupturing the shiny, unwrinkled surface of the beauty industry, and showing its raw, monstrous insides – its ugly self-obsessed face – in the broken mirror.

The very purposelessness and economic unviability of physical fights sabotages the system. Fight club as a concept, as a communitas, as a liminal organisation, denies the system's supremacy and the legitimacy of IKEA catalogues or lifestyle magazines. The bland urban *mise-en-scène* and muted colours make blood particularly noticeable as it becomes the symbol of rebellion and freedom from dependence on the capitalist system. Being in control lies at the base of feeling alive, it means being an actor and not a passive creature swayed by the big forces. When one cannot control other people or the circumstances of one's life, reclaiming control over the body is the last resort. Shame is the chains that the protagonist wants to shake off, and that Tyler does not have.

In fact, the narrative is structured to show the protagonist's gradual loss of shame: he starts appearing at work wearing dirty clothes, with his face scratched and covered in bruises. He daubs blood from the corner of the mouth when the boss is trying to shame him into thinking about his unprofessional appearance and suspicious behaviour. At some point, during a board meeting, the protagonist, instead of replying to a question, simply flashes his bloody smile, and the whole room goes silent. The office where everything is a 'copy of a copy of a copy' (as shown at the start of the film in the scene where the narrator dumbly stares at the working photocopier), suddenly becomes a darkly authentic, genuine place, where the masks are taken off and aggression is displayed openly. The world, Tyler teaches his friend, is not your mirror: 'You're not your job. You're not how much money you have in the bank. You're not the car you drive. You're not the contents of your wallet. You're not your fucking khakis. You're the all-singing, all-dancing crap of the world.'

Meanwhile, the state of being the 'all-singing, all-dancing crap of the world' – the trickster state – proves to be a dangerous and uncontrollable condition. It leads to hazardous over-inflation, which, without the framing and structuring functions of civilisation, quickly becomes the collective shadow actively working on Project Mayhem. The narrator's personal narcissism multiplies and becomes a narcissistic army – a big group of cold-blooded terrorists whose final aim is to topple the corporate system. In fact, the film's finale corresponds to Guy Debord's analysis of the corporate system as being essentially self-destructive and containing an internal time-bomb ready to explode at any moment. Debord predicts that the system will be destroyed by the trickster of change, which it enslaved and forced to toil:

> The things the spectacle presents as eternal are based on change, and must change as their foundations change. The spectacle is totally dogmatic, yet it is incapable of arriving at any really solid dogma. Nothing stands still for it. This instability is the spectacle's natural condition, but it is completely contrary to its natural inclination.
>
> *(2009: 53)*

The film's last scenes are ambiguous: the narrator kills Tyler thus also killing himself (the main rule of the doppelganger genre), survives, is reunited with Marla, and they profess their love for each other in an empty office with glass walls, while the buildings around them are exploding and crumbling. Apparently, through a series of extreme traumatic events he has finally learned to feel and to relate – he finally feels alive and genuine. Meanwhile, Tyler, like many tricksters, ends up being inoculated and disposed of – but his legacy remains. He did break the narrator's mirror, and did tear through his armour. He succeeded in – if not changing the protagonist – then at least giving him a degree of self-reflection and self-criticism.

Neither the narrator nor the buildings are allowed to survive because, after all, the corporate system is the very force that turned him into an unfeeling narcissist and repressed his humanity – suppressed his trickster. Like the narcissistic protagonist, the corporate system is tired of its own activities; it is tired of being barren and sterile; it is tired of masks. The system, it transpires from the finale, destroys itself.

When I was finishing this review, I stumbled upon a Calvin Klein advert for the perfume Downtown. It is in the form of a short 'film' made by David Fincher and featuring the actress Rooney Mara. Coincidentally, Calvin Klein was one of the many brands mentioned in *Fight Club*. I regard this advert as a sad proof that even the sincerest of tricksters cannot survive without the system.

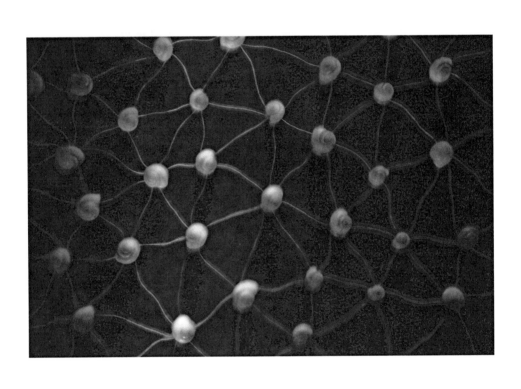

4

THE MEDIA TRICKSTER

Like many other contemporary tricksters, the mass media cannot be defined in absolute terms, as either supporting human identity or destroying and fragmenting it. It does both: on the one hand, the sheer volume and diversity of information generated by media disorientates the individual; while, on the other, the options it offers can be used to create a unique personality. The effect of the media's activity on us depends on our capacity for self-reflection, for seeing the world objectively, for perceiving others as separate from ourselves – it is closely linked to our ability to activate our 'civilised trickster' qualities. This chapter contains examples of 'bad' and 'good' tricksters using the media to challenge an unmoving structure or, by contrast, to meddle with phenomena that are best left alone; the tricksters uniting and dividing people; uncovering the truth or knowingly concealing it in the world in which the truth has become the proverbial needle in a haystack.

It has become commonplace to call postmodern culture fluid, traditionless, lacking in stable identities and meanings. It is characterised by a sense of 'unreality', identity confusion, and lack of psychological unity and completeness. The media trickster reflects the broken nature of modern lifestyles and the confusing diversity of choices. Like the trickster, the mass media is creative, and like the trickster, its creativity does not amount to a final result, to a complete product. It is creativity in rotation, aiming to destabilise, question and confuse any order or structure daring to impose its rules onto society.

New media and reality television particularly add to the identity confusion. As Alec Charles argues in *Interactivity: New Media, Politics and Society* (2012), 'new media appear at time[s] to make people and organizations lose all sense of themselves, and of proportion. It is as if their distance and relative anonymity or unaccountability release the users from their senses of reality' (Charles, 2012: 17). True to its trickster psychology, new media and reality television push the boundaries – and often completely erase the distinction between fantasy and reality. There are psychological consequences of this kind of border erasure:

> By translating it into the medium of the text message or the tweet, the event becomes at once real and unreal: it enters into the new paradigm of a hyper-mediated reality, which is at once detached from material reality (and therefore from traditional moral responsibility) and is also the only reality there now is.
>
> *(2012: 19)*

The ability to transgress boundaries does not in itself constitute freedom of expression or freedom of action – real freedom lies in the Millian combination of creativity and restraint, for the trickster without a framework is just pure destruction, pure chaos. Only the Millian 'civilised trickster', the balanced citizen, can appreciate autonomy in its creative form, and its use for identity-making purposes. In itself, fragmentedness is not a negative quality – it is only when human beings are unable to derive a meaning out of a range of alternatives that it becomes psychologically dangerous.

Writing in 1991, before the arrival of new media, Anthony Giddens emphasises that mass communications are the direct expression of the globalising, disembedding tendencies of modernity – and they are as much its mirror as its instrument. Although the media 'creates' news and stories, and compiles them into structural conglomerates such as newspaper columns, television programmes and interviews, the elements of information within each unit are forced together rather than forming a continuous narrative. A collage, Giddens writes, is not a narrative, yet

> the coexistence of different items in mass media does not represent a chaotic jumble of signs. Rather, the separate 'stories' which are displayed alongside one another express orderings of consequentiality typical of a transformed time-space environment from which the hold of place has largely evaporated.
>
> *(Giddens, 2012: 26)*

The media reflects the temporary nature of all modern constructions. In the ever-changing, fluid post-industrial world, with its endless consumer and personal choices, the only thing that is not on offer is the absolute truth, wholeness, meaning. However, even now that psychological fragmentation is the psycho-cultural norm, and the quest for wholeness has long been relegated to the 'mytho-religious' domain, the question of identity remains as acute as ever.

'Stable' identities grow in stable cultural environments with fixed meanings. In the absence of a fixed *habitus*, the mass media has begun to perform some of its functions. Television, newspapers and the internet offer alternative identities (or, rather, fragments of identities), which lead to the confusion between truth and fiction. In this liminal atmosphere, in the absence of permanent role models, the mass media reflects, embraces and contributes to the brokenness of culture. It acts as a kind of identity pimp providing the insatiable public with a rotation of inspiring public figures. On the positive side, the media can be said to be a community replacement as it ties people together with information; it creates a sense of unity and solidarity in the otherwise fragmented society. We are brought 'together' by a single piece of news, and we share the same television programmes, computer games and social networks.

However, due to the rapid rotation of information, identities thereby procured are often shallow and superficial. The entire cultural framework can be seen as narcissistic in the sense that it relies on the individuals *not* having, or sometimes not even *seeking* a stable individual character core. Instead, it manipulates consumer demand by introducing multiple choice and uncertainty.

Although they have 'unity of thought and consciousness' (Giddens, 2012: 26), these collections of fragmented information do not amount to a solid meaning. Any of the opinions and assumptions circulated in the mass media can be challenged by alternative opinions and assumptions. This quality, in fact, lies at the base of any democratic society and its efficiency depends on the presence of the 'civilised trickster' in each and every citizen. However, most individuals inhabiting such a culture do not feel psychologically safe, and their sense of identity remains mercurial, always keeping pace with the fast-moving life, always prepared to change direction. Marshall Berman highlights one of the principal dialectical features of modern existence: alongside the great emptiness of values ('God is dead') there exists 'a remarkable abundance of possibilities' (1983: 21). The psyche of the modern individual – and of society which he inhabits – consists of fleeting, flying, metamorphosing elements. Its very ephemeral character constitutes its anxiety, its neuroses and psychoses.

The search for a meaning

Much has been said about the postmodern culture's elusive tricksterism, mostly perpetuated and led by the mass media. Left-leaning philosophers and sociologists – Fredrick Jameson, Terry Eagleton, Marshall Berman and Guy Debord – tend to regard postmodern lack of ideological definition as highly pernicious for human identity, and the mass media as the shadow, as a narcissistic institution influenced by the capitalist culture. Most Marxist theorists assume that loss of structure is bad, and that it induces in the individual the feeling of being out of control (amounting, in the final instance, to shame).

According to Jameson, the features that characterise cultural products in late capitalism are pastiche and schizophrenia. By pastiche he means meaningless imitation of more authentic styles. Like Jung's theory of schizophrenia in modernist texts and paintings, Jameson's use of the word is meant to be descriptive, not diagnostic (Malpas, 2001: 29). Pastiche, Jameson writes

> is blank parody, parody that has lost its sense of humour: pastiche is to parody what that curious thing, the modern practice of a kind of blank irony, is to what Wayne Booth calls the stable and comic ironies of, say, the eighteenth century.
>
> *(Cited in Malpas, 2001: 25)*

Meanwhile, the cultural 'schizophrenia', the fragmented consciousness becomes visible when temporal continuities break down and

> the experience of the present becomes powerfully, overwhelmingly vivid and 'material': the world comes before the schizophrenic with heightened intensity, bearing a mysterious and oppressive charge of affect, glowing with hallucinatory energy. But what might for us seem a desirable experience – an increase in our perceptions, a libidinal or hallucinogenic intensification of our normally humdrum and familiar surroundings – is here felt as a loss, as 'unreality'.
>
> *(2001: 34)*

The culture that is deemed by Fredrick Jameson 'schizophrenic' in its hallucinogenic multiplicity and intensity, is also described by his British colleague Terry Eagleton as 'depthless, decentred, ungrounded, self-reflexive, playful, derivative, eclectic, pluralistic' (Eagleton, 1996: vii).

Jameson suspects that, in spite of its seeming variability, lack of stability, fragmentedness and pluralism, capitalism is a well-organised system. It skilfully imitates archaic rhythms in new ways and forms. It is simultaneously stable and destabilised, and this lack of security and constancy is largely self-inflicted and does not damage its working core. And even though images and fragments, with which capitalist organisations (including media and advertising giants) operate, do not amount to any verifiable or final 'truth', they nevertheless do not fall apart and are firmly kept together by the principle of profit fed and fuelled by consumption. Profit becomes the only truth; it is the base of the structure that is the capitalist system.

In fact, Marxist philosophers see mass communications as a dark trickster absorbed in its own delusional and narcissistic compulsive lying, completely detached from reality (including the reality of production), and unable to grasp the notion of truth altogether. The filmmaker and cultural theorist Guy Debord writes in his (rather disjointed) programmatic text, *The Society of the Spectacle* that the mass media is in no way neutral – this trickster is a fake, firmly rooted in the system:

> The concentration of these media . . . amounts to concentrating in the hands of the administrators of the existing system the means that enable them to carry on this particular form of administration. The social separation reflected in the spectacle is inseparable from the modern *state* – the product of the social division of labour that is both the chief instrument of class rule and the concentrated expression of all social divisions.
>
> *(Debord, 2009: 30)*

Meanwhile, the choices offered by the postmodern 'spectacular abundance' only conceal 'the unity of poverty' and 'develop into struggles between illusory qualities designed to generate fervent allegiance to quantitative trivialities' (2009: 49). This means that all the conflicting choices available in late modern societies are counterfeit. The battle of the choices is the battle of dead tricksters – the battle of ghosts, the war of shadows. Debord complains that the proverbial and elusive civilised trickster, the genuine personality, the citizen capable of making informed and responsible decisions does not exist: 'real adults – people who are masters of their own lives – are in fact nowhere to be found' (2009: 49).

Naturally, the difference between new and old gods is very significant, and primarily lies in the quality and 'longevity' of the new deities. Today image and information are as disposable as they are mercurial. Fixed meaning characteristic of the traditional *habitus* has transformed into the mutable, forever changing meaning prevalent in the age of the trickster. Jean Baudrillard does not bemoan the disappearance of the 'civilised trickster' (and does not, like Jameson, proclaim that such a creature never existed), but simply records the death of meaning and the triumph of (as the *Fight Club* narrator puts it) 'a copy of a copy of a copy'. As Baudrillard argues in *Simulacra and Simulation* (1981), 'we live in a world where there is more and more information, and less and less meaning' (Baudrillard, 2000: 79). Tricksters do not produce or even seek absolute meanings – their primary aims are movement, action, challenge and impulse. According to Baudrillard, the meanings temporarily (and endlessly) generated by the media cannot make up for the brutal loss of signification because innate finite meanings no longer exist (or, rather, are out of fashion). Sequences have become too fast for the viewer or reader to discern the signifieds behind the series of visual or linguistic signifiers. Signification has become an extraneous process, secondary to representation. Baudrillard writes:

> Despite efforts to reinject message and content, meaning is lost and devoured faster than it can be reinjected. In this case, one must appeal to a base productivity to replace failing media. This is the whole ideology of free speech, of media broken into innumerable individual cells of transmission, that is, into 'antimedia' (pirate radio, etc.).

> Or information has nothing to do with signification. It is something else, an operational model of another order, outside meaning and of the circulation of meaning strictly speaking. This is Shannon's hypothesis: a sphere of information that is purely functional, a technical medium that does not imply any finality of meaning, and thus should also not be implicated in a value judgment. A kind of code, like the genetic code: it is what it is, it functions as it does, meaning is something else that in a sense comes after the fact. [...]

> Or, very much on the contrary, there is a rigorous and necessary correlation between the two, to the extent that information is directly destructive of meaning and signification, or that it neutralizes them. The loss of meaning is directly linked to the dissolving, dissuasive action of information, the media, and the mass media.

> *(2000: 79)*

Meanwhile, there is no significant relation between 'the inflation of information and the deflation of meaning' (2000: 79). Television, being by its very nature what

Christian Metz would call a 'pluricodic medium' (cited in Stam and Flitterman-Lewis, 2008: 48), is particularly guilty of foregrounding representation at the expense of the signification process. This over-inflated representation, with its speed and immediate disposability, leads to the 'catastrophe of meaning' and, ultimately, to its implosion (Baudrillard, 2000: 83).

In fact, the 'catastrophe of meaning', when traditional signification is impaired by speed and technology, is quite in line with all the traditional trickster qualities. Mythological tricksters – including the message-bearer Hermes, the 'cunning' Odysseus and the chaotic Loki – are incurable liars. The flickering of television images and the instantaneous obsoletion of information plays tricks on the audience that has long ceased to expect any truth beyond the *participation mystique* of visual deception and linguistic simplicity. Hyper-representation is addictive; it becomes an obsession in which both the trickster and the tricked participate in an endless recycling of trivialities. While signification has traditionally stood for 'truth', representation has allied with the fantastic world of lies. The fragmentation and proliferation of images in the mass media reflects the broken, disorientated state of the postmodern self.

Compulsive lying of the mass media that seeks to disguise the fragmented, wounded inner core of the metropolitan individual, however, does not cancel the question of 'the real'. Neither can it make evaporate the problem of the wound itself, or exorcise the evil that had caused this wound. Perhaps, not surprisingly, popular culture obsessively returns to the physical aspect of human existence – particularly to metaphors of violence and destruction – for instance, in action films or body horror movies such as Ballard (1973)/Cronenberg's (1996) *Crash* or Palahniuk/Fincher's *Fight Club*. The return to the reality of the body, on the one hand, is a typical trickster move – after all, traditional trickster narratives emphasise the pre-conscious bodily fragmentedness and psychological disjointedness of trickster figures that is eventually overcome during ontogenesis. On the other hand, the reality of the body and of human sensations – particularly pain – remain the only signs of the proof of one's existence in the hyperreal world otherwise characterised by sensory overload and deferred signification. The disjointed body in popular culture echoes the catastrophe of meaning, the failure of the 'father' to provide a wholesome picture of the world.

Objects and people

The mass media has the dual function of confusing the individual and keeping his identity unstable while, at the same time, providing him with alternative (and temporary) identities and lifestyles. This function is often adjacent to both the production process and the advertising industry. Heinz Kohut's concept of selfobject can clarify the main mechanisms by which various media provide the individual with a rotation of temporary identities and fragments of identities.

In his book *Individuation and Narcissism*, Mario Jacoby argues that Jung and Kohut are ideologically close and rather compatible despite the fact that their sets of terminology differ significantly. He notes that 'modern psychoanalytic research on narcissism, especially that of Heinz Kohut, shows a clear convergence with the Jungian position' and Jung's concept of the individuation process 'may be paralleled with the lines of maturation in narcissism as postulated by Kohut' (Jacoby, 2010: 6). For instance, their views on individual development are not conflicting and can even be used to complement and enrich each other. Kohut's concept of selfobject, coupled with Jungian individuation, can illuminate the contemporary individual's struggle for identity and self-definition:

> [W]e do not see merely fixation on a small child's need for mirroring – the traumatic frustration of the normal need intensifies and distorts the need: the child becomes insatiably hungry for mirroring, affirmation, and praise. It is this intensified, distorted need which the child cannot tolerate and which it therefore either represses (and may hide behind pseudoindependence and emotional coldness) or distorts and splits off. [. . .]
>
> In the narcissistic transference, the infantile need for selfobject is remobilized.
>
> *(Kohut, 2009: 558)*

Kohut's analysis of narcissism and immature relationships that rest on mirroring and manipulation is applicable to cultural analysis. The psyche of the urban individual is living with a very old trauma – inflicted by industrialisation, social alienation, the weakening of community and intensification of city life – which was already apparent in the middle of the nineteenth century but became particularly acute at the start of the twentieth century. The trauma – of which Jung was a faithful historiographer – was catastrophically deepened by the two World Wars. The individual of today is suffering from a traumatic identity crisis brought about by the profound and irreversible changes in the social and relational structures of society.

The individual, torn from his roots, grows up thinking that the most responsible way of dealing with one's issues is trying to solve them on your own, without the involvement of your immediate or wider environment. These independent individuals who make up society, self-reliant and stoical, barraged with identity and lifestyle choices, separated from fellow human beings and isolated by the specifics of the urban environment, feel lonely and isolated. They feel out of control, insecure and lost. Anthony Giddens transposes the loss of 'the early sense of ontological security' (characteristic of narcissistic disturbances) onto contemporary culture and concludes that

> trust is a crucial generic phenomenon of personality development as well as having a distinctive and specific relevance to a world of disembedding mechanisms and abstract systems. [. . .] Trust in this sense is basic to a 'protective cocoon' which stands guard over the self in its dealings with everyday reality. It 'brackets out' potential occurrences which, were the individual seriously to contemplate them, would produce a paralysis of the will, or feelings of engulfment.
>
> *(Giddens, 2012: 3)*

Trust and the desire to have control over one's destiny go hand-in-hand.

A broken identity is always on the lookout for reparation and completion; for ways to achieve the mythical wholeness. As Christopher Lasch remarks, narcissism can be used as a metaphor to explain contemporary individual's fascination with fame and celebrity as well as the widespread 'fear of competition, the inability to suspend disbelief, the shallowness and transitory quality of personal relations, the horror of death' (Lasch, 1991: 59). The contemporary narcissist lives for himself and only for the moment: 'To live for the moment is the prevailing passion – to live for yourself, not for your predecessors or posterity' (1991: 5). Meanwhile, this man, 'the final product of bourgeois individualism', is permanently haunted by inner emptiness and anxiety as well as 'doubts the reality of his own existence' (1991: xvi). The contemporary narcissistic individual feels angry and distressed; he is constantly on the lookout for inner peace and meaning. He still seeks intimacy and mirroring – but in post-traditional cultures both are fleeting and impermanent.

This is when the mass media comes to the rescue by offering artificial means of control and other escapist and superficial solutions to identity brokenness. It offers the individual a variety of safe replacements – celebrities, cars, brand clothes – for the all-too-real and emotionally unsafe messiness of human connection and human relationships. Identities are produced, advertised and consumed in limitless quantities; they are offered in all shapes and sizes. Famous people are ready-made personality samples, complete with distinguishable lifestyles, beautiful faces and bodies, fashionable wardrobes and interesting, eventful lives. Caught in the eternal consumption process, participants are pushed into further destabilising their selves, deferring the process of maturation, of self-formation. One no longer knows what one wants – the only thing knowable, verifiable and, in fact, real – is the never-ending process of *wanting*.

The non-stop mirroring and copying process – the postmodern reaction to the trauma of modernity – has become obsessive-compulsive. Individuals caught in this process cannot stop consuming because constantly buying new things and altering their identities numbs the inner emptiness. The obsessive-compulsive element of shopping lessens the pain, dissolves the anger, and numbs the acute awareness of the trauma.

Because relationships of this kind are superficial, any individual development resulting from them can be considered fake. Deep down, under the persona (Jung) or the false self (Kohut), there is nothing – there dwells and broods the ubiquitous phenomenological chasm, the anger, the fear of non-existence. The impermanence, the high turnover of generated and debased objects effectively fuels the system – but pushes it out of balance. The media's typically tricksterish habit to impulsively (and unpredictably) debase and replace the objects of its manipulation is essentially self-destructive because it accelerates the whole process to dangerous proportions.

The media trickster provides a sense of ownership (and a feeling of being in control) by offering artificially constructed (but ephemeral) images for sale while, at the same time, leaving the consumer craving more. Mercurial media images aim to provide temporary satiation, a short-term satisfaction – a superficial masking of the narcissistic wound. Eventually the audience is left feeling even more powerless, immature and confused than they were before they had 'consumed' their first celebrity. The choice is too great and the temptation too strong. The very desire to consume selfobjects is imbued with powerful affect consisting of feelings of inferiority, rage, shame and embarrassment. In this way, the mass media's cure for injured narcissism is only temporary. The selfobject it offers is not genuine but prosthetic, replacing the void within.

Objectification is probably the easiest, and most psychologically accessible, type of relationship based on projective (less frequently – introjective) identification. Contemporary hectic lifestyles are not suitable for fostering authentic relationships but gravitate instead towards a rotation of partners, friends and role models. The phenomenon, which Zygmunt Bauman terms 'the messiness of real intimacy' (Bauman, 2001: 52), is unsuitable for the urban individual who expects to be in control of his objects lest their 'messiness' cause him to feel ashamed and out of control. Contemporary individuals expect objects in their environment to be easily-governed and predictable. There is simply no time for studying – or entering into – complex interactions with the objects that are too independent. The individual of the machine age expects things to happen at the touch of a button.

Baudrillard points out in *The System of Objects* that the contemporary individual's relationship with the outside world is both immature and manipulative. Technology, Baudrillard argues, only supports us in this immaturity and dependence on immediacy. We are no longer prepared to wait; we want things to happen quickly – we want things *here and now*. Only then do we feel in control – because quick satisfaction of our needs remind us of the omnipotent uroboric state of early childhood. This illusion of control, carefully orchestrated by consumer capitalism, keeps the individual in the constant state of dependency on the immediate availability of objects. This kind of manipulation makes consumers feel in control of many aspects of their lives. In a way, it also empowers them – but only temporarily, and only as long as they are prepared to pay for new products and devices.

Industrialisation made it possible for us to exercise our right to change the objective environment. For instance, one 'merges' with the automobile while driving. The car becomes our narcissistic extension, our ideal object. Thus, driving becomes a particularly attractive form of projective identification. Baudrillard writes:

> When it comes to material objects, however, and especially to manufactured objects complex enough to lend themselves to mental dismantling, this tendency has free rein. With the automobile, for instance, it is possible to speak of '*my* brakes', '*my* tail fins', '*my* steering wheel'; or to say '*I* am braking', '*I* am turning' or '*I* am starting'. In short, all the car's 'organs' and functions may be brought separately into relation with the person of the owner in the possessive mode. We are dealing here not with a process of personalization at the social level but with a process of a projective kind. We are concerned not with *having* but with *being*.
>
> (Baudrillard, 2005: 109)

The contemporary Western consumer-citizen, Baudrillard also points out, can be metaphorically seen as a 'collector' with a tendency to objectify everything, including people and relationships, and expecting obedience, mirroring and silent appraisal from his environment. For instance, for children 'collecting is a rudimentary way of mastering the outside world, of arranging, classifying and manipulating' (2005: 93). Collecting is a form of obsession; as an activity, it is both regressive and sublime and is based on 'serial intimacy' (2005: 94). Obsession with objects presupposes impermanence and fear of genuine, long-term intimacy. The collector only loves his objects 'on a basis of their membership in a series' while 'human relationships, home of uniqueness and conflict, never permit any such fusion' (2005: 94). The practice of collecting is based on the narcissistic illusion of mastery over the world. The tragedy of the consumer-citizen is that his delusion ('the IKEA flat') can easily crumble under both the tyranny of the system and the tricksterish confusion of postmodern life.

By contrast, Baudrillard argues, old-fashioned forms of communication and forming relationships involved *limited* choice – or did not give any choice altogether. In the traditionalist, socially rigid world of pre-individualism, in which the fragmenting trickster of freedom had limited power, people lived in communities that they could escape only of they were very lucky. People in pre-industrial societies had jobs to which they were bound for life. Their freedom of movement was restricted both socially and technologically. Any attempt to manipulate the world and/or change one's destiny involved confrontation with the social order.

Interaction with one's objective reality was not a form of aggressive mirroring – or the process of relishing and exercising the right for unlimited choice – but more of a fight for the right to have any choice at all. In the words of Giddens, 'tradition or established habit orders life within relatively set channels' whereas 'modernity confronts the individuals with a complex diversity of choices and, because it is non-foundational, at the same time offers little help as to which options should be selected' (Giddens, 2012: 81). Life with multiple lifestyle choices turns into a hall of mirrors; identities become mere reflections. In these circumstances, connecting with the outside world becomes an exercise in serial and ritualised objectification. But how to pick the right object? What to collect now? How to determine ways of connecting with the object(s)? What is in fashion today? Unfortunately, the absence of a rigid traditional framework does not automatically create independent thinking. Freedom of choice does not magic unique identities out of thin air. This is when the mass media becomes useful.

Today's Western individual would see this socially determined inability to control *most* objects and phenomena in one's surroundings as a form of madness, as a severe form of psychological impairment. Individuals in industrialised and post-industrial societies expect non-stop availability of objects suitable for projective identification. Lack of mechanical, dismantleable bodies is seen by the consumer-collector as a breach of contract; as if god(s) failed to supply them with (temporary) sources of (disposable) identities. The individual who cannot separate himself from an object – who sees his fridge as an extension of himself – would therefore perceive scarcity of projective material as unfair and cruel.

For instance, Baudrillard compares the car to the horse in his discussion of the failure of projective identification. Manipulation of non-manufactured 'objects' is difficult. In other words, we as consumers prefer the world to be as psychologically uncomplicated as possible because relationships with mechanical objects are not emotionally taxing. The behaviour of natural (non-manufactured) entities is disturbing for the consumer-collector because of their poorly manageable qualities such as temper and character:

> With the horse, despite the fact that this animal was a remarkable instrument of power and transcendence for man, this kind of confusion was never possible. The fact is that the horse is not made of pieces – and above all, that it is *sexed*. We can say 'my horse' or 'my wife', but that is as far as this kind of possessive denomination can go. That which has a sex resists fragmenting projection and hence also the mode of appropriation that we have identified as a perversion. Faced by a living being, we may say 'my' but we cannot say 'I' as we do when we symbolically appropriate the functions and 'organs' of a car. That type of regression is not available to us. The horse may be the recipient of powerful symbolic cathexes: we associate it with the wild sexuality of the rutting season, as with the wisdom of the centaur; its head is a terrifying phantasy linked to the image of the father, yet its calm embodies the protective strength of Cheiron the teacher. It is never cathected, however, in the simplistic, narcissistic, far more impoverished and infantile manner in which the ego is projected onto structural details of cars (in accordance with an almost delusional analogy with disassociated parts and functions of the human body).
>
> *(2005: 109)*

Celebrity culture, fed and shaped by mass media, cannot be seen as assisting individuals in finding themselves, in discovering their 'true selves'. Celebrities are treated by their makers and consumers as collectable and disposable prosthetic selfobjects created for the purpose of temporarily filling the gaping hole, of numbing the pain of brokenness. They are but pictures, images, two-dimensional things to be idealised, copied, manipulated, devalued, deposed, punished, shamed, stalked and projected upon in the endless repetition of the cycle. The hunger for compulsive collecting is a sign of the great emptiness within. Neither quality nor quantity of prosthetic selfobjects makes any difference as far as achievement of internal wholeness or freedom is concerned.

The biggest tragedy for an object is to realise that it has been used and abused – merely employed to temporarily fill the gap where the ego is supposed to be. The hapless psychological prostheses who believed themselves to be genuine – and genuinely loved and accepted – eventually realise to their own horror that they have been deceived by their former admirers. Debord describes the short shelf-life of an object as a tragic transition from being 'a unique creation', mediocre but inflated and sold as something prestigious, to becoming 'mundane' as soon as it is taken home, and its essential poverty is revealed (Debord, 2009: 53). However, celebrities are not the only victims of the cycle of collecting and discarding. The consumer-spectator remains unhappy at every stage of the cycle because the great emptiness remains unchanged and unchallenged – it cannot be healed or helped by the ever-proliferating stream of images.

The curse of the selfobject: Princess Diana

The sociological and psychological aspects of the Diana obsession (including the effect of her death on the public) have been the subject of numerous studies published in a variety of reputable academic periodicals, including the *British Journal of Psychiatry* and the *Journal of Communication*. The post-Jungians, too, took part in the debate. Their contribution includes a book section (Hauke, 2000) and a chapter in an edited collection (Bassil-Morozow and Anslow, 2015).

Diana remains the most iconic example of the selfobject used by the media and general public for identity-generating and meaning-making purposes. She was known, as Christopher Hauke points out, almost entirely through the photographic image yet 'seems to have attracted to her image aspects of the human self (not in Jung's sense, but self in the subject's sense of selfhood) which became embodied and personalized, in the individual known as "Princess Diana"' (Hauke, 2000: 68). It was estimated that around two and a half million people watched Diana's funeral, the service was broadcast live around the world, and the angry public reaction forced the Royal Family to fly the Royal Standard at half-mast. The UK came to a standstill to pay its respects, and over one million flowers were left at Kensington Palace, Buckingham Palace and St James's Palace. People expressed their grief very publicly – by crying during interviews, and by leaving touching cards, soft toys and candles at places of mourning. Hauke writes that, facilitated by the vast media coverage of her life and death, people 'suddenly found a range of human qualities condensed in Princess Diana which had been, and still are, lost to their own fragmented sense of themselves, and ambiguously valued, if not lost entirely, in the culture at large' (2000: 68).

It was as if people discovered a collective unity in grief – when they thought they had lost the susceptibility to *participation mystique*. Assisted by the media trickster, they were united by a single selfobject whose qualities prosthetically replaced their ability to feel, to be empathic and to be emotional. The effect of the selfobject lowered their 'civilised reserve', their narcissistic defences and the masks that separated them from each other fell off. The sense of connection, the craving to be 'in touch' with others, often hidden behind the defensive mask, is, as Kenneth Wright puts it, 'integral to the sense of being alive'. People take it for granted until they start to feel disconnected (Wright, 2009: 15). The media unites human beings in new ways – by providing selfobjects and by reaching large numbers of people simultaneously. It puts people 'in touch' with each other when attunement is the quality largely missing from today's hectic lifestyles.

It all sounds very romantic and sentimental, but objectification on a large scale has a serious shadowy side to it. It has consequences both for the person designated as the selfobject and for the mass consuming it. What the trickster releases (and the media trickster does it particularly well thanks to its ability to reach and unite a large number of people with one piece of information) is loneliness, shame and helplessness of the urban individual. Outpouring of public emotion on this scale is a trickster phenomenon – which, essentially, means that it manifests itself against the wishes of the framework and the frameworkers. It is liminal, which means that it interferes with the normal way of life, and is not always predictable even if one attempts to carefully control and frame it.

As Hawton et al. argue in the article 'Effect of Death of Diana, Princess of Wales, on Suicide and Deliberate Self-Harm', published in the *British Journal of Psychiatry*, loss of public figures may influence rates of suicide and deliberate self-harm (Hawton et al., 2000: 465). Unusually, there was an increase in suicide rates amongst females of Diana's age one month after the funeral, 'when depressive disorders may have amplified or precipitated in vulnerable individuals' (2000: 465). At the same time, cases of deliberate self-harm increased only in the first week following Diana's death (2000: 465). Most importantly,

> the increase in both suicide and DSH [deliberate self-harm] following the Princess's death was mainly found for females. The suicides occurred particularly in the age range which included the Princess's age (36 years), suggesting a specific modelling effect (Bandura, 1973), in keeping with findings for media influence on suicide (Schmidtke and Schaller, 2000).
>
> *(2000: 465)*

Some vulnerable minds could not cope with the wave of public emotion and were swayed by it: for instance, one woman, whose birthday coincided with the day of Diana's death, tried to take an overdose (Jackson, 2007).

This is the dark side of being in touch, of being attuned to the mood of the nation. This is the moment when the trickster, who had been hidden under the civilised façade, is allowed to come out, and his angry, anxious, unspent energy turns into self-destruction. This is also the dark side of the habit of using prosthetic selfobjects for the purposes of self-definition and identity-building. The emotional reaction is not to Diana-the-person, but to Diana-the-object, to the figure the grieving members of the public did not know personally. The media tricks its consumers into thinking that they own the selfobject. It provides people with 'porous' identity prostheses, capable of absorbing any issues silenced in individuals themselves.

The selfobject gives people's inner tricksters a voice, an outlet for self-expression. It becomes the mirror – and often a dark and dangerous one. The media trickster, with its intuition for all things popular, promises that the psychological prosthesis, which remains outside of the individual, will keep him alive – and make him feel human. Selfobject in this sense is a medium that serves as a replacement for the normal emotional life. It is a substitute for feelings of connectedness and emotional warmth, for which there is no space in late modernity. All the while, public figures of this scale remain but disposable toys, which, at any moment, can be replaced with a fresh supply of prosthetic drama.

The media trickster (or, rather, the media shadow) poses dangers for people used as selfobjects too. There is pressure on the selfobject to behave in certain ways and to perform certain things. Their star power can propel a product into being super-fashionable and cause it to sell out. Public figures are seen as 'originals', which are then cloned and replicated to produce 'a copy of a copy of a copy'. Ultimately, they embody the power of imitation and the (at least, partial) failure of the civilised trickster. Selfobjects of this scale signify the failure of Mill's dream of a 'genuine personality' who can make decisions independently from the crowd. Contemporary obsession with celebrity culture demonstrates the transformation process of the urban trickster into its narcissistic clone – the shadow.

Ultimately, celebrities are shame-absorbers 'living out' the drama that the ordinary man often misses in his own life. Often, significant selfobjects such as Princess Diana and Marilyn Monroe are bound to suffer under the weight of public attention and mass emotional reactions. In a way, the object whose life is public property becomes a sacrificial victim – it is expected to 'fail' because, by expiring, it absorbs the maximum amount of shame dwelling inside the soulless urban individual. As the devils escape, the playful media trickster becomes the dark media shadow.

After Diana's death, several editors admitted their role in creating the atmosphere of hysterical mass interest in Diana's life, which eventually led to the fatal chase in the Pont de l'Alma road tunnel in Paris, France. Phil Hall, the editor of the *News of the World* at the time of Diana's death, blames both the voracious public and the journalists in the Princess's death. He says in the ITV documentary, *Diana's Last Summer*:

> A big Diana story could add 150,000 sales. So we were all responsible. I felt huge responsibility for what happened and I think everyone in the media did. If the paparazzi hadn't been following her the car wouldn't have been speeding and, you know, the accident may never have happened.
>
> *(Pierce, 2007)*

His sentiments are echoed by another journalist, Stuart Higgins, who edited *The Sun*:

> The death of Princess Diana was the most tragic story during my period as editor. I have often questioned my role, the paper's role and the media's role generally in her death and the events leading up to it. The tabloids created a frenzy and appetite around Diana. But in the end I believe it was just a terrible accident, caused by a drunken driver and possibly because of the lack of the high level of police and security protection that she had enjoyed previously.
>
> *(Cited in Pierce, 2007)*

Ultimately, the effects and affects produced by the escaped trickster are not possible to predict and control. Chances are that what starts as a uniting emotion or common interest may eventually turn into the collective shadow. Meanwhile, the prosthetic selfobject cannot replace a genuine personality or genuine feelings – it can only mask the gaping emptiness, which will keep demanding new objects, new sacrifices, new drama and new extreme sensations. The neglect of the trickster leads to lives being lived externally – through objects, specifically designated for this purpose.

'Here's to the crazy ones, the misfits . . .'

In 1997 *Apple* launched an advertising campaign called 'Think Different', which, in its TV advert version, contained carefully montaged black and white footage of some of the most inspirational personalities of the twentieth century, and a narrative poem about the power of being 'crazy' and a 'rebel', narrated by the actor Richard Dreyfuss. The campaign was created by the Los Angeles office of advertising agency TBWA/Chiat/Day (Siltanen, 2011). The people listed in the clips and the posters were innovators, groundbreaking creatives – people who, in fact, *did* think differently and *were* different, just as the campaign claimed: Albert Einstein, Mahatma Gandhi, Thomas Edison, Martin Luther King, John Lennon, Pablo Picasso, Maria Callas and many others. The poem, in all versions, went on to become the widely popular hymn to tricksterism, originality, creativity – and even troublemaking. In fact, the original full text manages to describe every possible trickster attribute, and make them look like the most desirable qualities on earth. These are the heroic attributes of a fire-bringer – of someone who defied shame and the fear of 'being different', of someone who abandoned an easy path in the hope to discover something new. The language of the advertisement also emphasises the edgy and dangerous aspect of the trickster: madness, rebellion, trouble and inability to fit in with the rest of the 'crowd'. It fact, the poem starts with the 'negative' qualities and explores them further, revealing the true innovative nature of the trickster. What starts off as a list of the trickster's most archaic attributes, becomes a hymn to his creationist, meaning-making and progress-bringing abilities. The poem cannot be reproduced here due to copyright reasons, but it is widely available on the internet in all versions. Yet, it is also ironic and paradoxical that a poem that proclaims the supremacy of the trickster is protected by one of the most pervasive and important systems of modernity, the cornerstone of modern life – the intellectual property and copyright system. In this case, once more – the trickster is only a slave of the structure, although he is still at large somewhere in the vastness of the internet.

The poem is often mistakenly attributed to Jack Kerouac, and thought of as being lifted from his programmatic text, *On the Road* (1957) when, in fact, it was inspired by a postmodernist blend of other texts, including a song called 'Crazy' by the British singer-songwriter Seal, and the film *Dead Poets Society* (1989), directed by Peter Weir (Siltenen, 2011). The film's protagonist, played by Robin Williams, is an inspirational teacher with an unorthodox approach to life and poetry whose philosophy is 'looking at things in a different way' because 'the human race is filled with passion, which is waiting to be released'.

Rob Siltanen, one of the people who helped put the campaign together, describes his thought process during the final phases of its creation:

> I felt the opening was powerful because I designed it to sync up with the images of the geniuses and have a certain shock value. I thought about the brilliant people throughout history and the struggles they went through. Many lived tortured existences, and it was becoming clear to me that they shared a common thread. Like Apple, they all had amazing visions, but also like Apple, all of them at one point or another were given unflattering labels. Martin Luther King was seen as a troublemaker before he was universally seen as a saint, the rebellious Ted Turner was laughed out of town when he first tried to sell the concept of a 24-hour news channel, and it's been said that before Einstein was celebrated as the world's greatest thinker, he was thought to be just a guy with crazy ideas. Of course in 1997, Apple was being called a 'toy' that was only for 'creative types,' and it was being chastised for not having the same operating system as everyone else. But I felt this copy would speak to the fans and get people who weren't on our side to re-evaluate their thinking and realize that being different is a good thing. Ralph Waldo Emerson once said, 'To be great is to be misunderstood,' and I always believed that was the general concept behind the 'Think Different' campaign.
>
> *(Siltanen, 2011)*

Interestingly enough, Steve Jobs was initially disparaging about the text of the poem. Nevertheless, the campaign gave Apple the boost they so desperately needed at the time of its demise (Siltanen, 2011). What is more curious, however, is the fact that this poem, despite being written specifically to reflect the spirit and philosophy of Apple and its mastermind, can be applied to any other pioneer of new media, including Bill Gates (Microsoft), Mark Zuckerberg (Facebook) and Google's Sergey Brin and Larry Page. The text reflects the self-idealising, Romantic vision that new media's creators have of themselves and their products. After all, are not they the people who had invented something that had not existed before them? They are the people who spotted a gap in the market, and filled it with innovation and enterprise; the individuals who created the shining new world, redefined com-munication and united people in new and unexpected ways. Two of them, Mark Zuckerberg and Steve Jobs, now even feature as protagonists in biopics that depict their struggle to become the start-ups of the new media – *The Social Network* (directed by David Fincher, 2010) and *Jobs* (directed by Joshua Michael, 2013). This, surely, solidifies their status as tricksters, fire-bringers, visionaries, saviours of the masses and educators of the people?

In reality, the history of media giants, both old and new, shows that any fresh ideas and innovations, as soon as they attain a sizable influence, quickly solidify and transform from liminal phenomena, chaotic and unpredictable in their wild creativity, into well-structured organisations – essentially, well-functioning, normal aspects of the capitalist order. Turner notes that former communitates, once they become mainstream structures, tend to quickly solidify and forget that they used to be powered by tricksters: 'exaggeration of communitas, in certain political or religious movements of the levelling type, may be speedily followed by despotism, overbureaucratization, or other modes of structural rigidification' (Turner, 2009: 129). Put simply, these organisations employ people, spend resources and therefore have to find ways of earning money. Once they 'grow up', they tend to betray their trickster roots and become the 'normal' companies doing what all 'normal' companies do – maximise their profits. In this case, the fate of human identity in these new systems is uncertain. The only thing that can be said with absolute certainty is that identity is going to be used – if not to conform to the system – then as a resource to feed and expand it.

The solidification of the 'edgy' liminal into the 'mainstream' structural has affected a number of formerly revolutionary websites. Over the years, concerns have been raised about some of the policies of companies such as Facebook and Google – particularly about their privacy settings, their tendency to accumulate personal information that cannot be permanently deleted, and their tendency to use behavioural advertising, which uses information about consumers to tailor advertisements to their needs. The latter is particularly worrying because it smacks of both stalking and surveillance, and is purely manipulative.

Alec Charles argues in *Interactivity: New Media, Politics and Society* (2012) that a range of internet phenomena, which consider themselves to be the pioneers of freedom and the innovators in the field of social interaction, should be treated with caution. He writes that

> Facebook's vision of openness and connectedness could be interpreted in terms of data-mining strategy which categorizes and commodifies its users as packages of commercially valuable information [. . .] Facebook tends to expect rather more openness of its users than it is willing to provide to them.
>
> *(Charles, 2012: 119)*

Despite the fact that the internet has made our lives easier, its famed ability to liberate the individual is disputable. This is partially because an unrestrained internet trickster – the trickster at large – is both a dangerous and an idealistic idea. Absolute freedom in an essentially disembodied and anonymous sphere can be a double-edged sword (as internet trolls and numerous instances of abuse show). However, solidification of the former internet pioneers of individuality and freedom into companies primarily concerned with profit is deeply worrying; as is the increasing surveillance and policing of the internet. The question of individual agency, therefore, remains and is unlikely to be ever resolved because it involves the problem of balance between the trickster and the system.

The attack of the female trickster

This section discusses the female trickster and her ways of using the mass media to promote her message. The female trickster – particularly in the form of a feminist – is the ultimate kind of trickster. She is doubly anti-systemic because systems favour patriarchal properties: control, order, hierarchy and structure. As Ricki Tannen writes in *The Female Trickster: the Mask that Reveals* (2007), today the trickster-woman has come to create 'a new relationship with the historical adversity and hostility found in western consciousness toward females manifesting autonomy, agency, and authenticity as single, fulfilled, physically strong, and psychologically whole individuals' (Tannen, 2007: 10). Tannen goes on to discuss a range of real historical figures (female authors and comedians) and 'fictive female sleuths' who can be seen as female tricksters challenging the patriarchal discourse using their minds, bodies and texts.

Interestingly enough, my two examples of the female trickster using the mass media to publicise their message – the feminist Ukrainian protest group FEMEN and the Russian punk rock project Pussy Riot – are both from the Eastern Bloc. Both FEMEN and Pussy Riot are what I call 'gonzo trickster' projects in that they do not distinguish between fantasy and reality, between the mask of the trickster and its human vehicle, between performance and a political stance. Notable examples of gonzo tricksterism include the art of Sacha Baron-Cohen (*Borat: Cultural Learnings of America for Make Benefit Glorious Nation of Kazakhstan* (2006); *Bruno* (2009)) and the American comedian Andy Kaufman.

One most recent – and probably the most extreme – example of gonzo trickster is the Russian performance artist Pyotr Pavlensky who sacrifices his body for the sake of art and political protest. His most scandalous gonzo-installations include sewing up his mouth in support of Pussy Riot; stripping naked and wrapping himself in barbed wire in protest against the repressive actions of the government ('Carcass'); and, shockingly, nailing his scrotum to the cobblestones in Red Square ('Fixation'). The latter installation had a statement attached to it:

> The performance can be seen as a metaphor for the apathy, political indifference and fatalism of contemporary Russian society. As the government turns the country into one big prison, stealing from the people and using the money to grow and enrich the police apparatus and other repressive structures, society is allowing this, and forgetting its numerical advantage, is bringing the triumph of the police state closer by its inaction.
>
> *(Cited in Walker, 2013)*

Another of his statements reads: 'It's not the authorities who hold people by their balls. It's people themselves. The country will turn into a police state if people do nothing' (cited in Lally, 2013). Pavlensky's protests are powerful statements precisely because they involve one of the most effective tools of trickster influence – the body. They confuse both the authorities and the police because the punishment is administered by the artist himself, and not by the framework-ers. He reclaims the power that had previously belonged to the authorities. The body is no longer owned by them. It becomes the regenerating, and regener-ated, body of the trickster.

Thus, gonzo tricksters are prepared to take physical and legal risks to further their art. They often sacrifice personal safety and even health for creative purposes during their anti-systemic machinations. The mask of the clown is not enough to protect them, which means they are ultimately vulnerable in their fight with rigid and systemic phenomena (including prejudices). The task of the gonzo trickster is to uncover the hidden, the silenced and the shameful in a given culture; to bring the taboo subjects to light; to make people discuss them and re-evaluate their 'clas-sified' status. Gonzo artists of this kind embody the 'martyr' aspect of the trickster. Predictably, the system retaliates – and often in a physically violent manner.

Examples of female gonzo creativity include the artists Carolee Schneemann, Tracey Emin and Marina Abramović whose visual performances involved the female body and aimed to shock the audience. For instance, during her act *Interior Scroll* (1975), the feminist Schneemann gradually extracted a scroll of paper from her vagina, and read her speech from it. For her, this act symbolised the release of the female voice and the revelation of the knowledge women possess but are not allowed to express. Tracey Emin famously displayed her untidy sleeping place in *My Bed* (1999), and Abramović's visual experiments involved physical damage to her body, including letting the audience violate her with a range of objects in *Rhythm 0* (1974), and losing consciousness after running out of oxygen during the performance of *Breathing In/Breathing Out* (1977) with her partner and fellow artist Ulay.

Female gonzo acts are particularly transgressive because the trickster-woman breaks into the forbidden room and uncovers male shame – male weaknesses and fear – which she is not supposed to see because, if she does, the Bluebeard will lose his power. It is not surprising that female gonzo performers prefer 'physical' and sexual ways of delivering their messages: the body and its basic functions are the first targets of systemic control when the baby is being integrated into 'civilisation', and it therefore becomes the trickster's first line of attack. The female body in particular is the traditional target of patriarchal control and regulation. In shocking the audience with sexuality, nakedness or other transgressions, the trickster merely aims to provide the audience with an alternative view of things. Desacralisation thus becomes a political act.

FEMEN

FEMEN is an extreme feminist protest group founded in 2008. On their official website they call themselves a 'sextremist movement'. FEMEN members conduct their protests half-naked, which has nothing to do with traditional sexuality, but is meant to symbolise equality with men and freedom of expression. The official pictures displayed on the website are deliberately violent: a smiling pretty woman is holding a bloodied sickle in one hand and a male scrotum in the other; a woman dressed up as 'death' is announcing 'death for the patriarchy'; another model, wearing heavy make-up, has the word 'witch' written in black across her bare chest. All are half-naked.

The founder of the movement is Anna Hutsol, a Russian-born Ukrainian former economist and talent manager. By her own admission, she created the movement, which has since become international, in response to the growing Ukrainian sex industry, which was heavily dependent on foreigners coming to the country to enjoy accessible sex services. She says in an interview to the French channel France 24: 'I set up FEMEN because I realised that there was a lack of women activists in our society; Ukraine is male-oriented and women take a passive role' ('How They Protest Prostitution in Ukraine', 2009). Interestingly enough, Hutsol emphasises the sexual aspect of her chosen format: 'We thought we'd create an organization where young girls could come and help others like them and help society. And the format we picked was this extremely sexy, bright way of presenting ourselves' (Magnay, 2011).

In fact, underlying the format is a range of recognisable trickster qualities: crossing boundaries of public decency (perceived by 'the patriarchy' as aggression and penetration), visual shock, unpredictability and lack of unified agenda. Their aim is to shock the opponents out of their state of complacency and 'righteousness', to cause them to lose control over themselves and the situation. One of the ironies of FEMEN's principal tactics is that most policemen and security guards who arrest and remove them are male, and therefore have to deal with the embarrassment of handling naked women.

Over the years, the sextremists took part in a variety of political protests all over the world, from sex tourism and under-representation of women in politics to religious oppression to eating disorders in the modelling industry and the political situation in Russia. However, the fact that Hutsol relies on media attention and marketing strategies to publicise the movement's message, has led commentators to think that the whole thing is fake, and is just another colourful but meaningless media project. For instance, Diana Magnay argues that 'Gutsol [sic] came from the theater business and knows how to create a spectacle' (Magnay, 2011). Her doubts are echoed by Robyn Urback of the *National Post*, who writes in the aftermath of the FEMEN protesters' attack on the Paris Fashion Show in September 2013:

> FEMEN crashed the Nina Ricci fashion show, according to the FEMEN Facebook page, to protest the 'exploitative fashion industry,' which it called a 'dirty male business.' Paradoxically, however, much of the water cooler discussion about the stunt after the release of photos was of how the FEMEN activists were just as attractive, if not more, than the clothed models. The images were ogled, not understood.
>
> *(Urback, 2013)*

Urback criticises the lack of ideological cohesion in the sextremists' liminal activity, and argues that there is too much trickster and not enough politics in their messages.

The result is so confusing that the activists end up being as objectified as the victims of objectification they are trying to protect:

> FEMEN supporters may point to this superficial reception as further evidence of the notion that women are seen as sex objects in European and North American societies. Maybe so. But the onus is on FEMEN, not its audience, to make sure that its message is getting across.
>
> *(Urback, 2013)*

The jury is still out on the authenticity of this female trickster, which is accused of being an entertaining media project and not 'the real thing'. In other words, it is implied that, despite claiming otherwise, FEMEN and their mastermind are not employing their inner 'civilised tricksters' in order to deal with the rigidity of the patriarchal system. They are not rebels fighting for women's right to have non-systemically-constructed identities. Instead, they are just having fun for the sake of having fun, enjoying the attention and are, in fact, just destructive narcissists. As ever, the main problem with tricksters is that they defy definitions, and it is often difficult to tell the difference between 'meaningless destruction' and 'meaningful destruction' with absolute certainty.

Pussy Riot

The female punk band Pussy Riot is another example of female tricksterism publicised and supported by both Russian and international media. In fact, it can be said that it is various forms of media, from newspapers to blogs and social networks, that solidified them as a protest project after they had been arrested for their performance of the song 'Mother of God, Drive Putin Away' on 21 February 2013. The band is an offspring of another performance art project called Voina (meaning War), which specialises in highly controversial public stunts and uses technology to spread its message. Examples of Voina's stunts include a sex orgy at the Timiryazev State Biological Museum in Moscow (a metaphorically expressed protest against the Russian presidential elections of 2012) and drawing a gigantic phallus on the Liteiny Bridge in St Petersburg – right in front of the Russia's Federal Security Service headquarters. The latter action was titled 'Dick Captured by the FSB'.

Both the projects are not-for-profit, which allows them to sustain their purely liminal status. Being thus free of systemic influence, they have the total freedom of (trickster) expression. Notably many members of the projects are philosophy graduates or students of the Philosophical Faculty of the Moscow State University. Yet, despite its philosophical foundations, the tricksterism generated by the group is genuine in the Rabelaisian sense as it aims to break the best-guarded boundaries (the government, the police, the secret service) and involves the use of basic bodily functions to shock 'the mass' out of their slumber. The idea is to challenge the country's biggest narcissistic structures by doing embarrassing and unpredictable things. Their message is clear: the authorities cannot use shame to control members of the group because Voina disposed of the concept of shame altogether. It is difficult to imagine a more outrageous act of defiance than having group sex in a public place, documenting the whole thing and then publicising it on the internet. Like the artist Pavlensky, who sees his personal physical body as reflecting the body of the public, the members of Voina have become 'shameless' in order to free themselves from any systemic influence. When agency is taken away from the individual, the body is the only remaining area of control the individual still possesses. In performances like this, the violence received by the physical body becomes the metaphor for the state of society.

In February 2012, five members of the Pussy Riot band wearing brightly-coloured clothes and balaclavas, entered the Cathedral of Christ the Saviour of the Russian Orthodox Church in Moscow and performed a song in which they asked Mother of God to get rid of Vladimir Putin. The aim of the action was to sabotage the upcoming presidential elections, which were expected to be rigged. By staging the action at the Cathedral, the band attracted the public's attention to the widespread corruption in the Orthodox Church and to its close links with the Russian government. Three members of the band – Nadezhda Tolokonnikova, Maria Alekhina and Yekaterina Samutsevich – were arrested and put on trial for blasphemy and hooliganism. All three were sentenced to two years in a corrective penal colony on 12 August 2012. The judge defended her verdict saying that the three women 'crudely undermined social order' ('Pussy Riot Members Jailed for Two Years for Hooliganism', 17 August 2012). Tolokonnikova, who was sent to one of the tough penal colonies in Mordovia, continued her trickster activities in prison: in September 2013 she went on hunger strike in protest against the inhuman conditions and slave labour to which the inmates of the colony were subjected.

Interestingly enough, the verdict 'undermining the social order' sounds very similar to Socrates's crime of 'offending the gods of the state'. Offending state gods in all manners possible, from scatological pranks to philosophical discussions, is a traditional trickster pastime. Pussy Riot's trickster origins are visible in their motley clothes, which look like the traditional attire of professional clowns and fools. Their foolish façade, however, hides profoundly political agenda, which involves a range of issues including gender issues and social problems. The uncaptured members of the project outline it in an interview to *The Observer*, stating that 'Russia needs a feminist whip' and that it is time to expose the moral bankruptcy of the current political regime: 'It feels like a unique position to be in, but at the same time it's really scary. Because it's a great responsibility. Because we are not only doing it for us, we're doing it for society' says one of the girls (Cadwalladr, 2012). This is the social trickster in action – visible, bashful and brave, almost to the point of being careless and silly.

In the interview the girls also insist that the band's trademark balaclavas are a feminist-political statement – they mean being an anonymous superhero, *à la* Catwoman (Cadwalladr, 2012). The mask in this case means solidarity with all oppressed and silenced women. In a way, it also symbolises the tricksterish pre-individual state of unity with the world as it erases all individual distinctions and makes people omnipotent, it makes them braver. As one of the girls explains, the mask makes her believe that she can do everything and she believes that she can change the situation (Cadwalladr, 2012).

The mask of the trickster empowers the performers and makes them 'shameless' because it transports them to the state before the invention of shame and fear. In this deep, dark corner of the psyche no ideology or any other systemic construction can reach them. Structures have little access to the trickster's underworld, to its twilight state of mind. One cannot scare and threaten a Coyote or a Wakd-junkaga while an individual can be influenced, controlled and manipulated. Unless, of course, we are dealing with a trickster individual – the 'civilised trickster' who can switch off his sense of shame at times when the system employs it to control the rest of society.

5

CREATIVE REBELLION

In his book, *Sculpting in Time* (1989), the Russian filmmaker Andrey Tarkovsky outlines the operative principle of creativity – undermining the concept of 'normality' and challenging the boring stability, which holds the social fabric together. In other words, creativity is a trickster, a malicious but brilliant rebel, a bringer of fire who introduces progress into society impulsively and forcibly:

> Why is it that the artist seeks to destroy the stability sought by society? Settembrini in Thomas Mann's *The Magic Mountain* says, 'I trust, engineer, that you have nothing against malice? I consider it to be reason's most brilliant weapon against darkness and ugliness. Malice, my dear sir, is the soul of criticism, and criticism – the source of progress and enlightenment'. The artist seeks to destroy the stability by which society lives, for the sake of drawing closer to the ideal. Society seeks stability, the artist – infinity. The artist is concerned with absolute truth, and therefore gazes ahead and sees things sooner than other people.
>
> *(Tarkovsky, 2008: 192)*

It is not surprising that the creative trickster force is treated by society with caution. It is an impulse that is essentially anti-systemic as its aim is to alter the established practices and conventions. It is a raw energy born out of the depths of the psyche. The impulse is initially unstructured and unframed, but is eventually organised by its vehicle, the individual. Works of art and other products of human creativity are born when the trickster impulse, the exploring impulse, the individuating force, is allowed to express itself freely instead of being ignored, repressed or buried under the dead pile of everyday rituals. Releasing the trickster, setting it free, is the highest form of self-understanding – understanding through self-expression.

Schools of psychotherapy have traditionally differed in their assessment of the personal, social and spiritual impact of creativity. They have also disagreed about the psychological origins of the creative impulse and its role in human development. For instance, representatives of the Jungian school tend to have a more optimistic outlook on the tricksterish creative impulse. They regard it as a force that can be dangerous if unframed, used incorrectly or not controlled properly – and yet it is indispensable for the mental health of the individual. By contrast, the Freudian view has primarily centred on the Oedipal aspect of creativity as well as on the perils its activity poses for civilisation. Unlike Jung, who viewed creativity as a spiritual phenomenon and as a form of unconscious power, Freud regarded it as originating in human sexuality.

Sigmund Freud

For Freud, creative activity is a form of unspent sexual instinct. It has to do with the body and its 'discontents' (stemming from the past or the present) rather than the life of human spirit. For him, the urge to create largely has its roots in childhood problems. Creativity is the trickster that inevitably emerges out of the situation of repression and neglect of the physical side of life; it is a form of displacement. Freud writes in his essay, 'Leonardo Da Vinci and a Memory of His Childhood' (1910):

> We consider it probable that an instinct like this of excessive strength was already active in the subject's earliest childhood, and that its supremacy was established by impressions in the child's life. We make the further assumption that it found reinforcement from what were originally sexual instinctual forces, so that later it could take the place of a part of the subject's sexual life. Thus a person of this sort would, for example, pursue research with the same passionate devotion that another would give to his love, and he would be able to investigate instead of loving. [. . .]
>
> Observations of men's daily lives show us that most people succeed in directing very considerable portions of their sexual instinctual forces to their professional activity.
>
> *(Freud, 2001a: 77–78)*

To transpose our trickster paradigm onto Freud's ideas, the emerging sexual instinct is such a powerful force that its Oedipal encounter with civilisation leads to the accumulation of creative energy. Thus, sexual instinct is cornered by civilisation, locked within a certain behavioural framework, and buried under behavioural norms, social taboos and morality. If one is lucky, the repressed energy gets reincarnated as a creative impulse waiting for the right moment to come out and express itself. The human desire to explore the world and to find something new, according to Freud, is sexual in its nature.

Moreover, its presence in the psyche in the repressed, bottled-up state, inevitably causes neurotic illness. Once again, it is seen as dangerous, as something that can be cured or ameliorated with the help of a mental health professional. It is not a healthy energy, but a neurotic accumulation of unspent sexuality incidentally channelled into the production of something useful. Freud's discourse when he describes creativity is rational and measured – it is the framework aimed at capturing and branding the trickster. Seen from this perspective, intellect and rationality are the tools for framing and restricting its power, and moulding and shaping its energy into works of art and scientific discoveries. In a way, this view coincides with traditional mythological representations of the trickster as a creature that is promiscuous and oversexed:

> When the period of infantile sexual researches has been terminated by a wave of energetic sexual repression, the instinct for research has three distinct possible vicissitudes open to it owing to its early connection with sexual interests. In the first of these, research shares the fate of sexuality; thenceforward curiosity remains inhibited and the free activity of intelligence may be limited for the whole of the subject's lifetime, especially as shortly after this powerful religious inhibition of thought is brought into play by education. [...] We know very well that the intellectual weakness which has been acquired in this way gives an effective impetus to the outbreak of a neurotic illness. In a second type the intellectual development is sufficiently strong to resist the sexual repression which has hold of it. Some time after the infantile sexual researches have come to an end, the intelligence, having grown stronger, recalls the old association and offers its help in evading sexual repression, and the suppressed sexual activities of research return from the unconscious in the form of compulsive brooding, naturally in a distorted and unfree form, but sufficiently powerful to sexualize thinking itself and to colour intellectual operations with the pleasure and anxiety that belong to the sexual process proper.
>
> *(Freud, 2001a: 78–80)*

Freud's vision of creativity does not have much respect either for the power of this impulse or for the power of the unconscious where it originates. Freud adds to his assessment of the relationship between sexualised creativity and the intellect with its framing capacities, that the luckiest of artists (or, rather, their tricksters) avoid repression altogether, and let their talent flow unrestrained: 'libido evades the fate of repression by being sublimated from the very beginning into curiosity and by becoming attached to the powerful instinct for research and reinforcement', and even sexual urges pale into insignificance (2001a: 80). In the Leonardo essay Freud famously analyses the artist's childhood dream of being visited in his cradle by a vulture, which opened his mouth with its tail. Rather predictably, Freud interprets the dream in sexual terms – as a metaphor for fellatio – and expresses his amazement that 'phantasy is so completely passive in character' (2001a: 86).

Melanie Klein

The post-Freudians (save, probably, for Lacan whose vision of creativity is half-romantic and half-philosophical) drew on Freud's analysis of talent and imagination, and continued to analyse them in terms of mental health issues and childhood sexuality. For the Freudian camp, an artist is a sick person whose creative efforts, even when they lead to beautiful results, have their origin in the lack of understanding of 'the reality principle'. Melanie Klein's analysis of the creative process as a form of sublimation of aggression is particularly interesting. In her essay 'Infantile Anxiety Situations Reflected in a Work of Art and in the Creative Impulse' (1929), she recalls that one of her patients, a painter Ruth Kjar (Ruth Weber-Kiaer), had spent many years not knowing that she had artistic abilities. At the same time, the woman had always been an avid collector of art. One day her brother-in-law had to sell a painting that had previously been lent to her and occupied a prominent place in her living room. Looking at the blank space on the wall, where the picture had previously hung, made her particularly depressed until her husband found a solution – he suggested that she paint something herself. The result was a beautiful picture, which could have been the work of a professional artist.

Even though Klein witnessed a near-magical transformation of a depressed woman in mourning for a beloved painting into a gifted artist, the psychoanalyst's conclusions are far from metaphysical, religious or spiritual explanations that would be narratively and ideologically appropriate in such a case. She links the patient's creative success to the repressed feelings towards her mother. They include anger and death wish against the hated object. These aggressive impulses coexist with guilt and desire to restore the object that was ruined in a fit of anger. Kjar's paintings, Klein surmises, came out of this tension between the destructive and creative impulses in her attitude towards the difficult mother figure who was a complex and unfriendly object. Klein 'explains away' the miracle of the beautiful painting:

> In seeking the explanation of these ideas, it is instructive to consider what sort of pictures Ruth Kjar has painted since her first attempt, when she filled the empty space on the wall with the lifesized figure of a naked negress. Apart from the picture of flowers she has confined herself to portraits. She has twice painted her younger sister, who came to stay with her and sat for her, and, further, the portrait of an old woman and one of her mother. The last two are described by Karen Michaelis as follows: 'And now Ruth cannot stop. The next picture represents an old woman, bearing the mark of years and disillusionments. Her skin is wrinkled, her hair faded, her gentle, tired eyes are troubled. [...]
>
> This lady has a long time before she must put her lips to the cup of renunciation. Slim, imperious, challenging, she stands there with a moonlight-coloured shawl draped over her shoulders: she has the effect of a magnificent woman of primitive times, who could any day engage in combat

with the children of the desert with her naked hands. What a chin! What a force there is in the haughty gaze!'

'The blank space has been filled.'

(Klein, 1988b: 217)

Seen in this light, a work of art is born out of guilt and remorse, which are triggered by the civilising forces of society. The Kleinian trickster is an envious, greedy and angry child, furious at having his freedom restrained, and constantly looking for ways of escaping. Repressed, he no longer exists as a trickster and becomes the shadow brooding at the bottom of the psyche, accumulating energy and causing its carrier to be melancholic and unhappy. By discovering the magic box containing the angry and neglected jinni, the artist discovers a perfect way of releasing the internal psychic pressure. The destructive, hateful little gnome wants to escape, it wants to ruin the object, it wants attention, it wants to blow to pieces the framework so painstakingly crafted by the civilising influences of society. The task of the artist is to capture and utilise the pressure, to channel it in the right direction.

Creativity thus is a by-product of the war between childhood complexes and the irksome desire to get rid of the tension accumulated in the psyche. Klein has a formula for it: it is important that 'the fixations destined for sublimation should not have undergone repression too early, for this precludes the possibility of development' (1988b: 89). Moreover, any breakdowns in the flow of energy may lead to the symptom's repression rather than sublimation. In this case, the trickster (temporarily or forever) stays locked inside the psyche for a long time until it is discovered by chance. The story of Ruth Kjar is a good example of this happening: 'In my opinion we find that a fixation which leads to a symptom was already on the way to sublimation but was cut off from it by repression' (1988b: 89).

Thus, from Klein's view, the trickster of creativity is 'negative' energy fuelled by childhood angst. It is inadvertently 'genital' in character and its outbursts differ in intensity depending on the 'size' of the person's talent. Klein even has a theory about the similarities and differences between individuals who are merely talented, and geniuses: although their psychological layout is relatively similar, there is a range of significant qualitative and quantitative differences. The trickster residing in a genius is more powerful than the one inherited by an 'ordinary talent':

> Genius differs talent not only quantitatively but also in its essential quality. Nevertheless we may assume for it the same genetic conditions as for talent. Genius seems possible when all factors concerned are present in such abundance as to give rise to unique groupings, made up of units which bear some essential similarity to one another – I mean, the libidinal fixations.
>
> *(1988b: 89)*

Klein goes on to surmise that human creativity has its origins in the infantile wish to destroy the 'reality', and then rebuild it according to one's own vision. Creativity and the need for sublimation have their origins in the initial conflict between the child's natural narcissism and society's insistence that he follows the rules. In 'Infantile Anxiety Situations Reflected in a Work of Art and in the Creative Impulse', Klein describes a child who is bored and tired of doing homework. When his mother threatens to withdraw the usual treats, the child flies into a rage because his trickster (his freedom, his version of reality) is met with the wall of 'how things should be' – with the established and accepted framework. This kind of destructive-creative rage is not just aimed at the mother – it is aimed at the frameworkers as a class of beings, and at the notion of the framework itself. The infant's growing into the *habitus* is a violent affair full of mini narcissistic crises. After the mother leaves him alone in the hope that he would reconsider his behaviour, the boy

> jumps up, drums the door, sweeps the tea-pot and cup from the table, so that they are broken into a thousand pieces. He climbs on to the window-seat, opens the cage and tries to stab the squirrel with his pen. The squirrel escapes through the open window. The child jumps down from the window and seizes the cat. He yells and swings the tongs, pokes the fire furiously in the open grate, and with his hands and feet hurls the kettle into the room. A cloud of ashes and steam escapes. He swings the tongs like a sword and begins to tear the wallpaper. Then he opens the case of the grandfather-clock and snatches out the copper pendulum. He pours the ink over the table. Exercise-books and other books fly through the air. Hurrah!
>
> *(Klein, 1988b: 210)*

Yet, his happiness is short-lived. The system's message – planted into the child's head when the mother slammed the door – is starting to grow roots in the child's mind. Suddenly, the abused pieces of furniture start coming to life – the system retaliates. The picture of the birth of guilt that Klein paints – and the birth of the shadow externalised in the inanimate things – is conceptually and narratively very similar to the one depicted in Disney's famous animation, *Toy Story* (1995):

> The things he has maltreated come to life. An armchair refuses to let him sit in it or have the cushions to sleep on. Table, chair, bench and sofa suddenly lift their arms and cry: 'Away with the dirty little creature!' The clock has a dreadful stomach-ache and begins to strike the hours like mad. The tea-pot leans over the cup, and they begin to talk Chinese. Everything undergoes a terrifying change. The child falls back against the wall and shudders with fear and desolation. The stove spits out a shower of sparks at him. He hides behind the furniture. The shreds of the torn wallpaper begin to sway and stand up, showing shepherdess and sheep. [. . .]
>
> Half suffocated he takes refuge in the park round the house. But there again the air is full of terror, insects, frogs . . . a wounded tree trunk, which oozes resin in long-drawn-out bass notes, dragon flies and oleander-flies all attack the newcomer. The dispute as to who is to bite the child becomes a hand-to-hand fight. A squirrel which he has bitten falls to the ground, screaming

beside him. He instinctively takes off his scarf and binds up the little creature's paw. There is a great amazement amongst the animals, who gather
together hesitatingly in the background. The child has whispered 'Mama!' He
is restored to the human world of helping, 'being good'.

(1988b: 210–211)

The aim of the metaphorical 'terrifying room' is to show to the child that one
cannot destroy the existing framework without any (psychological or physical)
consequences. The budding human being ought to learn that crossing certain
boundaries is fraught with danger. Just when the boy imagines himself to be
omnipotent, the things that looked inanimate and harmless – in fact, the world that
looked subdued and easily controllable – suddenly become hostile and aggressive.
The trickster transforms into the shadow as the child starts to realise that the
framework is inescapable, and that it might make one conform against one's will.
This is the moment when shame and guilt are born, and they are born both internally and externally, in one's imagination and in real life.

At this moment the boy also realises that conforming to the system is a safer
choice than trying to deal on your own with the wild, dark, unpredictable imagination – with the darkness of the unconscious. Without systemic influence, the
world is out of control, it is hostile and disorganised. Moreover, without the
rational framework that educates him about the world and makes it looks less
dangerous and more transparent, the child's internal world, his psyche, collapses
with its external counterpart. In fact, the system protects the child from himself,
from the internal attack of pure narcissism. His destructive creativity is replaced
with guilt as he learns to restore and rebalance his personality after a bout of
aggression. His narcissistic reaction has met with the framework, and the energy
generated by the impact becomes creative and gives birth to a complex sublimatory narrative, which has a therapeutic ending – the child learns to regulate affect.
The framework, represented by the mother, takes away the boy's perfect omnipotent world, which results in the boy learning to limit and control his trickster.

The denial of mirroring gives birth to shame, internalisation of the system and
self-regulation. A new personality emerges amidst this violent and creative process.
In Klein's view, the battle of the omnipotent trickster with the framework and the
'early frameworkers' is tinged with anger, aggression and envy all of which are
eventually recycled into shame and remorse. Mythological tricksters, as we remember, lack a sense of identity and a sense of control over their own body. They lack
physical and psychological coherence. The boy in Klein's story learns to capture the
trickster and to organise parts of his personality into a coherent whole.

Heinz Kohut

Klein is not alone in thinking that creativity has its origins in primary narcissism, and
that it is also a remedy for narcissistic disturbances. By making something new, human
beings seize control over their environment. They also go back to the source of their

personality, to the moment when it was born, and draw the potentially explosive trickster energy (now securely tamed and controlled) from the well of the unconscious. Heinz Kohut directly links creativity to narcissistic fluctuations. His view is that, going back to the deep, dark well to ask the trickster for some creative energy means exposing yourself to mortal danger because the consequences of this quest are not always predictable. One may get overwhelmed by the jinni and end up struggling with 'severe procreative depression' or 'hypermanic overstimulation':

> During creative periods, the self is at the mercy of powerful forces it cannot control; and its sense of enfeeblement is increased because it feels itself helplessly exposed to extreme mood swings which range from severe procreative depression to dangerous hypomanic overstimulation, the latter occurring at the moment when the creative mind stands at the threshold of creative activity. [...] And when his discoveries lead the creative mind into lonely areas that had not previously been explored by others, then a situation is brought about in which the genius feels a deep sense of isolation. These are frightening experiences, which repeat those overwhelmingly anxious moments of early life when the child felt alone, abandoned, unsupported.
>
> *(Kohut, 2011: 818–819)*

Kohut does not write about the sublimated aggression and guilt that are part of the creative impulse, but talks about the creative power's ability to fragment and recreate the self. From the civilised individual's point of view, this energy is often felt as terrifying, as something much bigger than the humble human frame with its ordinary mind. This is the kind of power that takes us back to the pre-framed state of existence, back into the childish-narcissistic whirlwind of unrestrained emotions, unlimited drives and unbridled needs. Not surprisingly, artists and writers often create rituals around the creative process as a way of taming the wild beast, as a control-retaining strategy. As Kohut puts it, 'creative artists and scientists – the latter at times in striking contrast to their fierce rationality in the central area of their creative pursuits – often attempt to protect their creativity by surrounding it with superstitions and rituals' (2011: 819). Their obsessive-compulsive habits, silly as they look to an external observer, are makeshift mini-frameworks. The rituals constitute desperate ways of capturing and managing the trickster. Kohut goes on to analyse Thomas Mann's novella *Death in Venice* (1912), in which the main protagonist, the artist Aschenbach, had a difficult childhood and, as a result, has low self-esteem, obsessive nature and overwhelming creativity:

> [H]is childhood self has been insufficiently sustained by his environment and had been in danger of fragmentation – he had later become capable of providing himself with the needed experience of psychological perfection and wholeness – i.e., the experience of basic self-esteem – through the creation of works of art. Extensions or duplications of the self were now available which he could invest with narcissistic libido: he could give them formal perfection.
>
> *(2011: 821)*

Still a Freudian at heart, Kohut sees the creative 'return to the trickster' as a form of regression, as a way of distancing yourself from the limiting, restraining, framing influence of the external reality. In his essay 'Creativeness, Charisma and Group Psychology', Kohut gives Freud 'the taste of his own medicine', and examines the great man's writing and theory-generating talents. Kohut argues that his influential teacher experienced signs of psychological regression before and during the periods of intensive work. Kohut mentions that Freud smoked more when he felt creative (2011: 817). Following Freud, Kohut argues that this state of psychological regression – even followed by depressive episodes – is natural for a creative person. In this sense, the father of psychotherapy was no different from any other hapless artist afflicted by the trickster:

> [T]here is no doubt that . . . Freud had an enormous capacity for prolonged and concentrated attention to details in the service of the completion and perfection of his work. [. . .] Furthermore, one might hypothesise that that his intense oral-respiratory cravings (e.g., his increasing, unbreakable bondage to cigar smoking) were related to a depressionlike state of procreative inner emptiness, which was the manifestation of the decathexis of the self as the narcissistic energies detached themselves and became available for the creative task.
>
> *(2011: 816)*

Here Freud's cigar-smoking equals Leonardo's phallic fantasy. Freud, Kohut argues, was not better at managing his wild trickster than any other person in possession of a talent. He suffered from 'hypomanic overstimulation' and his discoveries led him 'into lonely areas' (2011: 818). As a result of these 'frightening experiences', he felt 'a deep sense of isolation' (2011: 818). Moreover, the terrifying feelings that come with being a pioneer of this kind 'repeat those overwhelmingly anxious moments in life when the child felt alone, abandoned, unsupported' (2011: 818).

In fact, Kohut replicates the anthropological formula which states that the system is only capable of self-renewal when the trickster and the system are of equal power. Kohut calls this process the conflict between the pleasure-seeking Guilty Man and the creative Tragic Man (who, by being proactive and socially useful, earns redemption for the regressive Guilty Man). The two represent the metaphorical tension between the primary narcissism and civilisation. Kohut postulates:

> My assertion is simply that the presence of disharmony and conflict between the two realms of the personality may not stifle a gifted individual's productivity; that it may perhaps serve as a stimulus for creative responses – even if the contest between the two realms for the dominance of one over the other remains unsolved throughout a whole (unhappy) lifetime.
>
> *(2011: 760–761)*

Kohut uses Tolstoy, who was famous for his painful creativity and turbulent self-searching, as a perfect example of such a trickster conflict. Tolstoy was notoriously difficult in interpersonal relationships, and his large family was directly affected by his mood swings, strange financial decisions, control issues, intermittent religiousness and lustfulness, heavy depression and suicidal thoughts. Tolstoy was also involved in a chronic conflict with a number of grand authoritarian structures – most famously, the Russian Orthodox Church. Kohut explains that this kind of 'creative hysteria' is the result of the conflict between Tolstoy's grand talent and the profoundly narcissistic, controlling aspects of his personality:

> Tolstoy's life was an endless struggle between pleasure-seeking, working Guilty Man and self-expression-seeking, creative Tragic Man. Luckily, Tragic Man predominated for sufficiently long periods to allow him to create novels which, like all great works of literature, revitalize those who are open to being affected by them. [...] But there was also another Tolstoy, clearly discernible both in the data of his biography and in some of his (lesser) writings. This is not only Tolstoy the gambler, drinker, and philanderer, but also, in the obverse, Tolstoy the man filled with disgust for the woman, guilt-laden with the need to expiate, to mortify the flesh.
>
> *(2011: 716)*

It follows from this assertion that a true talent is permanently at the mercy of the trickster force. It is always engaging in conflict with the prevalent order and arguing with the frameworkers. Talent only dies down – rather like a flame – when the artist joins forces with the system, or sells out and turns his work into a commercial mass product. Creativity, like any trickster born out of tension, happens on the border between the personal and the social; on the margin between guilt and self-flagellation, between tragedy and comedy; during the meeting of the opposites in one's personality. The trickster of creativity – uncontrollable and bringing excitement and pain – leads to flashes of self-realisation waiting to be transformed into flashes of realisation for the general public. Creative process becomes an act of self-crucifixion during which the shadow is turned into the trickster; dark matter is turned into gold.

To create, Klein and Kohut seem to imply, means to suffer. We create because we feel the need to connect with others; we create as a means of mending our broken inner world. We create because our universe is in pieces, and we need to construct a new one. Our trickster is angry because it has already met with restrictions to its freedom put up by the scheming frameworkers. We feel its steaming impatience inside – and it is this anger, it is this fury that drives the creative process. Works of art are born out of the conflict between the trickster and the framework; between the playful primitive energy and the social order; between intrinsic omnipotence and the Oedipal structure. The process of making new things can be both positive and negative, creative and destructive, because the trickster is trying to escape his box, the narrow cage of civilisation – and his angry screams and emotional pain translate themselves into beautiful creations. By creating, we get rid of this internal Oedipal tension. By creating, we release the trickster in a 'civilised' and properly framed fashion.

George E. Vaillant

One branch of the post-Freudian thought is particularly strict in its assessment of the creative trickster. The American psychiatrist George E. Vaillant devised a hierarchy of adaptive mechanisms and placed creative coping strategies – such as sublimation – on top of the pyramid. According to his scheme, sublimation is the most productive mature defence mechanism, and is a brilliant example of taming something as primitive and ancient as primary narcissism. It is the process of transforming a raw psychological, unresolved matter into tangible results. As such, sublimation is all about reorganising and controlling the trickster, about managing the problem using rational means. It is a particularly useful and fruitful form of impulse control. Sublimation is about 'framing' the impulse, perfecting it, shaping it, experimenting with it. Unlike suppression – another mature defence mechanism that mollifies the impulse but does not transform it – sublimation aims at re-making the trickster and re-forming it.

According to Vaillant, all defences are divided into four groups or levels. Level 1 includes psychotic mechanisms such as denial, distortion and delusional projection. Level 2 comprises defences that Vaillant labels as 'immature', and that are common in severe depression and personality disorders. They are fantasy (schizoid withdrawal, denial through fantasy), projection, hypochondriasis, passive–aggressive behaviour and acting out. Level 3 consists of neurotic mechanisms common in everyone: intellectualisation (isolation, obsessive behaviour, rationalisation), repression, reaction formation, displacement (conversion, phobias) and dissociation (neurotic denial). Level 4 is comprised of mature coping mechanisms such as sublimation, altruism, suppression, anticipation and humour (Vaillant, 1995: 80–81). While Level 1 is the most primitive end of the continuum, Level 4 mechanisms lead to successful resolution of conflicts, which is never achieved 'by sweeping distress under the rug, nor by arbitrary compromise between instinct and conscience, or by cowardly purchase of intimacy with masochistic sacrifice' (1995: 91).

Vaillant further argues that 'the sign of a successful defence is neither careful cost accounting nor shrewd compromise, but rather synthetic and creative transmutation [...] To solve important human crises, such creativity is critical' (1995: 91). Through sublimation human beings vent their most aggressive instincts – but it does more than just make instincts accessible. It makes ideas fun (1995: 94–97). Moreover, sublimation is a more successful coping mechanism than, say, intellectualisation:

> Many continued to value ideas more than feelings. But although intellectualisation may make for a brilliant academic record in high school, in adult life it must be tempered by a more flexible defence system – one that lets instinctual pleasure peek through.
>
> *(1995: 97)*

The artist is a man 'who can peddle his most private dreams to others' (1995: 101).

One might argue that the trickster is the ultimate sublimatory force. Whereas the maladaptive part of the defence mechanism spectrum – Levels 1 and 2 – may be said to correspond to the Jungian shadow, the two top levels coincide with a mature attitude towards human instincts. Creative solutions of conflicts allow one to make one's problems conscious while, at the same time, harvesting the affect and channelling it in the right direction. While the lower-spectrum defence mechanisms are counter-productive, regressive and destructive (including self-destruction) because they exclude the possibility of bringing the problem to the conscious level, sublimation is akin to psychological alchemy as it is capable of transforming the unconscious contents into gold.

Using the high end of the defence mechanism spectrum in order to alleviate the pain, the artist goes back to the darkest places in his soul – but then makes an effort and re-engages with society by elevating his problems to the social level. The trickster here is just a midwife assisting the individual in such a birth by generating – or rather, activating – a long-existing conflict. Psychological tension is vital for the creative impulse.

Carl Jung and the post-Jungians

The Freudian thought thus sees the creative aspect of the trickster as a by-product of the inescapable (Oedipal) tension – the war between the individual and the system. Creativity is always the result of strife; it indicates a problem. In any case, creative impulse occurs when something is wrong – and is in dire need of release. It is a way of escaping an unbearable situation. To sublimate means to transform, to transgress, to reshape both sides of the conflict – the internal and the external. It means to tame the conflict and to channel the destructive, oppressive energy into a positive – and more socially acceptable – project. Compared to regressive coping strategies, creativity is about the birth of something new instead of repeating old conflicts and making the same mistakes.

In contrast to Freud and the post-Freudians, Jung's additional 'layer' of the psyche – the collective unconscious – permitted him to detach the work of art from the Oedipal, sexual or any other personal issues the artist may harbour. The work of art grows out of its creator rather like a tree that draws its nourishment from the artist's psyche. It is a force 'that achieves its end either with tyrannical might or with the subtle cunning of the nature herself, quite regardless of the personal fate of the man who is its vehicle' (CW15: para. 114). The tree is a suitable and powerful metaphor to describe the creative process because it renders the sheer force with which the trickster impulse takes over the ego-consciousness of the artist. The work of art is a 'living thing implanted in human psyche' (CW15: para. 114).

Like this, the work of art is born out of its creator against his will, and in response to the current social climate. It may resonate in the author's personal unconscious, of course – or even come out of his personal problems. Yet, when he feels the need to create, the artist only answers the call of the collective unconscious; his issues only naturally grow out from the deepest problems of his society. Through the artist, the unconscious speaks and the collective expresses itself.

Unlike the Freudians who tend to regard the creative trickster as an evil spirit born out of the Oedipal dynamic (or even representing the Oedipal dynamic),

Jungians treat it as a spiritual phenomenon. Far from being the direct result of childhood problems, the psychological origins of a work of art are mysterious. The trickster energy is thus the energy of life rather than a harmful psychic atavism that needs to be restrained (or sublimated) in order for the individual to fully understand and accept the reality principle.

For instance, Leonardo's dream would have been interpreted by the Jungians in symbolic rather than literal ways. One such interpretation would be that the future genius already knew his predestination: the young artist is being force-fed by Mother Nature; or being suckled by the powerful creative force springing from the depths of the unconscious. The vulture is the unstoppable, uncontrollable, wild trickster pointing the young Leonardo in the direction of his future vocation. At the same time, the dream's symbolism has a violent aspect to it emphasising the narcissistic, darkish side of the trickster.

For Jung, the urge to create is a living thing, an *autonomous complex*, a split-off portion of the psyche. When activated, it can be so powerful that the artist is barely capable of controlling it. Creative people are mere vehicles for this unstoppable energy that demands to be let out. It is no wonder, then, that artists often forget reality altogether, and become wholly engaged in the process of harvesting the trickster impulse and rescuing it from the depths of the unconscious. The creative person's temporary madness is not subject to his conscious control: 'The divine frenzy of the artist comes perilously close to a pathological state, though the two things are not identical' (CW15: para. 122).

Similarly, Tarkovsky describes the creative process as something springing from the totality of the psyche, but which also involves the artist as a whole person. When one hears its call, one has no other choice but to answer it:

> The artist's inspiration comes into being somewhere in the deepest recesses of his 'I'. It cannot be dictated by external, 'business' considerations. It is bound to be related to his psyche and his conscience; it springs from the totality of the world-view. If it is anything less, then it is doomed from the outset to be artistically void and sterile. It is perfectly possible to be a professional director or a professional writer and not be an artist: merely a sort of executor of other people's ideas.
>
> *(Tarkovsky, 2008: 188)*

Meanwhile, the energy coming out of the artist may feel to him as disturbing or even tyrannical: 'Depending on its energy charge, it may appear either as a mere disturbance of conscious activities or a supraordinated authority which can harness the ego to its purpose' (CW15: para. 115). The process of taming the trickster is so intense that the creators may not fully realise what is happening to them when they are inside the affective state:

> As long as we ourselves are caught up in the process of creation, we neither see nor understand; indeed we ought not to understand, for nothing is more

injurious to immediate experience than cognition. But for the purpose of
cognitive understanding we must detach ourselves from the creative process
and look at it from the outside; only then does it become an image that
expresses what we are bound to call 'meaning'.

(CW15: para. 121)

The process of conversion of this autonomous complex into a finished work of art
can be very draining for the ego-consciousness. The human frame may happen to
be too fragile for the power of the trickster, and the artist's mental heath may suffer in the process of filtering out the raw material coming out of the unconscious
and squeezing it into a lucid framework that is the work of art. Naturally, this
process may even temporarily 'infantilise' the artist (cf. Freud's 'regressive state'):

> How does an autonomous complex arise? For reasons which we cannot go into
> here, a hitherto unconscious portion of the psyche is thrown into activity, and
> gains ground by activating the adjacent areas of association. The energy needed
> for this is naturally drawn from consciousness – unless the latter happens to
> identify with the complex. But where this does not occur, the drain of energy
> produces what Janet calls *abaissement du niveau mental*. The intensity of conscious
> interests and activities gradually diminishes, leading either to apathy – a condition
> very common in artists – or to a regressive development of the conscious func-
> tions, that is, they revert to an infantile and archaic level and undergo something
> like a degeneration. [...] The autonomous complex thus develops by using the
> energy that has been withdrawn from the conscious control of the personality.
>
> *(CW15: para. 123)*

While the human form is fragile, creativity is something that can make it immortal. In his essay, 'On the Relation of Analytical Psychology to Poetry', Jung
describes creativity in terms of the 'loss of control' and being possessed by 'an alien
will'. In this sense, creativity is akin to the trickster taking over its carrier:

> They [works of art] come as it were fully arrayed into the world, as Pallas
> Athene sprang from the head of Zeus. These works positively force them-
> selves upon the author; his hand is seized, his pen writes things that his mind
> contemplates with amazement. The work brings with it its own form; any-
> thing he wants to add is rejected, and what he himself would like to reject is
> thrust back at him. While his conscious mind stands amazed and empty
> before this phenomenon, he is overwhelmed by a flood of thoughts and
> images which he never intended to create and which his own will could
> never have brought into being. Yet in spite of himself he is forced to admit
> that it is his own self speaking, his own inner nature revealing itself and utter-
> ing things which he could never have entrusted to his tongue. He can only
> obey the apparently alien impulse within him and follow where it leads,
> sensing that his work is greater than himself, and wields a power which is

not his and which he cannot command. Here the artist is not identical with the process of creation; he is aware that he is subordinate to his work or stands outside it, as though he were – a second person; or as though a person other than himself had fallen within the magic circle of an alien will.

(CW15: para. 110)

The post-Jungians tend to discuss creativity in the similar 'spiritual trickster' vein. The archetypal psychologist James Hillman echoes Jung's ideas in that he describes the creative impulse as a wild energy that poses potential psychological dangers for its bearer. Since this energy originates in the collective rather than the personal psyche, it is tricksterish in its nature and may start behaving in a number of uncontrollable ways. Also – very much like the trickster – it is neutral rather than purely positive. So great is its power over the individual that it might easily overwhelm him – and even make him suicidal. In fact, Hillman argues – the negative feelings and mood fluctuations experienced by the artists under the influence of creativity are normal for someone who is trying to deal with the impulse of this scale. It is not at all surprising that the artist is struggling to keep the impulse in check, to manage it in some way. It is born deep within the psyche, and when it escapes, the delicate human frame is not always capable of holding and stabilising it:

> The creating Gods are the destroying Gods. As Jung said, 'Creation is as much construction as destruction' (CW3: para. 245). The ectopsychic instinctual force, because it comes from beyond the psyche, is more than human and mightier than its possessor. Its possessor is, in fact, always in danger of possession. Working as a compulsion, the force is always 'too much'. One spends one's life trying to slow it, tame it, give it enough time and space, because its haste is the destructive devil within the creative impulse itself. Suicide always remains the fundamental possibility of psychological creativity, as its reversal, since the destruction of soul is the counterpart of the creation of the soul.
>
> *(Hillman, 1998: 36)*

Tarkovsky confirms Hillman's view that the creative trickster is neither good nor bad, but neutral. The impulse is so powerful that it can overwhelm the creative person – which is a relatively small price to pay for the honour of being a vehicle used by the unconscious for delivering such a precious treasure to the masses. Someone who looks less normal than the rest of the people, and therefore is prepared to sacrifice his life to his art, is a hero:

> True artistic inspiration is always a torment for the artist, almost to the point of endangering his life. Its realisation is tantamount to a physical feat. That is the way it has always been, despite the popular misconception that pretty well all we do is tell stories that are as old as the world, appearing in front of the public like old grannies with scarves on our heads and our knitting in our hands to tell them all sorts of tales in order to keep them amused. The

tale may be entertaining or enthralling, but will do only one thing for the audience: help them pass the time in idle chatter.

(Tarkovsky, 2008: 188)

In this sense, Hillman's definition of creativity is even more radical than Jung's. His position implies that suicidal thoughts are almost 'normal' in creative people. Unrestrained – and in full swing – the power becomes so overwhelming that it turns into the shadow. The line between the trickster and the shadow in this case is often invisible – and it is particularly indistinguishable from the point of view of society, which values beautiful works of art but has difficulty dealing with the darkness of their origins: with the (collective) unconscious; with the fact that art is fed by a vulture. Hillman's creative and destructive trickster gods do not care about the mental state of the carrier of the talent – they use him as a vehicle for their own expressive purposes. Like jinnis, they escape through the mortal frame and leave the artist exhausted, broken, obsessed, mad or even dead. The artist's task is to build some kind of internal dam in order to contain the powerful flow of the energy that wells up in the unconscious and threatens to drown its vehicle during its wild escape.

Donald Winnicott

Winnicott linked human creativity to personality development. Like any trickster, the creative impulse's starting point is messy. Unframed and unguided, it is a pure hurricane of destruction and change for the sake of change. In fact, it is paradoxically creative in its destructiveness. This impulse, as it manifests itself in small children, may consist of 'faeces smearing' and 'prolonged crying' because these actions are bound to disturb the system (or attract its attention) (Winnicott, 1992: 69). Meanwhile, the system, in the form of the baby's immediate environment (including the primary caregiver), responds to these outbursts by soothing the baby, by paying attention to it. In this sense, creative mess initiates human contact and has the task of attracting and managing emotional connections.

For Winnicott, even simple everyday activities are creative, such as cooking and cleaning, for creativity lies at the core of what it means to be human:

> The creative impulse is therefore something that can be looked at as a thing in itself, something that of course is necessary if an artist is to produce a work of art, but also as something that is present when *anyone* – baby, child, adolescent, adult, old man or woman – looks in a healthy way at anything or does anything deliberately, such as making a mess with faeces or prolonging the act of crying to enjoy a musical sound. It is present as much in the moment-by-moment living of a backward child who is enjoying breathing as it is in the inspiration of an architect who suddenly knows what it is that he wishes to construct, and who is thinking in terms of material that can actually be used so that his creative impulse may take form and shape, and the world may witness.
>
> *(1992: 69)*

Winnicott also relates creativity to transitional objects – the baby 'creates' the object when it cannot control the situation of mirroring (i.e. interaction), or when the original object is unavailable (the mother is absent and the baby grabs a blanket or a teddy bear to soothe itself). Transitional objects – blankets, teddies and dolls – constitute the first expression of imagination at work; they are the first 'created', 'imagined' objects. Winnicott writes in *Playing and Reality* (1971):

> Perhaps some soft object or other type of object has been found and used by the infant, and this becomes what I am calling a *transitional object*. This object goes on being important. [...]

> When symbolism is employed the infant is already clearly distinguishing between fantasy and fact, between inner objects and external objects, between primary creativity and perception. But the term transitional object, according to my suggestion, gives room for the process of becoming able to accept difference and similarity. I think there is use for a term for the root of symbolism in time, a term that describes the infant's journey from the purely subjective to objectivity; and it seems to me that the transitional object (piece of blanket, etc.) is what we see of this journey of progress towards experiencing.
>
> *(1992: 3–7)*

It transpires from Winnicott's argument that the trickster is born out of distress, out of the necessity to survive, and by its nature is primarily an act of attracting attention. The baby imagines that the blanket is the breast, or the primary caregiver, and since this act is urgent and spontaneous, it is bound to be 'messy' and disorganised at first. It is only later in life that people learn to apply various frameworks (language, musical composition) to these spontaneous acts in order to take them beyond the tricksterish 'faeces-smearing'.

Fusing Winnicott's idea that creativity is linked to 'feeling alive' with Hynes's definition of creative activity as 'excreta' (Hynes, 1993b: 216), one gets the picture of creative products as being blemished, as something that is eternally in motion yet never reaching the ideal. The artist always sees his creation as 'imperfect' for two reasons. First, as a transitional object, it replaces the ideal mirroring connection, and therefore is only a substitute and not the 'perfect' original. Second, the origins of creativity are messy. The drive, the impulse itself is pre-civilised, and therefore – from the point of view of consciousness – impure. No amount of framing can remove all traces of its origins. By definition, the unconscious cannot be 'clean'. Anything that comes out of it, including the trickster impulse, is bound to be 'tainted' (or regarded as 'tainted') because of its nature and origins.

The psychotherapist Kenneth Wright applies Winnicott's concepts of transitional objects and mirroring to explain human creativity. He postulates that being creative enhances the feeling of being alive and that adult creativity is an extension of early maternal mirroring. The artist rebuilds himself, recreates his personality and his world by performing for himself the activities which 'the adaptive mother once provided' (Wright, 2009: 62). Metaphorically and psychologically, a work of art is a mother's face,

> a complex derivative of the transitional object, or as Winnicott says in his paper on mirroring, 'a complex derivative of the face' [...] In this sense it is also heir to the mother whose responsive forms were never quite sufficient, and like the transitional object, a 'not-me' extension of the artist, which contains important element of his affective being. In this sense, the art object is a narcissistic structure that serves the artist's own need for recognition, containment and integration.
>
> *(Wright, 2009: 53)*

Seen in this light, creativity is a way of re-creating the lost connection with the primary caretaker in childhood, as a replacement for the lost warmth, understanding and feeling of being attuned and connected to the mother (2009: 69). For instance, Wright argues, the creative artist is someone who 'has suffered a relative deficiency in mirroring and attunement – perhaps a disruptive loss of the mother's responsiveness – which has made him feel that security lies in becoming one's attuning "other"' (2009: 69).

To use our trickster paradigm, the trickster is the creative voice residing in the artist's psyche and lacking expression. It has to be discovered, accessed, framed, channelled and nurtured in order for a work of art (or even 'everyday creativity') to appear. It is also responsible for the individual's 'genuineness', for self-expression and creativity make us feel alive and unique. Human identity is born out of this voice. Wright gives as an example the poet Rilke, whose mother used to dress him as a girl to make up for the disappointment of having a son instead of a daughter. However,

> Rilke succeeded in keeping himself alive and discovered in himself a means of creating and finding the forms that he needed. His poetic calling can be seen as a recognition that this was his most important task: to create and recreate the responsive mother he had lacked.
>
> *(2009: 69)*

Meanwhile, as members of the audience, we seek to consume someone else's created symbols and transitional objects ('works of art') because we wish to experience 'contact with our own dormant sentience, and through it carefully contrived and resonant forms responding to it' (2009: 53). This means that, by looking at a work of art, by enjoying it, together with the artist we go back to the trickster state; we revive our tricksters. By making strange, different, unfamiliar things, the artist provides alternative views on ordinary phenomena, thus helping to renew society from within. The creative trickster 'refreshes' our vision of ourselves and the social processes. Without this impulse, society is at risk of stagnation, tyranny and extinction. The loss of the trickster is the beginning of the system's demise.

Case study: creativity in the Soviet Union

Creativity is an invaluable element of the social climate. One of its key roles is managing stagnation and providing cultural renewal. It keeps social mechanisms healthy and vibrant while also challenging and questioning the political processes. Society in which the creative trickster is repressed suffers from stagnation and eventually its elements start dying off. Damage to the trickster equals damage to the freedom of expression. Without the creative impulse, which is responsible for the singularity of each individual, mass thinking may give birth to a monstrous version of systemic narcissism. The trickster foregrounds voices of dissent whereas the collective shadow emerges from the depths of the national psyche and rolls like a wave, sweeping away everything in its path.

The Soviet Union is a good example of a regime with some serious 'trickster problems'. Creativity had always been a big threat to the uniformity of its mass thinking. Various ways of limiting the creative impulse were invented while the remaining creative elements were tightly controlled and significantly curbed. For instance, all Soviet art was to be done in the style of 'socialist realism' – a representational mechanism whose aim was authentic rendition of the everyday life of the common people. It became state policy in 1932. Its rules applied to both literature and the arts, and incorporated a range of stylistic and ideological elements. In order to 'reflect the truth of life' (in contrast to the inflated artificiality and pretentiousness of the bourgeois art), a painting or a work of fiction was only allowed to use basic stylistic tools, and eschew any complexity or excessive adornment in its depiction of workers and peasants. The works of the writers Maxim Gorky, Alexander Fadeev and Alexander Sholokhov, and sculptors such as Vera Mukhina (author of the famous sculpture group 'The Worker and the Peasant Woman') were shining examples of the socialist realism genre. These authors cooperated with the frameworkers and managed the trickster in accordance with the current ideology.

Meanwhile, socialist realism was a very narrow framework, and inside it the trickster was almost stifled to death. Artists who did not wish to comply with the rules, or only accepted them partially, had trouble finding funding and audience for their work – even after Stalin's death and during the so-called 'thaw era' when Soviet ideological and cultural restrictions were relaxed. For instance, Andrey Tarkovsky's film *Andrey Rublev* (1965), which tells the story of a famous Russian icon painter struggling to survive amidst the cruelty of medieval Russia, had to be edited several times before the authorities agreed to release it; his other masterpiece, *The Mirror* (1974), received a limited distribution. Tarkovsky's films were regarded in the Soviet Union as elitist, bizarre and ideologically corrupt. Tarkovsky, who openly proclaimed his trickster to be free and unrestrained by the 'state gods', was accused of deliberately neglecting the norms of the socialist realism genre:

> In the course of my career in the Soviet Union I was frequently accused . . . of 'having cut myself off from reality', as if I had consciously isolated myself from the everyday interests of the people. I must admit in all candour that I never understood what these accusations meant.
>
> (Tarkovsky, 2008: 165)

Representatives of the so-called 'creative intelligentsia' were treated in the Soviet Union as dangerous tricksters. In fact, the intelligentsia was regarded with suspicion both in pre-and post-revolutionary Russia as a motley group of people united by independent thinking and desire for change. Their fate was often far more violent than the aforementioned limited exposure or shortage of funding. During the Stalin years, many representatives of the 'creative intelligentsia' died in prison camps or were executed (including the poets Nikolai Gumilev (1886–1921) and Joseph Mandelstam (1891–1938), the novelist Isaak Babel (1894–1938) and the theatre director Vsevolod Meyerhold (1874–1940)). Some – such as the authors Anatoly Solzhenitsin and Varlam Shalamov, and the historian Lev Gumilev (the son of the poet Anna Akhmatova) – were lucky enough to survive the horrors of labour camps.

The novelist Mikhail Bulgakov (1891–1940) probably had the most mysterious fate of all Soviet tricksters: although his novels and plays, including *The Master and Margarita* and *A Dog's Heart* were too 'phantasmagorical' to be printed or staged, he was nevertheless inexplicably liked by the 'principal frameworker' – Joseph Stalin. In Bulgakov's case, Stalin's sadistic 'love' did not mean anything good – the writer was locked in a limbo, not being able either to publish or go abroad. He stayed in this stifling trickster state up until his death from nephrosclerosis on 10 March 1940.

In the 1960s and 1970s a new trickster phenomenon emerged in the Soviet Union – the 'buried alive' trickster force, the dissident movement. Not surprisingly, many members of the movement, including the poet Joseph Brodsky, the writer Sergey Dovlatov and the musician Mstislav Rostropovich, were eventually thrown out of the country and settled abroad. The regime had a range of ways of suppressing the intelligentsia and keeping the hazardous trickster in check. They included harassment, censorship, persecution, imprisonment (including in mental health institutions) and exile. The trickster could either be stifled with the help of prisons, psychiatric hospitals and other authoritarian institutions, or – when everything else failed – expelled from the country altogether as a foreign body.

For instance, Joseph Brodsky went through every harassment imaginable organised by the frameworkers, but still refused to conform to the 'norm' or to cooperate with them. A gifted poet and translator, he was arrested in 1964 and put on trial for 'social parasitism', vagrancy, corruption of youth and distribution of prohibited materials. After the trial he went through the most powerful 'trickster silencing' ordeals the frameworkers had: psychological and physical torture at two different psychiatric clinics, imprisonment and internal exile with hard labour (Haven, 2002: xviii). Brodsky's survival skills matched those of the mythological Prometheus, and his ability to restore himself after a significant trauma could rival those exhibited by Coyote or Wakdjunkaga: in these conditions he kept writing poems and learning foreign languages (2002: xviii–xix). Seeing that all their efforts to crush the trickster failed, and that he still kept writing and being proactive, in 1974 the Soviet authorities announced their decision to expel Brodsky from the country. True to himself, Brodsky told them that he did not wish to go anywhere, to which the reply was that he would still have to leave because 'the coming winter was going to be very cold' (2002: xix). He travelled to Vienna where he was met by W.H. Auden, then to London, and finally to the United States.

The role of the 'creative intelligentsia' in the Soviet (and also now Russian) society corresponds to the martyr aspect of the trickster impulse emphasised by Jung and Turner. Taking on a structure – and particularly a large-scale narcissistic-ideological monster – is bound to be a painful experience. In foregrounding their role as tricksters and 'tellers of truth', Soviet (and Russian) writers and artists have often forgotten that they were also human beings – fragile and mortal. Without much regard for their own physical wellbeing or psychological comfort, they expressed, and keep expressing, their disdain for the stupidity, cruelty and shallowness of the structure.

In the Soviet Union, the revolutionary optimism and elation of 1917 soon transmogrified into a controlling, trickster-bashing nightmare, which lasted for seven decades and, finally, devoid of renewing energy, ran out of steam and fell apart like a house of cards.

Genuine creativity vs. narcissism: *Amadeus* (1984)

Film director Miloš Forman tends to choose narratives in which trickster protagonists fight for their freedom of expression against a clique of narrow-minded and cold-blooded frameworkers. Forman's parents died in a Nazi concentration camp, which probably influenced his choice of narrative material. Mozart falls in line with the other courageous rebels from Forman's catalogue of tricksters: R.P. McMurphy (Jack Nicholson) in *One Flew Over the Cuckoo's Nest* (1975); Moses Gunn (Booker T. Washington) in *Ragtime* (1981); Larry Flynt (Woody Harrelson) from *The People vs Larry Flynt* (1996); and the artist Goya (Stellan Skarsgård) in *Goya's Ghosts* (2006).

Forman does not idealise his tricksters. Despite their heroic intentions, they are far from being angels. McMurphy is a criminal and a rather careless joker whose tireless activity at the psychiatric hospital in which he is confined result in a patient's death; the talented black jazzman Moses Gunn resorts to terrorism to prove his cause; and Larry Flynt is a pornographic magazine publisher and drug addict. Their methods of dealing with the hegemony of rules and restrictions are often dubious, and at times outright dangerous. All the while, their dark side is inseparable from their struggle for the freedom of speech and the right to possess an identity. Many of Forman's trickster-protagonists (McMurphy, Moses Gunn) die fighting with the frameworkers while others have their life ruined and art neglected or destroyed. At the end of *Ragtime*, Moses comes out of the library in which he and his co-terrorists are hiding only be gunned down by the police. Meanwhile, McMurphy is lobotomised by the hospital staff. Both the tricksters lose the fight with the powerful frameworkers.

Forman is also interested in the tricksterish power of creativity – in the ability of the creative impulse to challenge the existing order of things with its warped logic and propensity to limit the freedom of the individual. Both Goya and Mozart do not like their art to be influenced by the recommendations and threats of the frameworkers, who would rather they paint more conventional pictures and write a more conformist kind of music with 'fewer notes'. These two representatives of the 'creative intelligentsia' are primarily interested in what they see as 'truth', by which they mean the truth of their vision. Both wish to apply to their internal tricksters their own frameworks rather than those offered by the representatives of the system – the Inquisition in Goya's case, and Emperor Joseph II of Austria and his fatuous and envious advisors in the case of Mozart. Goya's terrible drawings actually reveal the truth about the Inquisition, and Mozart keeps writing beautifully complex music despite the fact that the stupid and talentless Emperor thinks that it contains 'too many notes'.

In *Amadeus* Forman employs a traditional framing device in order to render Mozart's personality and talent. The film is a third person 'narrative within a narrative'. The fact that the narrator is limited-omniscient suits the theme of obsession with an object and infatuation with its properties. The film opens with the elderly Salieri going insane and attempting to commit suicide. He is admitted to an asylum where he is visited by a young and naive priest trying to tease out the demons in the elderly composer's head. From this point on, the central part of the narrative unravels, which centres around Mozart's personal and creative life, and ends with his untimely death in poverty.

This framing device justifies Forman's depiction of Mozart as a silly, giggling childish personage. Salieri is the principal focaliser in the film, which means that all people are filtered through his perception and his imagination. He envies Mozart so much that he desperately wants to see him as a buffoonish individual unworthy of the noble title of composer. Unfortunately for Salieri, even when he manages to devalue and humiliate his rival as a human being, Mozart's genius and his music remain as brilliant as ever.

Salieri is an unreliable narrator, and we cannot determine to what extent his fantasies about Mozart's death are true. In fact, the audience suspects that the Italian's account is seriously distorted and blurred by his narcissistic hysteria. The priest also refuses to believe that the patient carefully orchestrated his rival's death, thinking that the elderly composer is influenced by his unstable mental condition. However, as the interview progresses, the young man stops smiling as he gradually realises that the darkness of the human soul may lead to terrifying obsessions and thoughts of murder.

Salieri may not have killed Mozart physically, but he instigated a smear campaign, which led to Mozart losing his good name, his income and the opportunities to display his work. All this time Salieri was surreptitiously watching his rival's demise and consuming the energy generated by the burning, bleeding talent. He did not do this on his own, but took advantage of the best tools of oppression and control offered by the system: spreading malicious rumours about Mozart and upholding the view that his music was too complex for a normal person to enjoy.

Forman's message in the film is deliberately anti-systemic. In an interview with Peter Culshaw in *The Telegraph*, the director says that he has no illusions about either the communist or the capitalist systems. Both have their oppressive moments, and both limit the artist's freedom. One simply cannot trust the structure:

> Having worked under both a Communist system and a free-market system, Forman is aware of the pitfalls of both. 'You either have commercial pressure

or ideological pressure. I prefer commercial pressure, otherwise you can be at the mercy of one or two idiots'.

I ask if repression might have some advantages, in that artists are provoked to use their ingenuity. 'I don't think you should imply that dictatorship is good for art, but it's a complicated subject. There are some times when a dictatorship is weakened, which happened for four or five years in the 1960s in Czechoslovakia, which were very fruitful. The Communists had lost total control, but there was no commercial pressure, so some great films were made. But I would always prefer freedom'.

In Amadeus, Mozart is up against the mediocrity of Salieri and the old guard and the court system. It's ironic, I suggest, that his film, while boosting Mozart, enabled millions to hear of Salieri. Finally he achieved a measure of the immortal fame he wanted. 'Well, mediocrity never goes away – but neither, I hope, do those who are willing to challenge it'.

(Culshaw, 2002)

Salieri's obsession with Mozart boils down to his desire to possess a fully-fledged trickster impulse. The court composer's creative power is weak and undeveloped; he is repressed and religious, and his oppressive and gloomy personality stifles the creative flow of the unconscious. He applies to his creative trickster too stringent and stifling a framework. As a result, the impulse cannot escape and he fails to write beautiful and memorable music.

Salieri's dreams of omnipotence clash with reality, which keeps reminding him that his talent is only moderate and incomparable with that of his rival. Reality makes him feel powerless and ashamed of his moderate abilities. He grieves the fact that he is too ordinary, too mediocre. Salieri wants to have the divine spark his rival possesses, but in his narcissistic imagination the possession of such a spark is transformed into the experience of being 'God'. He dreams about being omnipotent through music; he strives to become perfect; he imagines himself to be great; he craves control over minds and souls. However, his 'grandiose self' (to use Kohut's term) proves to be too strong for his very ordinary frame. As Mario Jacoby observes, sometimes the grandiose self 'exerts too much pressure to follow its demands for perfection' and the ego becomes aware that its achievements are rather meagre. This is the start of a narcisstic crisis:

As Kohut correctly observed, such demands can spur a naturally gifted person on to great heights of achievement, but usually they simply have the effect of overtaxing him. [. . .]

The grandiose self is behind the impulse to strive for perfection and is thus an energising force. If one is able to set realistic goals, this can be a genuine air to achievement. But as soon as one becomes driven, needing to attain 'greatness' at any price, it becomes destructive. In pathological cases, it can drive the person to fraud, chicanery and deceit.

(Jacoby, 1996: 44)

Moreover, often its demand for perfection 'results in a devastating critique of one's shortcomings':

> Only a few individuals affected by this problem are aware that the roots of their merciless self-deprecation lie in their own grandiose fantasies. Most feel only pain and a sense of inferiority. [...] Because such fantasies are heavily laden with shame, interpreting them in analysis requires great tact and sensitivity on the part of the therapist. [...] The limitless demands of the grandiose self inhibit all creative endeavours, because they subject every attempt at expression to merciless criticism. Feelings of inferiority and shame do not promote expression of one's ideas.
>
> *(1996: 44)*

Forman gives us an insight into the (fictional) Salieri's childhood and shows us in flashbacks why his creative impulse is impaired. Salieri's father – unlike Mozart's – never wanted his son to study music, but expected him to join the family business. Salieri grew up with his spirit restrained by a combination of Oedipal systems (the patriarch, religion and commerce), and he never learned to set it free. When the father suddenly dies, Salieri's dream comes true – he escapes the rural home and goes away to study music. Unfortunately, it is too late to teach his fully formed trickster new tricks – it refuses to rise and fly, and turns down the offer to leave the cage. Although Salieri is diligent, moderately gifted and professionally successful (he becomes a court composer for the Austrian king), the vital component is missing from his life, and this vital component is unimpeded – wild creativity. A narcissist in love with himself yet suffering from profound self-hatred, Salieri fails to be creative because creativity presupposes understanding 'the soul of things', it requires the ability to venture outside one's subjectivity, to immerse oneself into the world, to merge with the other. Creativity means becoming someone else, if only for a brief period of time. Salieri cannot be anyone but himself – and, paradoxically, he does not enjoy being himself. He wants to be someone else, someone more gifted. He wants to be Mozart. His problems form a vicious circle.

Mario Jacoby traces the 'blocked trickster' syndrome back to the use of shame as a controlling tool by early representatives of frameworks in the life of the infant. He argues that sometimes

> the child's feelings of 'omnipotence' are met too early with a 'knowing better' attitude on the part of his unempathic parents, resulting in the basic feeling that 'I cannot really live up to the demands of life, and it is hopeless to try to change the situation'.
>
> *(Jacoby, 1996: 45)*

Likewise, Salieri is afflicted by narcisstic depression whereby he is so ashamed at his powerlessness that he feels that he does not have the right to exist:

The psychological effect of such an omnipotent, deprecating authority is more than a feeling of nameless guilt. It also means being ashamed at every turn. If one has no right to exist, it would be better not to be seen. One feels one is somehow leprous, needing to be ashamed of even wanting to belong to the human race, let alone making any claims on life or other persons. Of course, claims cannot be repressed completely, and so they come out in indirect, complex, and ambivalent ways, such that one's partner can hardly fulfil them.

(1996: 45)

Meanwhile, his rival is in full possession of a perfectly functioning trickster. He is a rather mad-looking, giggling genius partial to silly clothes. Even his personality is a fountain of creative energy. In one of the scenes he is trying on different wigs at a hairdresser's – including a particularly stupid pink one – and laughing happily in the process as he witnesses his transformations in the mirror. In yet another scene, Mozart is late for a court performance (which he is supposed to direct) because he is chasing a girl. In his appearance the director puts an emphasis on relativity of 'the norm', be it fashion, hairstyles, music or behaviour. Forman's Mozart swears, tells scatological jokes and shows little respect for, and little knowledge of, the concept of authority. At the start of the film he is so naive that he is completely unaware of the dark side of human nature. He is someone who has so much faith in the trickster that he does not notice anything else. Peter Culshaw writes:

> When the film was first released, some Mozart lovers objected to Shaffer and Forman's portrayal of Mozart as a barely house-trained idiot savant, a genius yob. Forman remains unmoved: 'Some specialists in Mozart claim ownership of him but it's all there in the letters – his scatology, his foul language, his childishness. Even his giggle – one lady wrote to her niece in Prague, shocked to hear this animal-like sound coming from the mouth of the divine composer.
>
> *(Culshaw, 2002)*

What Freud writes about Da Vinci is also true of Forman's Mozart:

> Indeed, the great Leonardo remained like a child for the whole of his life in more than one way; it is said that all great men are bound to retain some infantile part. Even as an adult he continued to play, and this was another reason why he often appeared uncanny and incomprehensible to his contemporaries. It is only we who are unsatisfied that he should have constructed most elaborate mechanical toys for court festivities and ceremonial receptions, for we are reluctant to see the artist turning his power to such trifles. He himself seems to have shown no unwillingness to spend his time thus, for Vasari tells us that he made similar things when he had not been commissioned to do so: 'There (in Rome) he got a soft lump of wax, and made very delicate animals out of it, filled with air; when he blew into them they flew around, and when the air ran out they fell to the ground. [...] The same playful

delight in harmlessly concealing things and giving them ingenious disguises is illustrated by his fables and riddles. The latter are cast into the form of "prophesies": almost all are rich in ideas and to a striking degree devoid of any element of wit.'

(Freud, 2001a: 127)

Like Leonardo, the protagonist of *Amadeus* does not see the boundary between work and play, between perfection and creative chaos, between the private and the public. Unlike Salieri, Amadeus (Mozart) does not wear masks (including social masks) and does not hide in the shadows. In fact, this lack of respect towards the given, rigid, official frameworks is what annoys Salieri most. The court composer cannot help but conform because his internalised father found his external reflection in the rules outlined by the Viennese musical clique. The absence of creative freedom seems to fit in with Salieri's views on life and his vision of himself both as a composer and as a person. The start of his narcissistic crisis coincides with the arrival of Mozart onto the Viennese musical scene. He says in a flashback about his pre-Mozart days: 'Everybody liked me. I liked myself.'

Salieri is his own harshest critic. He hates the fact that he cannot generate music as light, joyful and tricksterish as that of Mozart, but does not realise that Mozart's talent – as well as his ways of framing it – comes out of childish naivety, out of the rejection of established frameworks, free from any systemic influence. Mozart is mad and free – that is why he is visited by God every time he sits down to compose. By contrast, Salieri is aware of his own powerlessness and shame. Much as he seeks to identify with God, God does not seem to hear his voice or his prayers. As Salieri explains to father Vogler in the frame narrative, all he ever wanted was to speak to God. God, he says, gave him that longing, and then made him mute. Why? If God did not want Salieri to praise him with music, why implant the desire, like a lust in his body, and then deny him the talent?

When Salieri realises that God is no better than his father in that neither of them is prepared to look after him or make him 'perfect', he becomes destructive. What could have been the trickster impulse of creativity becomes the shadow impulse of destruction. When Salieri's father suddenly dies, he feels as if he had caused his death, and rejoices in it. In fact, he hates in God the same qualities he hates in Mozart. When he hears the genius laughing and telling obscene jokes to his fiancée, he cannot believe his ears. He had thought that geniuses are made by systems, and that talents are born out of obedience.

Most importantly, he promised God to glorify his name through beautiful music. By confusing fame and popularity with love for God, Salieri clearly cannot tell the difference between himself and the world; between himself and the primary omnipotence; between his identity and the mirror provided by the crowd. The court composer confuses the playful trickster with the envious, self-obsessed, eternally hungry shadow. He had thought that talent was a form of narcissistic transaction, and attempted to barter with God by offering him his 'chastity', 'industry' and 'deepest humility' every hour of his life in return for immortality and fame. To Salieri's honour, before Mozart's arrival to Vienna, he had observed his part of the contract. At the same time, he is unsure whether this transaction was validated by God at all. 'I was a model of virtue' – he says to Father Vogler. 'If you had been me, wouldn't you have thought God had accepted your vow?'

Having promised God his life in return for fame, Salieri is very curious about the narcissistic exchange between Mozart and God. What did Mozart offer God in exchange for his prodigious abilities? When did this transaction happen – when Mozart was four? When he was six? What kind of person is he? Salieri's own prayers are deeply narcissistic – they smack of a trade agreement instead of genuine spiritual devotion. The court composer desperately wants to know how much his rival paid God for the goods. Maybe, he, Salieri, did not offer enough, perhaps he should consider raising the stakes? He desperately wants to know if 'talent like this is written on his [rival's] face'.

To his horror, the court composer soon realises that Mozart got his talent for free. There was no narcissistic transaction between Mozart and God. Even worse – 'talent like this' is not written on his face at all – apart from the moments when he is writing music, his face has a silly and clownish expression. Mozart can behave like an idiot, and the precious talent is still his. He swears, he tells inappropriate jokes – and is not punished for his misdemeanours. The 'obscene, dirty creature' defies frameworks, insults the frameworkers, creates his own rules – and he is still not disciplined. On the contrary – he is rewarded for his mad and dangerous behaviour.

Salieri gets the answers to all his burning questions at the residence of the Prince Archbishop of Salzburg where Mozart is invited to play some of his music. The court composer hides in a room where the food for the feast is stored, and inadvertently sees Mozart crawling on the floor, inappropriately grabbing his future wife Constanze (Elizabeth Berridge), telling her playful obscene jokes about 'people farting backwards' and making her say 'kiss my arse' out loud.

Salieri is scandalised. This is totally unfair. God is laughing at Salieri, for God is not how the court composer imagined him to be – a serious man, the pinnacle of justice, a father figure. God is an obscene trickster, a clown, and Mozart is his son, created in his father's true likeness. Both are creators. Yet he, Salieri, is not.

Enraged, Salieri annuls his narcissistic transaction. He wants his 'money' back from God because the deity failed to observe his part of the contract. Salieri is no longer going to be chaste, just or treat people well. He is not going to praise God's name in his music. Instead, he is going to be ruthless. From now on Salieri and God are going to be enemies because God chose for his instrument 'a boastful, lustful, smutty, infantile boy', and gave Salieri for reward only 'the ability to recognise the incarnation'. God, as Salieri sees him now, is unjust, unfair and unkind, and deserves to be rejected and blocked. Salieri also promises to 'hinder and harm' God's 'creature on earth' – Mozart.

When Father Vogler explains to the elderly Salieri that all human beings are equal in God eyes, Salieri asks in a very irritated manner: 'Are they?!'

The envious Salieri tries to catch the trickster by the tail; he wants to know where this beautiful music comes from. He desperately wants to discover the roots of genuineness, the birthplace of talent, the origins of the trickster. What he does not understand is that a trickster of this kind is born out of spontaneity; it does not follow the rules of narcissistic exchange, and it does not work within the walls of ideological or conceptual prisons. Salieri tries to copy Mozart, he starts analysing Mozart's music, he unpicks it note by note, but still cannot see where its brilliance come from because on the page it looked nothing. The beginning was simple, 'almost comic'. It was just bassoons and russet horns – like a rusty squeezebox'. And then suddenly 'high above it' an oboe came in, 'hanging there unwavering', and then a clarinet took over and turned it into 'a phrase of such delight!'. This was the kind of music Salieri had never heard. It made him tremble. This music was amazing, filled with unfulfillable longing, it was the very voice of God. And yet it was composed by Mozart – the madman, the performing monkey!

What Salieri actually admires in this piece is its wholeness, innovativeness and freshness. Mozart's unstoppable creativity shows itself in every aspect of his life whereas Salieri's life – as well as his proposed exchange with God – is based on limitation, prohibition and strict framing. Salieri wants a regular employment and plays by the rules. By contrast, Forman's Mozart has very little idea about the existence of frameworks – or the frameworkers. He is happy to oblige his patrons the Cardinal and the King, but only obeys them so much as it does not stifle the flow of his creative energy.

Forman's Amadeus lives without any notion of a 'given' external reality: he plays with realities; he denies the existence of a permanent order. When he meets the King for the first time, he fails to observe the protocol correctly. He is so removed from the external reality that he does not even know which one is the King when he is finally allowed to enter the room. Amadeus is not concerned with the building bricks of narcissism such as status, money and fame. All he values in life are spontaneity and originality – trickster qualities – whereas fame and money belong to the realm of the shadow. The latter are human and man-made whereas the former are pre-civilised and 'unconscious' phenomena.

It is not the shape or the colour of the wig that matters, and not the correct way of greeting the King, but the fact that Mozart can sit down at the piano and immediately turn Salieri's clumsy and boring 'Welcome March' into the sparkling *Non Piu Andrai Farfallone Amoroso*. It is true abilities that matter, and not contracts, exchanges or formalities. By trying to buy talent from God, Salieri assumed that God was part of the human system; that he was one of the frameworkers. And he was not – God was the ultimate trickster because anyone who creates is a priori a-systemic – if not anti-systemic.

Salieri's obsession with Mozart is a curious combination of shame and admiration, love and hate, the unstoppable desire to *be* Mozart and to destroy the object. Mozart is Salieri's idol; the court composer can't think of a time when he 'did not know his name'. Salieri wants to be the object, he wants to control the object and, failing that, to destroy the object, to crush it under the mass of humiliation and shame – which he does by gradually driving Amadeus to poverty and finally by asking him to write *Requiem*. Yet, Salieri nearly cries when he describes to the priest the beauty and innovativeness of *Don Giovanni*. It was the music of true forgiveness filling the theatre, conferring absolution onto everyone in the audience. Clearly, God was singing through this little man, making Salieri's defeat even more shameful, bitter and unbearable with every passing bar.

Ultimately, Salieri is betrayed by his very obsession with perfection and control. He is a model of virtue – yet his own music is bland. Mozart is a dirty buffoon, but his music is divine. He wants Mozart to become his ideal mirror – and he is so desperate in his hysterical narcissism and his desire to merge with the object, that he stays with the genius during his last hours, soaking up Mozart's creativity, transcribing *Requiem*, feverishly trying to get a glimpse into the working principles of the genuine trickster.

Yet, the perfectionist Salieri fails to understand how Mozart's mind works because the true creative process is never perfect. It is always an inspiredly messy affair. Amadeus's creative process is as unconscious as it is unpredictable. Mozart seems to believe that it is his God-given right to create new frameworks instead of fitting into existing ones. Moreover, in his view, his ways of shaping the trickster energy are better and more efficient than the ones invented and upheld by the King and his courtiers. Salieri's tragedy is that nothing in this world can reach the stages of ideal completion and perfect wholeness. In fact, the whole thing was created by a trickster God who magicked order out of chaos, but forgot to finish it – forgot to fix it in a permanent position. Thus he left holes in the contraption, through which chaos flows in from time to time. Salieri does not know that it is this state of temporariness and impermanence – the creative state – that keeps the world functioning and alive.

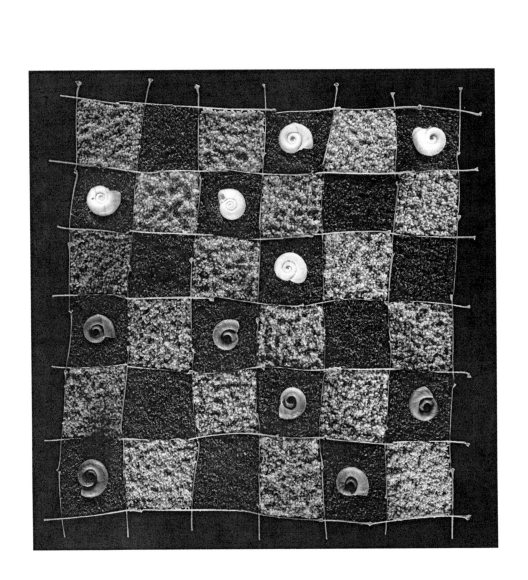

CONCLUSION

My aim in this book was to create an analytical paradigm with a broad scope and good applicatory potential. I have applied the paradigm to a range of psychological, cultural, social and political phenomena, from personal issues to the highest level of society's functioning: self-esteem and shame, lifestyle and relationships, creativity and self-expression, media, advertising, economy, political ideology and, most importantly, human identity and authenticity.

The paradigm is by no means complete, and everyone else is welcome to improve and expand it. Many more different applications are possible. For instance, it can be used for the analysis of the mass media's relationship with politics and politicians, from the Watergate affair to the Leveson Inquiry and the British parliamentary expenses scandal of 2009. I believe that it can be relevant to a wide range of contemporary issues such as internet tricksterism (including 'trolling' and the problem of identity on social media), which is the subject for a whole separate book. The trickster metaphor is also applicable to a number of historical and political phenomena, including race, gender and sexuality, religion, freedom movements, street riots, political correctness, human conflict and even organisational politics.

Most importantly, despite claims that individuals in Western societies are free to choose their path in life, it is clear that the contemporary world the crammed with systems of all shapes and kinds. Today we cannot escape the structure even if we want to – we are all monitored, branded, catalogued and supervised by a variety of systems and sub-systems. For, to escape systemic control, one needs to leave work, close one's bank account, throw away one's passport and other forms of identification, and go live in the woods without a mobile phone, radio, TV or internet access – and even this liminal condition is no guarantee of complete freedom from systemic influence. For better or for worse, structures are an integral part of the social experience.

The trickster paradigm's wide applicability is due to the fact that it concerns a very general and almost archetypal issue – the relationship between change and the system; between new and old; between laughter and seriousness; between freedom and control. It describes the life and functioning of the framework, which, despite its restrictive influence on the individual, is necessary for the very survival of civilisation and society. The trickster impulse, which is responsible for change and renewal, also contributes to the progress and success of the system – only the system does not always appreciate its help, efforts and energy.

The trickster is often seen as the adversary of the order because it uncovers systemic failures, reveals faulty functions and laughs at outdated or biased rules. It drags to the surface everything that is hidden, repressed, shameful or outlawed. When it is prevented from accomplishing its function, the repressed energy accumulates under the surface of the (personal or social) phenomenon, and draws in anger, shame and fear. The trickster can be said to be participating in the process of acknowledging and managing this energy; recognising its existence and dealing with the underlying feelings of shame and ambition. Although, left unguarded, the trickster impulse can do more harm than good, its importance for both human development and the psycho-social processes is indisputable.

Moreover, being aware of the trickster is our civil duty because any society that neglects or represses its tricksters usually ends up dealing with the collective shadow.

BIBLIOGRAPHY

Abrahams, Roger (1983) *African Folktales*, New York: Pantheon Books.

Afanasiev (1994) *Russkie Zavetnye Skazki*, Saint Petersburg: Boyanych.

Babcock-Abrahams, B. (1975) 'A Tolerated Margin of the Mess: the Trickster and his Tales Reconsidered', in *Journal of the Folklore Institute*, 11, pp. 147–186.

Bakhtin, Mikhail [1965] (1984) *Rabelais and His World*, Bloomington, IN: Indiana University Press.

—— (1997) *The Dialogic Imagination: Four Essays*, Austin, TX: University of Texas Press.

Balint, Enid (1993) 'On Being Empty of Oneself', in J. Mitchell and M. Parsons (eds), *Before I Was I. Psychoanalysis and the Imagination*, London: Free Association Books, pp. 57–62.

Ballard, J.G. (1973) *Crash*, New York: Farrar, Straus and Giroux.

Bassil-Morozow, Helena and Anslow, James Alan (2015) 'Faking Individuation in the Age of Unreality', in Lucy Huskinson and Murray Stein (eds), *Analytical Psychology in the Changing World*, London: Routledge.

Bateson, Gregory (1936) *Naven: a Survey of the Problems Suggested by a Composite Picture of the Culture of a New Guinea Tribe Drawn From Three Points of View*, Stanford, CA: Stanford University Press.

Baudrillard, Jean [1968] (2005) *The System of Objects*, London and New York: Verso.

—— [1981] (2000) *Simulacra and Simulation*, London: Routledge.

Bauman, Zygmunt (1989) *Modernity and the Holocaust*, Oxford: Polity Press.

—— (2000) *Liquid Modernity*, Cambridge: Polity Press.

—— (2001) *Community. Seeking Safety in an Insecure World*, Cambridge: Polity Press.

Beaumarchais, Pierre-Augustin [1773] (2008) *The Figaro Trilogy: The Barber of Seville, The Marriage of Figaro, The Guilty Mother*, Oxford: Oxford University Press.

Beck, Aaron T. (1991) *Cognitive Therapy and the Emotional Disorders*, London: Penguin.

Beebe, J. (1981) 'The Trickster in the Arts', *San Francisco Jung Institute Library Journal*, 2 (3), pp. 21–54.

Belmonte, Thomas (1990) 'The Trickster and the Sacred Clown: Revealing the Logic of the Unspeakable', in Pellegrino D'Acierno and Karin Barnaby (eds), *C.G. Jung and the Humanities: Towards a Hermeneutics of Culture*, London: Routledge, pp. 45–66.

Benko, Georges and Strohmayer, Ulf (1997) *Space and Social Theory: Interpreting Modernity and Postmodernity*, San Francisco and Indianapolis: Wiley-Blackwell.

Berger, John (1977) *Ways of Seeing*, London: Penguin.

Berman, Marshall (1983) *All that Is Solid Melts into Air: The Experience of Modernity*, London: Verso.

Bertens, J.W., Bertens, Hans and Fokkema, D.W. (eds) (1997) *International Postmodernism: Theory and Literary Practice*, Amsterdam: John Benjamins Publishing Co.

Boas, F. (1898) 'Introduction', in J.A. Teit, *Traditions of the Thompson River Indians of British Columbia*, Boston, MA: Houghton Mifflin.

Bourdieu, Pierre [1977] (2002) *Outline of a Theory of Practice*, London: Cambridge University Press.

—— [1990] (2003) *The Logic of Practice*, Cambridge: Polity Press.

Boyle, Frankie (2009) *My Shit Life So Far*, London: HarperCollins.

—— (2011) *Work! Consume! Die!*, London: HarperCollins.

Bull, Sarah (2013) 'Frankie Boyle Booed by Comic Relief Crowd as He Makes "Jokes" about the Queen and Duchess of Cambridge so Revolting that His Entire Sketch Is Axed from BBC3 Broadcast', *Daily Mail*, 7 March 2013.

Cadwalladr, Carole (2012) 'Pussy Riot: Will Vladimir Putin Regret Taking on Russia's Cool Women Punks?', *The Observer*, 29 July 2012.

Campbell, Joseph (1959) *The Masks of Gods: Primitive Mythology*, New York: Viking.

—— [1968] (2008) *The Hero with a Thousand Faces*, Novato, CA: New World Library.

Charles, Alec (2012) *Interactivity: New Media, Politics and Society*, Oxford: Peter Lang.

Cook, Guy (1992) *The Discourse of Advertising*, London: Routledge.

Cotterell, Arthur (ed.) (1999) *Encyclopaedia of World Mythology*, London: Paragon.

Crossley-Holland, Kevin [1980] (1993) *The Penguin Book of Norse Myths: The Gods of the Vikings*, London: Penguin.

Culshaw, Peter (2002) 'Improving on Perfection', *The Telegraph*, 11 July 2002.

Debord, Guy [1967] (2009) *Society of the Spectacle*, Eastbourne: Soul Bay Press Ltd.

Dee, Jack (2009) 'Jack Dee: I Was a Depressed Alcoholic in a Dead-end Job . . . then I Told My First Joke', *Daily Mail*, 5 October 2009.

Defoe, Daniel [1722] (1993) *Moll Flanders*, Ware: Wordsworth Editions.

Dorje, Rinjing (1997) *Tales of Uncle Thompa*, Barrytown, NY: Station Hill Press, Inc.

Doty, W. (1993) 'A Lifetime of Trouble-making: Hermes as a Trickster', in W.J. Hynes and W. Doty (eds), *Mythical Trickster Figures: Contours, Contexts*, Tuscaloosa, AL and London: University of Alabama Press, pp. 46–65.

Doueihi, A. (1993) 'Inhabiting the Space between Discourse and Story in Trickster Narratives', in W.J. Hynes and W. Doty (eds), *Mythical Trickster Figures: Contours, Contexts*, Tuscaloosa, AL and London: University of Alabama Press, pp. 193–201.

Douglas, Mary [1968] (1996) *Purity and Danger: An Analysis of the Concepts of Pollution and Taboo*, London: Routledge.

Douglas, Mary and Isherwood, Baron C. (1996) *The World of Goods: Towards an Anthropology of Consumption*, London: Routledge.

Durkheim, Emile [1893] (1964) *The Division of Labour in Society*, New York: The Free Press.

Eagleton, Terry (1996) *The Illusions of Postmodernism*, Oxford: Blackwell.

—— (2003) *After Theory*, London: Allen Lane and Penguin.

Easterling, P.E. and Hall, Edith (2002) *Greek and Roman Actors: Aspects of the Ancient Profession*, Cambridge: Cambridge University Press.

Erdoes, Richard and Ortiz, Alfonso (1999) *American Indian Trickster Tales*, London: Penguin.

Erikson, Erik [1950] (1995) *Childhood and Society*, London: Vintage.

Evans-Pritchard, E.E. (1967) *The Zande Trickster*, Oxford: Clarendon.

Franklin, Bob (2005) *Key Concepts in Journalism*, Thousand Oaks, CA: Sage Publications.

Freud, S. [1910] (2001a) 'Leonardo da Vinci and a Memory of His Childhood', in J. Strachey (ed. and trans.), *The Standard Edition of the Complete Psychological Works of Sigmund Freud* (Vol. 11), London: Vintage, pp. 59–139.

—— [1914] (2001b) 'On Narcissism: an Introduction', in J. Strachey (ed. and trans.), *The Standard Edition of the Complete Psychological Works of Sigmund Freud* (Vol. 14), London: Vintage, pp. 73–105.

Fromm, Erich (2010) *Authority and the Individual*, London: Harper Perennial.

Frosh, S. (1991) *Identity Crisis: Modernity, Psychoanalysis and the Self*, London: Macmillan.

Geertz, Clifford (1964) 'Ideology as a Cultural System', in D. Apter (ed.), *Ideology and Discontent*, New York: the Free Press of Glencoe, pp. 47–76.

—— (1973) *The Interpretation of Cultures*, London: Hutchinson.

—— [1974] (1984) 'From the Native's Point of View: On the Nature of Anthropological Understanding', in Richard A. Shweder and Robert LeVine (eds), *Culture Theory: Essays on Mind, Self and Emotion*, Cambridge: Cambridge University Press, p. 126.

Giddens, Anthony [1991] (2012) *Modernity and Self-identity: Self and Society in the Late Modern Age*, Stanford, CA: Stanford University Press.

Goldman, L.R. (1998) 'A Trickster for All Seasons: the Huli Iba Tiri', in L.R. Goldman and C. Ballard (eds), *Fluid Ontologies: Myth, Ritual and Philosophy In the Highlands of Papua New Guinea*, Westport, CT: Bergin and Carvey, pp. 87–124.

Hauke, Christopher (2000) *Jung and the Postmodern. The Interpretation of Realities*, London and Philadelphia: Routledge.

—— (2005) *Human Being Human: Culture and the Soul*, London: Routledge.

Haven, Synthia (ed.) (2002) *Joseph Brodsky: Conversations*, Jackson, MS: University Press of Mississippi.

Hawton, K. et al. (2000) 'Effect of Death of Diana, Princess of Wales, on Suicide and Deliberate Self-Harm', in *British Journal of Psychiatry*, 177, pp. 463–466.

Headrick, Daniel R. (1988) *The Tentacles of Progress: Technology Transfer in the Age of Imperialism, 1840–1950*. New York: Oxford University Press.

Hesiod (2004) *Theogony; Works and Days; Shield*, translated by Apostolos N. Athanassakis, Baltimore: Johns Hopkins University Press.

Hillman, James [1975] (1992) *Re-visioning Psychology*, New York: Harper Perennial.

—— (1998) *The Myth of Analysis: Three Essays in Archetypal Psychology*, Evanston, IL: Northwestern University Press.

Hirschkop, Ken and Shepherd, David [1989] (2001) *Bakhtin and Cultural Theory*, Manchester: Manchester University Press.

Hockley, Luke (2001) *Cinematic Projections: The Analytical Psychology of C.G. Jung and Film Theory*, London: University of Luton Press.

—— (2007) *Frames of Mind: A Post-Jungian Look at Cinema, Television and Technology*, Bristol and Chicago: Intellect.

Hoffman, E.T.A. [1819] (2006) *The Life and Opinions of Tomcat Murr*, London: Penguin.

Humboldt, Wilhelm Von [1850] (1993) *The Limits of State Action*, Indianapolis, IN: Liberty Fund.

Huskinson, Lucy and Stein, Murray (2015) *Analytical Psychology in the Changing World*, London: Routledge.

Hyde, Lewis (1999) *Trickster Makes this World: Mischief, Myth and Art*, New York: Farrar.

Hyers, Conrad (1996) *The Spirituality of Comedy: Comic Heroism in a Tragic World*, New Brunswick, NJ and London: Transaction Publishers.

Hynes, W.J. and Doty, W. (eds) [1993] (1997) *Mythical Trickster Figures: Contours, Contexts*, Tuscaloosa, AL and London: University of Alabama Press.

Hynes, William (1993a) 'Inclusive Conclusions: Tricksters – Metaplayers and Revealers', in W.J. Hynes and W. Doty (eds), *Mythical Trickster Figures: Contours, Contexts*, Tuscaloosa, AL and London: University of Alabama Press, pp. 46–65.

—— (1993b) 'Mapping the Characteristics of Mythic Tricksters: a Heuristic Guide', in W.J. Hynes and W. Doty (eds), *Mythical Trickster Figures: Contours, Contexts*, Tuscaloosa, AL and London: University of Alabama Press, pp. 202–217.

Iyengar, Sheena (2010) *The Art of Choosing*, London: Little, Brown.

Jackson, Marie (2007) 'Did Diana's Death Change Us?', BBC News website, 31 August 2007.

Jacobi, Jolande [1942] (1973) *The Psychology of C.G. Jung* (Eighth Edition), translated by Ralph Manheim, New Haven and London: Yale University Press.

—— (ed.) (1953) *Psychological Reflections. An Anthology of the Writings of C.G. Jung*, London: Routledge and Kegan Paul.

—— (1964) 'Symbols in an Individual Analysis', in Carl Gustav Jung and Marie-Louise von Frantz (eds), *Man and His Symbols*, London: Picador, pp. 323–374.

Jacoby, Mario (1996) *Shame and the Origins of Self-esteem*, London: Routledge.

—— (2010) *Individuation and Narcissism*, London: Routledge.

Jameson, Fredric (1975) *The Prison-house of Language: a Critical Account of Structuralism and Russian Formalism*, Princeton, NJ: Princeton University Press.

—— (1991) *Postmodernism, or the Cultural Logic of Late Capitalism*, London: Verso.

—— (2009) *The Cultural Turn: Selected Writings on the Postmodern, 1983–1998*, London: Verso.

Johnston, Sheila (1998) 'The Clevering Up of America', *The Independent*, 20 September 1998.

Jung, C.G. [Except where a different publication is cited, all references are to the hardback edition of C.G. Jung] (1954) *The Collected Works* (CW), edited by Sir Herbert Read, Dr Michael Fordham and Dr Gerhardt Adler, and translated by R.F.C. Hull, London: Routledge.

—— [1963] (1995) *Memories, Dreams, Reflections*, London: Fontana.

—— (1975) *Letters, II, 1951–1961*, Gerhardt Adler (ed.), in collaboration with Aniela Jaffé, translated by R.F.C. Hull, Princeton, NJ: Princeton University Press.

—— and Kerenyi, Karl (2002) *Science of Mythology: Essays on the Mythology of the Child and the Mysteries of Eleusis*, London: Routledge.

—— and von Franz, M.-L. (eds) (1964) *Man and His Symbols*, London: Picador.

Kalabin, Aleksei (2013) 'Time Lines', *British Vogue*, July 2013, p. 163.

Kalsched, D. (2010) *The Inner World of Trauma*, London: Routledge.

Kerényi, Karl (1956) 'The Trickster in Relation to Greek Mythology', in Paul Radin *The Trickster: A Study in American Indian Mythology*, New York: Schocken Books, pp. 173–191.

Klein, M. (1988a) *Envy and Gratitude*, London: Vintage.

—— (1988b) *Love, Guilt and Reparation*, London: Vintage.

—— (1997) *The Psycho-analysis of Children*, London: Vintage.

Knox, Jean (2010) *Archetype, Attachment, Analysis: Jungian Psychology and the Emergent Mind*, London: Routledge.

Kohut, Heinz [1977] (2009) *The Restoration of the Self*, Chicago, IL and London: University of Chicago Press.

—— [1978] (2011) *The Search for the Self*, London: Karnac.

Kopp, Sheldon (1974) *The Hanged Man: Psychotherapy and the Forces of Darkness*, Palo Alto, CA: Science and Behaviour Books.

Lally, Kathy (2013) 'Russia Pursues Performance Artist Who Nailed Himself to Red Square in Protest', *The Washington Post*, 15 November 2013.

Lambek, Michael (ed.) (2002) *A Reader in the Anthropology of Religion*, San Francisco and Indianapolis: Wiley-Blackwell.

Lasch, Christopher [1979] (1991) *The Culture of Narcissism: American Life in an Age of Diminishing Expectations*, New York: W.W. Norton & Co.

Leeming, David Adams (1998) *Mythology: the Voyage of the Hero*, Oxford: Oxford University Press.

Lesage, Alain-René [1715–1735] (2005) *The Adventures of Gil Blas of Santillane*, Whitefish, MT: Kessinger Publishing.

Lewis, C.S. [1958] (1988) *The Four Loves*, Orlando, FL: Harcourt.

Lukács, Georg [1938] (2002) 'Realism in the Balance', in Fredrick Jameson (ed.), *Aesthetics and Politics*, New York: Verso, pp. 28–60.

McCaughrean, Geraldine (1999) *One Thousand and One Arabian Nights*, Oxford: Oxford University Press.

McHale, Brian (1992) *Constructing Postmodernism*, London and New York: Routledge.

—— (1997) *Postmodernist Fiction*, New York and London: Methuen.

Magnay, Diana (2011) 'Topless Feminist Protesters Show What They Are Made of', CNN website, 21 January 2011.

Maier, Sonja (2010) *The Death of A Dream – Hunter S. Thompson and the American Dream*, München: GRIN Verlag.

Makarius, Laura (1993) 'The Myth of the Trickster: the Necessary Breaker of Taboos', in W.J. Hynes and W. Doty (eds), *Mythical Trickster Figures: Contours, Contexts*, Tuscaloosa, AL and London: University of Alabama Press, pp. 66–86.

Malpas, Simon (ed.) (2001) *Postmodern Debates*, London: Palgrave.

Mann, Thomas [1936] (1992) *Confessions of Felix Krull, Confidence Man*, London: Vintage Books.

Marx, Karl [1848] (2004) *The Communist Manifesto*, London: Penguin.

Metz, Christian (1974) *Film Language: a Semiotics of the Cinema*, New York: Oxford University Press.

Mill, John Stuart [1859] (2001) 'On Liberty', in Michael Morgan (ed.), *Classics of Modern and Politics Theory*, Indianapolis, IN: Hackett Publishing Company.

Miller, J.C. (2004) *The Transcendent Function: Jung's Model of Psychological Growth through Dialogue with the Unconscious*, New York: State University of New York Press.

Mills, C. Wright [1951] (1967) *White Collar: the American Middle Classes*, New York: Oxford University Press.

Morgan, Michael (ed.) (2001) *Classics of Modern and Politics Theory*, Indianapolis, IN: Hackett Publishing Company.

Morris, Colin [1972] 2004) *The Discovery of the Individual*, Toronto and London: University of Toronto Press.

Neumann, Erich [1949] (1969) *Depth Psychology and a New Ethics*, translated by Eugene Rolfe, London: Hodder & Stoughton.

—— [1959] (1974) *Art and the Creative Unconscious: Four Essays*, Princeton, NJ: Princeton University Press.

Nietzsche, Friedrich [1889] (2012) (translated by Walter Kaufmann and R.J. Hollingdale), *The Twilight of the Idols, How to Philosophise with a Hammer* [e-book], n.p.: CreateSpace Independent Publishing Platform.

Palahniuk, Chuck (1996) *Fight Club*, New York: W.W. Norton & Company.

Pelton, Robert D. (1980) *The Trickster in West Africa: A Study of Mythic Irony and Sacred Delight*, Berkeley, CA: University of California Press.

Pierce, Andrew (2007) 'Princess Diana: Editors Admit Guilt over Death', *The Telegraph*, 21 August 2007.

Rabelais, François (2004) *Gargantua and Pantagruel* [e-book], New York: Digireads.com Publishing.

Radin, Paul (1972) [1956] *The Trickster: A Study in American Indian Mythology*, New York: Schocken Books.

Ricketts, Mac Linscott (1966) 'The North American Trickster', *History of Religion*, 5 (2), pp. 327–350.

—— (1993) 'The Shaman and the Trickster', in W.J. Hynes and W. Doty (eds), *Mythical Trickster Figures: Contours, Contexts*, Tuscaloosa, AL and London: University of Alabama Press, pp. 90–106.

Robb, David (ed.) (2007) *Clowns, Fools and Picaros*, Amsterdam: Rodopi.

Rose, Nikolas (1998) *Inventing Our Selves*, Cambridge: Cambridge University Press.

Rosenberg, Donna [1994] (1999) *World Mythology: an Anthology of the Great Myths and Epics*, Lincolnwood, IL: NTC Pub. Group.

Russell, Bertrand [1949] (2010) *Authority and the Individual*, London: Routledge.

Samuels, Andrew (1985) *Jung and the Post-Jungians*, London: Routledge.

—— (1993) *The Political Psyche*, London: Routledge.

—— (2001) *Politics on the Couch: Citizenship and the Internal Life*, London: Carnac Books.

——, Shorter, Bani and Plaut, Fred (1992) 'Trickster', in Richard P. Sugg (ed.), *Jungian Literary Criticism*, Evanston, IL: Northwestern University Press, pp. 273–274.

Schwartz-Salant, N. and Stein, M. (eds) (1991) *Liminality and Transitional Phenomena*, New York: Chiron Publications.

Sennett, Richard (1978) *The Fall of the Public Man*, London: Penguin.

Shakespeare, William (2007) *The Complete Works of William Shakespeare*, London: HarperCollins.

Shelley, Mary [1818] (1999) *Frankenstein*, Ware: Wordsworth Classics.

Sherman, Josepha (1996) *Trickster Tales and Folk Stories From Around the World*, Little Rock, AR: August House Publications Inc.

Siltanen, Rob (2011) 'The Real Story behind Apple's "Think Different' Campaign"', *Forbes*, 14 December 2011.

Simmel, George [1903] (2004) 'The Metropolis and the Mental Life', in Vanessa Schwartz and Jeanne M. Przyblyski (eds), *The Nineteenth-century Visual Culture Reader*, London: Routledge, pp. 51–56.

St John, Graham (ed.) (2008) *Victor Turner and Cultural Performance*, New York: Berghahn Books.

Stam, R. and Flitterman-Lewis, Burgoyne (2008) *New Vocabularies in Film Semiotics*, London: Routledge.

Stearns, Peter N. (2006) *Consumerism in World History: The Global Transformation of Desire*, London: Routledge.

Stein, Murray (1993) *In MidLife: A Jungian Perspective*, Dallas: Spring Publications.

Stevenson, Robert Lewis [1886] (2003) *The Strange Case of Dr. Jekyll and Mr. Hyde*, London: Penguin.

Stoker, Bram [1897] (2004) *Dracula*, London: Penguin.

Stoppard, Tom (1991) *Rosencrantz and Guildenstern Are Dead*, New York: Grove Press.

Strachey, J. (ed. and trans.) [1960] (2001) *The Standard Edition of the Complete Psychological Works of Sigmund Freud*, London: Vintage.

Sugg, Richard P. (ed.) (1992) *Jungian Literary Criticism*, Evanston, IL: Northwestern University Press.

Tannen, Ricki Stefanie (2007) *The Female Trickster: the Mask that Reveals*, London: Routledge.

Tarkovsky, Andrey [1989] (2008) *Sculpting in Time: Reflections on the Cinema*, Austin, TX: University of Texas Press.

Turner, Victor [1969] (2009) *The Ritual Process: Structure and Anti-Structure*, New Brunswick, NJ and London: Aldine Transaction.

—— (1974) *Dramas, Fields, and Metaphors: Symbolic Action in Human Society*, Ithaca, NY: Cornell University Press.

—— (1975) *Revelation and Divination in Ndembu Ritual*, Ithaca, NY: Cornell University Press.

—— (1979) *Process, Performance and Pilgrimage*, New Delhi: Naurang Rai.

—— (1992) *Blazing the Trail: Way Marks in the Exploration of Symbols*, Tucson, AZ and London: University of Arizona Press.

Ullman, Walter (1966) *The Individual and Society in the Middle Ages*, Baltimore: Johns Hopkins Press.

Urback, Robyn (2013) 'FEMEN Puts on a Good Show. That's All', *National Post*, 2 October 2013.

Vaillant, George E. [1977] (1995) *Adaptation to Life*, Cambridge, MA: Harvard University Press.

Van Gennep, Arnold [1909] (2004) *The Rites of Passage*, London: Routledge.

Velie, Alan R. [1979] (1991) *American Indian Literature: an Anthology of Traditional and Contemporary Indian Literature*, Norman, OK: University of Oklahoma Press.

Von Frantz, Marie-Louise [1970] (1973) *An Introduction to the Interpretation of Fairytales*, Zurich: Spring Publications.

—— (1964) 'The Process of Individuation', in Carl Gustav Jung and Marie-Louise von Frantz (eds), *Man and His Symbols*, London: Picador, pp. 159–254.

Waddell, Terrie (2006) *Mis/takes: Archetype, Myth and Identity in Screen Fiction*, London and New York: Routledge.

—— (2009) *Wild/Lives: Trickster, Place and Liminality on Screen*, London: Routledge.

Walker, Peter (2010) 'Frankie Boyle Meets His Match in Mother of Down's Syndrome Child', *The Guardian*, 8 April 2010.

Walker, Shaun (2013) 'Artist Nails His Scrotum to the Ground in Red Square', *The Guardian*, 11 November 2013.

Walker, Stephen F. (2002) *Jung and the Jungians on Myth*, New York and London: Routledge.

Weber, Max [1930] (2005) *The Protestant Ethic and the Spirit of Capitalism*, London: Routledge.

Welsford, Enid (1936) *The Fool: His Social and Literary History*, London: Faber and Faber.

Wilde, Oscar [1890] (1992) *Picture of Dorian Gray*, Ware: Wordsworth Editions.

Willeford, William (1969) *The Fool and his Sceptre: A Study in Clowns and Jesters and Their Audience*, Evanston, IL: Northwestern University Press.

Winnicott, Donald (1965) *The Maturational Process and the Facilitating Environment*, London: Hogarth Press.

—— [1971] (1992) *Playing and Reality*, London: Routledge.

Wright, Kenneth (2009) *Mirroring and Attunement*, London and New York: Routledge.

Wyatt, Daisy (2013) '"I Wish the Queen Had Died": Offensive Frankie Boyle Jokes Cut from BBC Comic Relief Broadcast', *The Independent*, 7 March 2013.

Wu, Cheng'en [1590] (1993) *Journey to the West*, Beijing: Foreign Languages Press.

Young-Eisendrath, Polly and Dawson, Terence (eds) (1997) *The Cambridge Companion to Jung*, Cambridge: Cambridge University Press.

Unauthored articles

'Frankie Boyle's Top 10 Controversial Jokes: From Katie Price to Madeleine McCann', *Metro*, 7 March 2013, http://metro.co.uk/2013/03/07/frankie-boyles-top-10-controversial-gags-from-katie-price-to-madeleine-mccann-3530889/.

'How They Protest Prostitution in Ukraine', France 24, 28 August 2009, http://observers.france24.com/content/20090828-how-they-protest-prostitution-ukraine-femen-sex-tourism.

'Pussy Riot Members Jailed for Two Years for Hooliganism', BBC News website, 17 August 2012, www.bbc.co.uk/news/world-europe-19297373.

INDEX